The
Opening
Mind

Morris
Weitz

A Philosophical Study of Humanistic Concepts

**The
Opening
Mind**

The University
of Chicago Press
*Chicago
and London*

Morris Weitz is the Richard Koret Professor of
Philosophy at Brandeis University.

The University of Chicago Press, Chicago 60637
The University of Chicago Press, Ltd., London

Printed in the United States of America
82 81 80 79 78 77   9 8 7 6 5 4 3 2 1

Library of Congress Cataloging in Publication Data

Weitz, Morris, 1916–
    The opening mind: a philosophical study of humanistic concepts

    Bibliography: p.
    Includes index.
    1. Concepts.   I. Title.
    BD181.W38   121   77-7387
    ISBN 0-226-89240-9

For my
parents

Contents

Concepts are fundamental in philosophy, the sciences, and the humanities and in many human and animal activities. What they are and what roles they play have been of perennial concern to philosophers in their efforts to provide an adequate account of the conceptual life. Perhaps philosophers alone employ concepts and proffer theories of them: what they are and what they do. Even though a particular philosopher's range of concepts can be as narrow as he pleases—he may devote his life to an investigation of the one concept of entailment—any philosophical theory of concepts, if it is to do justice to the ostensible variety of conceptualization, must accommodate at least the major distinguishable uses of concepts, whether the concepts themselves are ordinary, scientific, or humanistic.

It is just here, I think, that philosophy is inherently interdisciplinary, since the adequacy of our understanding of concepts depends primarily on our appreciation of the diversity of concepts as they are found, not only in philosophy, but in all disciplines.

It has long seemed to me, as it has to others, that a central task of philosophy is the exploration of the conceptual life. One important region to be mapped—certainly as important as the sciences—is the humanistic disciplines. During the past ten years or so, especially in *Hamlet and the Philosophy of Literary Criticism* and in various essays in the philosophy of art, I have tried to elucidate some of the basic concepts of literary criticism and art history. Instead of beginning with preconceived theories of drama, tragedy, interpretation, evaluation, and criticism of works of art in literary criticism or of period-style concepts in art history, I studied the roles of these concepts in a rich and living tradition of criticism and art history. This examination, whether finally correct or not, uncovered three radically different kinds of concepts, hitherto unnoticed by philosophers: the perennially debatable (*tragedy*); the perennially flexible (*art, drama*); and the irreducibly vague (*Mannerism*). All of these seem to me indisputable examples of open concepts: that is, concepts and their conveying terms that function under no definitive sets of criteria. These concepts, I concluded, are not ambiguous, nor are they vague in the traditional sense of "obscure" or "without boundaries"; and, more important, they are not closed in the classical platonic sense of being governed by necessary and sufficient criteria.

These discoveries of the logical character of certain concepts were, of course, anticipated as well as inspired by others, especially Waismann and Wittgenstein. But I also realized that their probings into open texture and family resemblances do not

sufficiently clarify the logic or range of open concepts. More is needed on the logic of different kinds of less-than-definitive sets of criteria for certain concepts if these diverse open concepts are to be sorted out.

It is precisely this task of sorting-out that I have set myself in this book. I begin with the relation between words, concepts, and things or, in grander, traditional terms, the relation between language, conceptualization, and the world. In particular, I ask whether concepts are words, meanings of words, or uses of words; whether concepts are abilities or entities, either sensible or supersensible; whether talk about concepts is reducible to talk about uses of words; and whether the having of concepts is the same as the having of certain skills, including being able to wield certain expressions. I attempt to formulate and defend the only theses I am able to support regarding these questions: that there are concepts, irreducible to anything else, and that any theory of concepts, whether explicit or implicit in a particular philosopher's use of concepts, entails a corresponding theory of language—specifically, a theory about the logical nature of the sets of criteria governing the intelligible, correct use of certain words.

Having articulated these two theses, I go on to present a survey of the recent critique of closed concepts among some contemporary philosophers, along with their various conceptions of open concepts.

These first two chapters introduce the next five, devoted to certain basic concepts in aesthetics, art history, psychology, and ethics, in which I argue that these concepts are open, in varying degrees of openness, rather than closed, as they are traditionally and commonly assumed to be. Unfortunately, I have not

canvassed as many varieties of open concepts as I wished; there
is much to be done on the detailed explorations of concepts,
especially in the social and natural sciences and in mathematics,
which, had I attempted them, would have required another
volume. However, having established my main contention, that
the underlying assumption of Western philosophy, expressed or
embodied in its various theories of concepts, namely, that all
concepts are and must be closed—beautifully put by Frege's "A
concept that is not sharply defined is wrongly termed a concept"
—is false, I am satisfied with the results of this volume. What I
have done, I have tried to do thoroughly. That there are
concepts other than closed ones, of varying degrees of openness,
I think I have shown. What I have not established or even
ventured is a general theory of concepts: open and closed. The
reason I have not is that my lingering suspicion that there is no
such theory may be justified; if so, we are left in philosophy with
an ever-incomplete sampling of their great diversity. In place of
a conclusion, then, I offer only afterwords: about what is no
longer questionable or deniable, that there are irreducible and
respectable varieties and even vagaries of conceptualization; and
about what can be done in this area of inquiry, where what can
be done is not to be understood as what remains to be done. I
know the answer to the one, but not to the other.

Throughout the book, I attempt not only to establish foundations for concepts in the humanities, by disclosing their varieties
of openness, but, equally as important, to dispel the myth that
the respectability of the humanities rests on the determination of
closed concepts and their definitions, supposedly modeled on the
precision and definitive sets of conditions governing scientific
concepts. In showing that some of the basic concepts of the
humanistic disciplines are governed by open, not closed, sets of
criteria, without which they do not and perhaps cannot function, I celebrate rather than continue to apologize for the
irreducible varieties and vagaries of the conceptual life.

Chapters 2, 4, 5, and 6 have appeared in other versions
elsewhere. I have reworked these extensively and have tried to
integrate them with the wholly new materials of the other
chapters. An earlier version of chapter 2 appeared in my article
"Open Concepts" in the *Revue Internationale de Philosophie*,
no. 99 (1972), pp. 86–110. Parts of chapter 4 have been
reworked from my article "Tragedy," which appeared in volume
8 of *The Encyclopedia of Philosophy*, edited by Paul Edwards,
copyright © 1967 by Crowell Collier and Macmillan, Inc.
Chapter 5 is a much-revised and expanded version of my article
"Genre and Style," published in *Perspectives in Education*,

xii   *Religion, and the Arts*, edited by Howard Kiefer and Milton Munitz, copyright © 1970 by the State University of New York Press, Albany. And an earlier, quite different version of chapter 6, "Human Action," appeared under the same title in the *Annual Proceedings of the Center for Philosophic Exchange*, vol. 1, no. 3 (1972).

  Finally, I wish to express my gratitude to my colleagues, Douglas Stewart and David Wiesen, for aid in certain matters Greek and Latin, and to Henry David Aiken for invaluable conversations in the language of philosophy; to The National Endowment for the Humanities for a Senior Fellowship that enabled me to devote the academic year 1973–74 to the writing of this book (as well as a companion volume on the history of philosophical theories of concepts, to be published, I hope, in the not too distant future); and to La Fondation Camargo and, especially, its director, Russell Young, who graciously and generously accommodated myself, my three children, and my wife—a Resident Fellow—in the Fondation.

**The
Opening
Mind**

The history of philosophical theories of concepts, from Plato to Gilbert Ryle and Peter Geach, reveals an indisputable variety of explicit theories that range from concepts as supersensible entities (universals, meanings, abstract objects, definitions, predicates, and relations), mental entities (innate ideas, images, thoughts, or conceptions), neutral intermediaries between words and things, and abstractable items, ranging from families of sentences to an assortment of mental abilities or capacities.

Implicit theories of concepts, derived from the particular uses of concepts employed by individual philosophers, exemplify a similar diversity regarding the nature and roles of concepts.

There is also a range of overt or covert disagreement among philosophers over explicit or implicit theories about the possession of concepts, from views that we are directly aware of them to opposing claims that concepts are the same as having them, where this consists of habits, skills, or abilities to wield words or to perform certain nonlinguistic or linguistic tasks.

There is even variety in the few traditional repudiations of concepts: that there are none; that concepts are misguided and harmful ontological projections of the names of classes or of the meanings of certain words; or that concepts are harmless stylistic conveniences for certain uses of words or even for words all by themselves, i.e., concepts are attractive visual substitutes for eye-aching inverted commas.

However varied the traditional explicit and implicit and (some) recent theories of concepts may be in their doctrines about the nature and roles of concepts, they are nevertheless uniform and homogeneous in assuming the closed character of all concepts. For implicit beneath all the ostensible diversity between the entity theories and the dispositional theories and

Words, Concepts, and Things

3

among the entity, intermediary, or abstracted-items theories themselves is the supposition that concepts, when complex, and their conveying terms, whether of simple or complex concepts, are and must be governed by definitive sets of necessary and sufficient properties, conditions, or criteria. It is this assumption—about the logical character of the properties, conditions, or criteria and of the corresponding terms that express them—that is basic in traditional and in some recent theories of concepts.

Are all concepts closed, governed by definitive sets of properties or criteria? Or are some concepts open in the sense that they are governed by less-than-definitive sets of criteria? It is only an affirmative answer to this last question that could establish the logical variety among concepts, not among theories of concepts, that I shall be seeking.

Every theory of concepts implies a corresponding theory about their conveying terms. To talk about concepts—their nature and roles—or to employ certain concepts is necessarily to talk about certain words or to employ these words under certain specified or implicit conditions or criteria. To show that a concept is open, therefore, is to elucidate the use of its conveying expression and to ascertain that the criteria of its correct use are less than definitive.

Concepts, however, are not words, even if they turn out to be harmful or harmless substitutes for words; nor do concepts imply words. And the use of concepts is not the same as the use of words; nor does the use of concepts imply the use of words. My contention is only that talk about concepts (including talk about theories of concepts) implies corresponding theories of uses of words. But this entailment does not render equivalent the having of concepts and the correct employment of certain expressions; nor does it countenance the reduction of concepts or talk about concepts or of uses of concepts to words or to the uses of words. Contemporary theories that identify concepts with employments of certain expressions and identify the having of concepts with abilities to wield these expressions, or that reduce concepts to words or eliminate concepts altogether, contrast sharply with the only thesis about the relation between concepts and language that I am able to support: that talk about concepts, whether in explicit or implicit theories of concepts, entails talk about words and their uses. This entailment, if it can be validated, not only falsifies equivalence, reduction, and elimination theses about the relation between concepts and language; it also suffices to establish open concepts, provided that there are words which convey these concepts that do not have definitive sets of criteria for *their* correct use. To say, for example, that the concept of x is governed by a specific set of necessary and sufficient properties, conditions, or criteria is to entail that the word "x" that expresses the concept is similarly governed. If it turns out on examination that the word is not so governed, it follows by simple *modus tollens* that the concept is not closed.

A theory of concepts, whether explicit or implicit, rests on the assumption that there are concepts. But suppose, now, that there are no concepts. Then all explicit theories of them are philosopher's fabrications, and all implicit theories of them are erroneous interpretations of their employments of words. If, thus, there are no concepts, there can scarcely be theories about what they are. And we have no proper subject: no thesis to reject about all concepts being closed, no thesis to proclaim about some concepts being open.

Are there concepts? This surely must be our first question. Since Ryle is the first to articulate the distinction between the questions Are there concepts? and What are concepts? let us begin with his answers:

> By "concept" we refer to that which is signified by a word or a phrase. If we talk of the concept of *Euclidean point* we are referring to what is conveyed by this English phrase, or by any other phrase, Greek, French, or English, that has the same meaning.
>
> So far this indication is entirely neutral between different philosophical theories about what sort of things concepts *are;* whether, e.g. they are Lockean ideas or Platonic Essences.[1]

Although Ryle expresses doubts about, followed by a rejection of, concepts as meanings of words or phrases and defines concepts as auxiliary meanings of whole sentences, he persists in his distinction between the affirmation of concepts and competing statements about what they are. Now, however debatable his theory of concepts, even as auxiliary meanings, may be, his claim that there are concepts that are neutral between different ontologies of them is unobjectionable. But we are still left with the question Does his doctrine of neutrality establish that there are concepts? "There are universals" or "There are propositions" is also neutral between conflicting theories about what universals or propositions are, as, indeed, is "There are words" or "There are sentences" neutral between different theories about what these are. Yet, for many, "There are universals" and "There are propositions" are as suspect as the theories about what they are; whereas "There are words" or "There are sentences" seems to be dubious for no one.

Words, Concepts, and Things

More than Ryle's neutrality in relation to theories is required, therefore, to show that there are concepts. Is "There are concepts" like "There are words and sentences," or is it like "There are universals and propositions"? Perhaps the affirmation resembles neither. Let us look again at Ryle's example.

Whether there are Euclidean points or not, we can nevertheless talk about them, as we can intelligently talk about Shakespeare or Shakespeare's Hamlet, even though the first existed, the second did not. When I talk about a Euclidean point, then, according to Ryle, I employ the concept by means of the English phrase "Euclidean point," which conveys this concept. A French-speaking person can also talk about a Euclidean point. He uses French words; but he talks about the same thing and he uses the same concept (though conveyed by different words) as I do. So, too, with a German or a Russian, even if either of them (and here

I improvise on Ryle's example) should invent a new geometry, with its new concepts expressed by additional German or Russian words. What more natural than to say that all four of us employ the same concept of a Euclidean point and that two of us employ other concepts as well, each of which is conveyed in our own languages? We surely agree that Euclidean and non-Euclidean geometry are neither French, English, German, nor Russian. So the concept of a Euclidean point is not a phrase in any language, not even in the language of geometry. Nor is it a point, which may or may not exist. The concept of a Euclidean point is precisely that neutral intermediary between our words, thoughts (or conceptions), and thing (whatever it is or whether it is) that is needed in order to make this cross-referring among different phrases (or different utterances of the same phrase) intelligible. In talking about a Euclidean point, all four of us use different words to express the same concept to talk about the same thing. We do not employ two things: a concept and a phrase; rather, each employs one thing: a concept by means of a phrase. Without the concept of a Euclidean point, we can use different words to talk about the same thing; but there is nothing to determine whether it is the same talk or different talk. The concept mediates different words, same thing, and same talk about it. That it does does not render the concept a projected meaning of a word or phrase or the projected content of a translation. The concept is a neutral intermediary, not a neutral entity, whatever that is; nor is it Ryle's neutral as between opposing ontological theories of it.

If we turn from the concept of a Euclidean point to a more homely example, the concept of a dog, we encounter the same neutrality in concept talk and employment. There are certainly dogs in the world; and it is beyond question that there are the words "dog," "*chien*," and "*Hund*," among others. Is there also the concept of a dog? To say that there is—once again—in no way affirms, implies, or presupposes that the concept is an entity, supersensible or sensible, a disposition, an abstracted item from families of sentences about dogs, or even an extracted common feature of dogs. If "There is the concept of a dog" implies anything, it implies only that the concept of a dog is, so far, neither a dog nor the word "dog." "There is the concept of a dog," thus, seems to resemble neither "There are words" ("There are dogs") nor "There are universals" ("There is dogness"). The latter two sets are affirmations of entities: the first set is as true as can be—since there really are words and dogs; the former two, though also affirmations of entities claimed to be true by some, are suspect for many, since it is not obvious that there are universals, including dogness. "There is the concept of a dog," however, affirms no entity at all; rather it serves to deny that concept talk is reducible to word talk or to thing talk. The concept of a dog, like the concept of a Euclidean point, is needed to mediate different words or different utterances of the same word, the same (kind of) thing, and the same (kind of) talk—that is, talk of dogs and not, say, of cats.

If dogs and Euclidean points are not sublime enough, take God. Here, too, we talk about God, and we may ask, for example, Does He exist? or Is He benevolent? In our talk, queries, and arguments about God, we use "God," "*Dieu*," or "*Gott*," again among many other words. And especially because it is God, we also talk about the concept of God. Does the Frenchman, philosopher or not, have the same concept of God—or, if you prefer, *le même concept de Dieu*—as the Englishman? Or, for that matter, do two Englishmen who debate about God, using the same word "God" in doing so, have the same concept or not? How can we tell? How could we even try to tell if there were not the concept of God that is other than God or "God" or "*Dieu*" or "*Gott*," etc?

So there are things and words and concepts. Words are things—they are surely identifiable items in the world; but they have a special relation to other things that other things do not have to each other. "Dog" relates to dogs as dogs do not to cats. What this special relation is is of fundamental concern to philosophy of language but not to philosophy of concepts.

Are concepts, like words, things in the world, albeit with a special relation to other things, including words? Is the concept of a dog like a dog or like "dog"? If it is like a dog, it is a very special dog; if it is like "dog," it is a very special "dog," for it excludes *"chien"* and *"Hund."* Concepts are neither words nor things; they are neutral intermediaries between words and things. And to say that there are concepts—these intermediaries—is not yet to say what they are, whether entities, sensible or supersensible; items, abstractable or extractable; or dispositions, capacities, or abilities. "Concepts are neutral intermediaries," therefore, like "There are concepts," affirms the irreducibility of concepts, not a theory of them. Neither is a minimally ontological claim like "There are words and sentences" or a maximally ontological claim like "There are propositions and universals." Instead, both "There are concepts" and "Concepts are neutral intermediaries between words and things" disclaim the reducibility of concept talk to word talk and thing talk as they affirm the indispensability of concepts in our coherent talk about the world. In his essay "Logical Atomism" (1924),[2]

Bertrand Russell returned to his doctrine of external relations and to Bradley's criticism of it that it rendered relations extra terms that must be related ad infinitum. The doctrine of external relations, Russell sums up, is not a doctrine about the ontology of relations but about the irreducibility of all relational propositions to subject-predicate ones. For Russell, "There are external relations" also serves primarily to disclaim reducibility of relational talk to subject-predicate talk and to claim the indispensability of relations in our coherent talk and understanding of the world. If "There are concepts" resembles other seemingly existential assertions, it resembles "There are external relations" as Russell interprets it more than it does any of its putative models that we have considered, such as "There are words and sentences" or "There are propositions and universals."

"There are no concepts" contradicts "There are concepts." But it need be no ontological disclaimer either, as it serves to deny that concepts are indispensable or that concept talk is irreducible if we are to retain coherent, intelligible talk and understanding of the world. "There are only words and objects," thus, need be no more ontological than "There are words and objects and concepts."

Can talk about concepts be reduced to talk about words? Are concepts mere substitutes for words? Does "the concept of x" reduce to "the word 'x'"?

If we separate words from their meanings or roles—no mean feat—then the most stringent affirmative answer to our three questions offers more than a reduction of concepts to words, it eliminates them altogether: There are no concepts, only words. Concepts, then, are not mistaken projections of the meanings or uses of words but are simply egregious proliferations of words.

Now, although this rejection of concepts is without its avowed
exponents, it is at least intimated by some of the obiter dicta of
philosophers as far apart as Ryle and W. V. Quine, both of
whom sometimes seem to identify "the concept of x" with "the
word 'x'" in their sporadic admonitions to forego concept talk
except as a stylistic or typographical convenience. Of course, I
exaggerate their remarks—found, in Ryle's case, especially in
The Concept of Mind and, in Quine's case, in his persistent
semantic ascent from concept talk to word talk—remarks that
are themselves no doubt exaggerated and, in any case, are not
compatible with their authors' more moderate opinions that
concepts reduce to roles of expressions (Ryle, occasionally) or
that concepts are paraphrasable by talk about words, specifically, contextually defining them (Quine).

But, however aberrant, the thesis that concepts are eliminable
substitutes for words—words by themselves, without their
meanings or uses—deserves consideration, if only to be demol-
ished because it is incoherent. If the concept of x is nothing but
the word "x" and the word "x" is separated from its meaning or
role, what, then is "x"? A mark or a sound, a class of similar
noises or shapes (as Russell once defined it), or a kind of physical
item that can be employed in linguistic communication? According to the thesis, it cannot be a piece in a language game, since
that would make a word a physical item plus its meaning or role,
and it would identify a concept with a word together with its
meaning or role. Apart from this difficulty about the nature of a
word, involved in any attempt to eliminate concepts in favor of
words, what has the thesis to say about the concept of a word?
To be consistent, it must say that the concept of a word is an
eliminable substitute for the word "word." What, then, about
"*mot*" or "*Wort*," among many others? These are surely words
for "word." So, once more, we have at least three different
words for one thing—a word—as well as the concept of a word
that is not a word yet is required if we are to ensure the same
talk—word talk about a word—and not different talk about
anything else. Here, too, without the concept of a word to
mediate the different words for word, our conceptions or
thoughts about words, and words as things, we cannot even talk
about words and, a fortiori, of a concept as an eliminable
substitute for a word. A condition of the truth of the thesis that
concepts are eliminable by words, that they reduce to words, is
therefore the falsity of the same thesis: that at least the concept
of a word cannot be the word "word."

Can sentences in which the word "concept" appears be
paraphrased (without loss) by sentences in which the word

"word" appears instead—although not necessarily as simply a substitute for "concept"?

Russell was the first to provide an affirmative answer to this question about the reduction of talk about concepts to definitional talk of words in their sentential contexts. His answer was the second of his theories of concepts—that concepts are logical fictions or are replaceable by logical fictions—which, after 1914, supplanted his earlier theory that concepts are ontological entities. Russell did not succeed in his attempt to resolve all talk of concepts into talk about contextual definitions because these definitions, which he construed as existential claimers or disclaimers about the values of certain propositional functions, presupposed an ontology of concepts: the predicates and relations of *The Principles of Mathematics*, without which the propositional functions remain purely verbal.

Quine also gives an affirmative answer to our question about the reduction of concept talk to talk about words in their sentential contexts. Quine often introduces "concept" or "notion" in his texts—for example, "an absolute concept of objective information," which appears in one of his recent books, *Philosophy of Logic* (p. 4), along with talk about the notions of grammaticality, word, truth, synonymy, equivalence, meaning, and lexicon, among others. Neither "concept" nor "notion" appears in the index of that book, nor does "concept" occur without a cross-reference to "attribute" in any of his other books. Nevertheless, like "intentional objects," a term which also appears in his texts and sometimes, in one form or another, in his indexes, it is safe to assume that concepts, like intentional objects, are on Quine's Index: forbidden objects, no reputable, prospective values for any variables.

According to Quine, all talk about concepts divides into discourse about properties and discourse in which "concepts" are verbal substitutes for "terms." The first is ideally paraphrasable into talk about certain classes of things. The second is always paraphrasable by talk about words. In neither case is "concept" to be tolerated in austere renderings of the discourse in which it occurs. There are no concepts; and all references to them or talk about them must be eliminated by paraphrasing them away, except when they are kept as stylistic conveniences. Thus, "an absolute concept of objective information" is to be read as "the term 'objective information' applies absolutely," where this term is defined in a context. The context here is particle physics and its matrix of alternatives; "objective information" replaces "concept of objective information" and is defined as follows: "Two sentences agree in objective information, and so express the same proposition, when every cosmic distribution of particles that would make either sentence true would make the other true as well" (*Philosophy of Logic*, p. 4). To say, then, that the term "objective information" applies absolutely—and thereby to paraphrase the whole of "an absolute concept of objective information"—is to say that the term can be applied without our having on each occasion to reiterate what features are going to count.

Both the concept of objective information and its conveying words, whether applied absolutely or not, are terms of art— technical terms; I have neither the competence nor the desire to question their definitional resolutions in context or Quine's specific contextual definition or paraphrase. My concern, rather, is whether all concepts can be eliminated by paraphrase, whether all talk of concepts can be reduced to talk about contextual definitions. Russell did not successfully eliminate all concepts by paraphrase or reduce all talk of concepts to con- textual definitions. Quine admits that the elimination of talk about concepts as properties is an ideal as yet unrealized but devoutly to be pursued; but he insists that all uses of "concept," including "the concept of a property," can be paraphrased away. Is even this thesis about concept talk true? Can we paraphrase "the concept of x" by "the definition of 'x' in its sentential context"? We have already seen that "the concept of x" cannot be paraphrased by "the word 'x,'" either alone or in its sentential context, since we need "the concept of x" to mediate different linguistic values of "x" in same talk about xs.

Central in this version of reduction of concept talk to word talk are the concepts of paraphrase and contextual definition. We cannot claim that all talk of concepts can be paraphrased by contextual definitions of their conveying words without employ- ing the concepts of paraphrase and contextual definition. Do these concepts reduce to words or paraphrases or contextual definitions? Does "the concept of a paraphrase" reduce to "the paraphrase of 'paraphrase'"? Does "the concept of a contextual definition" reduce to "the contextual definition of 'contextual definition'"? That they do follows from the thesis that all talk of concepts is eliminable by paraphrase into their contextual defini- tions.

Now, whatever contextual definition is or is stipulated to be, the concept of such a definition cannot be equated with the words "contextual definition" in a proper sentential context.

The paraphrase of "paraphrase" is "to say the same thing in other words"—its dictionary definition. The contextual defi- nition of "contextual definition" would be the definitional restatement of each of the sentences in which "contextual definition" occurs, and in such a manner that the phrase, because it is putatively defective, would disappear in its new sentential context, just as "the present king of France" or "the present queen of England" no longer appears when sentences containing these phrases are contextually defined.

The concept of a paraphrase involves what it is to say the same thing in other words; it relates to, but must differ from, the concept of a translation, which also concerns saying the same thing in other words, however ambiguous "saying the same thing" may be. The concept of a contextual definition also is concerned with saying the same thing in other words but, in every case, of saying it better, where the criteria of "better" have been those of correct logical or factual form. Both Russell, who invented (or discovered?) the concept, and Quine, who employs

it rigorously, agree that quantificational talk about the values of the variables, say, "x is king of France" or "y is queen of England," is better than—is not merely saying the same thing in other words as—our ordinary talk about these regal personages. So Quine must mean that talk about definitions of words in use is not only the same as talk about concepts but is better talk because it reveals in certain important ways something about concept talk that concept talk conceals or disguises.

What does concept talk conceal, according to Quine? That it is talk about words in use and nothing more (to be contextually defined), not talk about dubious entities (to be inspected and, if complex, to be given real definitions). Talk about concepts, like similar talk about round squares, centaurs, witches, and intentions, among other strange objects, is to be silenced by resolutions of their corresponding terms in newly formed sentential contexts, not merely muted or purified by paraphrase.

Does concept talk conceal or disguise talk of dubious entities? "There are concepts" is about no things: hence, no entities, dubious or not. It is only because Quine conflates "Are there concepts?" with "What are concepts?" so that answers to both become ontological assertions, to be formulated canonically as quantified affirmations or denials of values of variables, that he regards concept talk as inevitably talk about entities. But, as I have already argued, "There are concepts" is not, if I am right, like "There are tables," even though "Concepts are sensible entities" may be like "Tables are collections of material particles" or "Concepts are supersensible entities" may resemble "Tables are ideas in the mind of God." Whatever we may say about these claims, "to be a concept" need not conform to Quine's

"To be is to be the value of a variable"; and to insist that it does is
to foreclose on the difference between the disclaimer to reducibility of "There are concepts" and the claimer, "There are tables."
It is simply not true, then, that all concept talk conceals or disguises entity talk. "There are concepts" conceals or disguises
nothing. Further, neither "The concept of a paraphrase is distinct
from the paraphrase of 'paraphrase'" nor "The concept of contextual definition is distinct from the contextual definition of
'contextual definition'" need be about an entity, dubious or not.
So neither is defective, to be replaced by a paraphrase or a contextual definition.

The concept of a paraphrase involves saying the same thing in
other words. If this concept reduces to the paraphrase of
"paraphrase" or the contextual definition of sentences in which it
disappears, we render not only the concept inoperative, which
Quine would welcome, but the activity of paraphrasing incoherent, which Quine would not accept; for without the concept
of saying the same thing in other words—a concept that needs
analysis or elucidation, not paraphrase—we have nothing to
debate about the very possibility of paraphrase, nor have we
any way of deciding purported cases of paraphrase.

With the concept of a contextual definition, we have as part of
its content the concept of a restatement that is better in certain
specified ways than the original statement that prompts the
contextual definition. As we used to say, before Quine exposed
the difficulties about meanings, the concept of a restatement
which is better than the one it replaces is part of the meaning of
"a contextual definition." In any case, the plausibility, slim as it
is, of the concept of a paraphrase being reduced to the paraphrase of "paraphrase" vanishes as we turn to the possibility of
the concept of a contextual definition being reduced to the
contextual definition of "contextual definition." For, in order to
effect such a reduction, we must assume that "contextual
definition" is defective—as is, for example, "round square"—
and requires a resolution that eliminates it in a sentential
context. Such an assumption is absurd, for its truth would
render incoherent the practice of contextual definition where it is
needed and salutary. If "the concept of contextual definition" is
reducible to "the term 'contextual definition' contextually defined," on the model of, say, "the concept of a property" is
reducible to "the term 'property' contextually defined," then
there can be no contextual definitions, since there can be no way
of determining or even understanding what is a better restatement of a prior statement with its defective term. Once again,

the attempt to dispense with talk of concepts has as a necessary condition of its success the indispensability of at least one concept and, in this case, the concept of a contextual definition.

Talk about concepts, then, is not eliminable, paraphrasable, or contextually definable. What about the equivalence thesis: that all talk of concepts implies and is implied by talk about uses of words? The most impressive variant of this thesis is the doctrine that concepts are the having of them and that the having of them is the same as the ability to wield certain expressions. To have a concept of x, on this view, is to be able to employ "x" correctly, that is, according to the standard criteria and rules governing the use of "x."

Are concepts abilities? Is the having of a concept being able to use language? Is talk about concepts the same as talk about the uses of certain expressions? Since I am especially concerned here with the relation of concept talk to word talk and the putative reducibility of the one to the other, I shall concentrate on the third of my three questions: Is talk about concepts equivalent to talk about uses of language?

Recent philosophers in Oxford and Cambridge, including Ryle and the later Wittgenstein, suspicious of traditional "What is the nature of x?" questions as the very model of philosophical questions, and equally wary of their counterpart "What does 'x' mean?" questions, turn instead to "What is the role of 'x'?" In regard to concepts, they shift from what they are or what they supposedly mean or name or denote to what it is to have a particular concept. There are dogs, there is "dog," "*chien*," or "*Hund*," and there is the concept of a dog. But to know what the concept of a dog is is, for them, to understand what it is to have this concept. And to have this concept, they claim, is to be able to use the word "dog" or "*chien*" or "*Hund*" correctly. On this view, there are words and things and concepts; but concepts are abilities to use certain words, not extra, special things.

Whatever the merits of this dispositional theory of concepts are—and they are considerable—other philosophers, both recent and past, deny that being able to use certain words correctly is the same as the having of certain concepts or is even a necessary feature of them. Behaviorists and cognitivists in psychology, as well as philosophers, such as H. H. Price, argue that the possession of concepts can be truly attributed to nonlanguage-using animals, since they engage in recognizably discriminatory behavior; and Geach, along with other philosophers, dissociates the having of concepts from the ability to use language, at least in the case of the aphasic.

Being able to use certain words correctly may be a sufficient

condition of the having of certain concepts. But even this
criterion of the dependence of concepts on the use of language
has been rejected by many philosophers, from Plato to Russell
and Moore, who insist that any correct use of language depends
on a prior apprehension or possession of concepts which can be
achieved without language. According to them, at least for
certain crucial words (such as "piety" for Plato, "good" for
Moore, or "number" for [early] Russell), being able to use them
correctly presupposes the having of certain concepts. Having a
concept, thus, is a necessary condition for being able to use
language correctly. However, if this is so, then it does follow on
this view that our ability to use words correctly is a sufficient
condition for our having certain concepts. How, then, can Plato
or Russell or Moore reject the doctrine that being able to use
language correctly is a sufficient condition for the having of
concepts? Only by claiming that the criteria for this correctness
are not the conventional rules that govern our uses of words but
are, rather, the properties or constituents of the concepts
themselves, at least when these concepts (as skills for Plato [on
one interpretation of Plato's theory of concepts] or as entities for
Russell and Moore) are not simple. Thus, it is the definitive
properties or constituents or the indefinable character of the
concept (for example, Moore's concept of good) that determines
whether we have a particular concept and are thereby able to use
a particular word according to its correct criteria. We may be
able to use certain words in accordance with their convention-
ally accepted rules—with established usage; but in the platonic
tradition, unless we can intuit a form or can state the definitive
properties or can apprehend the simplicity of a particular
concept, we do not have the concept. All we have is an ability to
use words which may or may not be in accordance with their
true criteria.

There is, then, fundamental debate, among both historical
and contemporary philosophers, about whether concepts, or the
having of them, in all cases involve uses of language, abilities to
employ certain expressions correctly, or even to be able to
perform a number of relevant tasks; and there is similar disagreement whether certain correct uses of language or certain
abilities to use language or to do other things are exhaustive of
the putative class of having concepts. The conditions, both
necessary and sufficient, differ for the having of concepts and for
the correct employment of certain expressions; for abilities to
wield these expressions; and for skills of one sort or another,
shared by animals and humans. However close, therefore, talk
about concepts is to talk about uses of words, and however close

the having of concepts is to being able to wield words or to perform other tasks, they are not the same. Talk about concepts, then, whatever it is or implies, is not equivalent to talk about language uses and skills: neither mutually implies the other. In any case, no one has yet shown that they are equivalent; and many have argued convincingly that they are not equivalent, however intimately related they may be.

What, then, is the relation between talk about concepts and talk about words? If it is not elimination, paraphrase, contextual definition, or equivalence—each a form of reduction—what is the relation? Concepts or the having of them—whatever they are or are said to be by the contending theorists—do not imply words, uses of words, or abilities to use words, or abilities in general. Moreover, the employment of concepts does not imply uses of words; yet, because it is employment (though not employment of concepts), it does imply skills. But this entailment yields nothing for the understanding of the relation between concepts and words. We must look elsewhere.

My thesis is this: Talk about concepts entails talk about words —the words that convey these concepts; but talk about these words entails no talk about concepts. The relation between talk of concepts and talk of words is one-way entailment, not mutual. Every theory of concepts implies a corresponding theory of the words that express the concepts. Consider the following schema, suggested by Wittgenstein (*Philosophical Investigations*, Part 1, § 370):

(a) What is (the nature of) x?
(b) What does "x" mean or name?
(c) What is the role of "x"?

Now, in the sense that an answer to (c) does not entail an answer to (b), and an answer to (b) does not entail an answer to (a), an answer to (a) does entail an answer to (b), and an answer to (b) entails an answer to (c).

On this schema, which I take to be impeccable, it is possible to talk about "imagination" without talking about imagination, just as it is not possible to talk about imagination without talking about "imagination" or some synonym (Wittgenstein's example). So, too, it is possible to talk about "concept" without talking about concept or to talk about "x" without talking about the concept of x; but it is not possible to talk about concept or the concept of x without talking about "concept" or "x."

Talk about concepts entails talk about words. But not all talk about anything entails talk about the words we use to talk about it. So we cannot generalize this from our schema: that we can talk about words without talking about objects but cannot talk about objects without talking about the words we use to talk about them, since it is obvious that we talk about most things by using words, not by talking about words the way we talk about objects. "Talk about" is therefore too loose. Our thesis about the relation between talk about concepts and talk about words needs tightening up.

A theory of concepts—whether explicit or implicit—implies a corresponding theory of the role (or use) of the words employed to convey its particular concepts. Thus, answers to "What is a concept?" or "What is the concept of x?" entail answers to "What is the role of 'concept' or 'x'?"; but answers to "What is the role (or use) of 'concept' or 'x'?" do not entail any answers to "What is a concept?" or "What is the concept of x?"

In any adequate discussion of the relation between things, words, and concepts or, in grander terms, of the problem of conceptualization, at least seven major questions deserve scrutiny:

(1) Are there concepts?
(2) What are concepts?
(3) What is it to have a concept?
(4) Is correct use of language necessary or sufficient for the having of concepts?
(5) Is the having of concepts necessary or sufficient for the correct use of language?
(6) Does a theory of language and of its functioning imply a theory of concepts?
(7) Does a theory—explicit or implicit—of concepts (the having of them, conceptualization) imply a theory of language?

In regard to these seven questions, the correct answer to (2), What are concepts? seems as remote today as ever. And competing answers to (3), (4), (5), and (6) leave these questions as debatable as answers to (2). For my part, I am confident only of affirmative answers to (1), Are there concepts? and (7), Does a theory of concepts imply a corresponding theory of language? In saying that there are concepts, that is, that they are not reducible to words, things, paraphrases, contextual definitions, uses of words, or abilities to wield words or perform other tasks, I have already said all I have to say about my affirmative answer.

My affirmative answer to (7), however, requires further amplification and argument. A theory of concepts implies a theory of language; but a theory of language does not imply a theory of concepts. If, to revert to our homely example, we distinguish, as—I hope we now agree—we must, between dogs, "dog," and the concept of a dog, what I am claiming is that a theory about the concept of a dog implies a theory about the role (or use) of "dog" in such a way that an elucidation of that role (or use) implies nothing about the concept of a dog. Indeed, one may hold, as Ryle once did (in "Systematically Misleading Expressions"),[3] that a correct reading of the correct uses of words renders concepts and theories of them otiose.

A theory of concepts implies a theory of language; but a theory of language includes much more than I intend to deal with. All I wish to concentrate on is one part of a theory of language, the functioning of those words that logicians have traditionally called "general terms." About these, at least two important questions arise: What do we do with these terms? and What are the prevailing conditions under which we do it? Indeed, my major concern is with the second and, in particular,

with an assumption that I believe traditional theories of concepts have made and which many modern theories share, in their implicit theories of the functioning of language: that general terms are and must be governed by sets of necessary and sufficient criteria that are determined by the definitive properties discovered in the analysis of the relevant concepts or by the intuited simplicity of those concepts that are found to be unanalyzable, hence indefinable. This assumption is tied to a metaphysical doctrine of essences—according to which doctrine concepts, at least those that are complex, have necessary and sufficient properties or constituents—and to a correlative doctrine that the primary pursuit of philosophy is the formulation of the real definitions of these essences. It is these essences that secure the corresponding sets of certain general terms. Concepts, thus, are either complex or simple. Complex concepts are closed in the sense that they have essences: sets of definitive properties, constituents, or criteria. However, whether they are simple or complex, our intuition, apprehension, analysis, or even elucidation of these concepts, so this theory implies, yields the thesis that all our general terms are governed by sets of definitive criteria derived from our knowledge of their corresponding concepts.

In the platonic tradition, including Plato and Aristotle, Russell and Moore, this thesis about the logic of general terms becomes a necessary overall condition for the intelligibility of discourse. In spite of the fact that many philosophers have repudiated the specific doctrines that there are essences and, consequently, that there are forthcoming real definitions of them, the platonic tradition persists in those who still seek the necessary and sufficient conditions of concepts or the necessary and sufficient criteria of general terms. It is therefore not true that the assumption of the closure of criteria as a necessary condition of the intelligibility of discourse does not remain sacred, even among some distinguished contemporary sacrilegious nominalists. How else are we to interpret the demand for the necessary and sufficient conditions, for example, of synonymy as a basis for nonlogical analytic truth?

It is this assumption about the necessity of the closure of criteria, derived from a theory of concepts, that I wish to center on. Is it true, as many philosophers, from Plato to Russell and Moore, and beyond, to some of the very recent greats, have claimed or implied, and as Frege so beautifully summed it up, that "a concept that is not sharply defined is wrongly termed a concept" (Frege, *Grundgesetze der Arithmetik*, § 56)? If it is true that our concepts are and must be sharply defined, then, as I have argued, it follows from this doctrine that the definition of the concept must govern the set of definitive criteria of the corresponding general term in order for it to be employed correctly.

But is it a necessary condition of our correct use of general terms that they are governed by these sets of necessary and sufficient—definitive—criteria? Here, I think, we come to the heart of conceptualization as it involves language. I shall try to show in the ensuing chapters that at least some of our general terms do not, in some cases cannot, and in many cases need not depend on sets of definitive criteria for their intelligibility or correct use. Therefore, the traditional assumption of a closed, definitive set of criteria as a necessary condition of correct discourse, together with the theory of concepts from which this assumption follows, is false. Not all concepts are closed. Some are open in the precise sense that their corresponding general terms or words perform their roles under open sets of criteria rather than closed or definitive sets. Thus, some concepts or their conveying words, implied by their concepts but not implying them, rest on necessary but on no sufficient conditions or criteria; others, on disjunctive sets of nonnecessary, nonsufficient conditions or criteria; still others, on no necessary, no sufficient, yet some undebatable, or no necessary, no sufficient, and no unrejectable, or no necessary but some sufficient conditions or criteria.

That some of our general terms are not and need not be governed by closed sets of necessary and sufficient criteria, therefore, that not all concepts are and must be closed if discourse is to be intelligible, is, it seems to me, of the greatest importance. First, because the discovery of open concepts—not just ambiguous, vague, or woolly words, which open concepts and their conveying words are not—throws new light on the whole problem of conceptualization. Concepts are present in thinking, talking, perceiving, communicating, and perhaps even in sensing and feeling. That some of these concepts are open, not closed, invites us to look afresh at the roles these concepts play in these activities. To conceptualize, to have concepts, to be able to use language correctly—each of these, as well as thinking, talking, perceiving, and communicating, may be much less rigid and precise than traditional philosophy has supposed. That conceptualization includes rather than excludes that which is not sharply defined as a condition of some intelligible discourse enlarges our understanding of the actual functioning of conceptualization. The recognition of open concepts forces us to see the varieties of conceptualization and in that way provides a truer account of it than the traditional one.

Perhaps I can make this general reason for the importance of open concepts clearer by turning to a second reason for their importance. Concepts are involved in all intellectual disciplines, including the sciences and the humanities. Each of the sciences revolves around its central concepts, including that of science itself. Here, concept formation and conceptual change have been recent topics for discussion and debate. But the logical character of, and the differences among, the various concepts of the sciences and of science itself have not yet had the scrutiny they deserve. The assumptions that these concepts are homogeneous, at least in their conventional stipulative or contextually defined character, and that their intelligibility of use requires sets of definitive criteria, remain unchallenged so far as I can judge, in spite of the seeming and seemingly endless disputes about scientific concepts. Precision continues as the semantical goal of the reconstruction and, latterly, of the description of scientific concepts in the demand for closed concepts: that is, concepts governed by sets of definitive criteria.

Is it true that all the concepts in the sciences and the concept of science are logically homogeneous, closed? Are they, must they be, governed by necessary and sufficient criteria to perform their assigned roles? Surely, here is one extremely important area of investigation for philosophy, and especially for philosophy of science, as the elucidation of concepts.

The humanistic disciplines, which include history and certainly border on the social sciences, contain many concepts of crucial practical as well as theoretical importance. Karl Popper has argued that these disciplines, especially history, politics, and sociology, suffer from an obsession with essences and real definitions, an obsession that the natural sciences exorcised long ago and that must be cured if there is to be progress in the social sciences. Methodological nominalism, with its relegation of all definitions to conventional stipulation, must replace methodological essentialism and its futile search for real definitions.

As powerful as Popper's attack against essentialism is, he has missed another, and I think more basic, methodological feature of the social sciences and the humanistic disciplines: that these disciplines are still beholden to the ideal of closed concepts, of concepts whose criteria are precise and complete. It seems to me that the social sciences and the humanities are suffering, not from essentialism, but from this putative model of the natural sciences and mathematics. The assumption prevails in the social sciences and the humanities that their central concepts must be defined by clearly formulated sets of necessary and sufficient criteria if these disciplines are to achieve the respectability they attribute to the natural sciences and mathematics.

It is this assumption—which *is* an obsession—that respectable disciplines rest on closed concepts, along with the entailed search for real definitions and theories, that the discovery and exploration of open concepts dispel. Why must sociology define "society"; politics, "the state"; anthropology, "man"; literary criticism, "poetry" or "tragedy" in order to talk about these things? If it is the case, as I believe it is, that these concepts, as well as the concepts of democracy, religion, or education, like those of morality or art or those of game or contract, are each governed by open sets of criteria, where these sets cannot be rendered definitive without foreclosing on the use of the concept, then this logical feature of openness must be accommodated in any adequate elucidation of conceptualization. To reject open concepts as genuine concepts or to castigate them as ambiguous or vague is not to describe their roles but is instead to promote a theory of concepts that makes our actual use of language unintelligible. The humanities and the social sciences, perhaps even the natural sciences, must, if they are to do justice to their own concepts, no longer excuse or apologize for the varieties and even the vagaries of the conceptual life but must instead come to celebrate them; for without the variety and the vagaries, they are no more.

Two questions remain before we can explore open concepts: Are concepts basic in philosophy? and Are theories of concepts basic in individual philosophies? That concepts are basic in philosophy follows from the fact that, though one can philosophize without talking about, say, morality, beauty, or even reality, one cannot philosophize without concepts and language even if one ends up by mistakenly holding that there are no

concepts or that they are reducible to something else or, as some
have done, by saying that language is ultimately self-defeating.
Thus, whatever else it includes, philosophy is conceptualization
in language. One can philosophize about anything: the existent
or the nonexistent, the ought-to-be or the ought-not-to-be, or
even concepts (as entities or dispositions). Concepts and theories
of them, even when one philosophizes about concepts, are
embodied in the language employed to philosophize and, in
particular, in the functioning of the general terms. It is in this
employment of general terms that one finds the implicit theory
of concepts: of their nature, their role, and the logic of the
conditions for that role. Explicit theories of concepts, like
explicit theories of morality, beauty, or reality, must also be
tested by comparing or contrasting them with the implicit
theories of concepts inevitably present in the language of

philosophizing. An explicit theory of concepts, thus, may be one
aspect of a philosopher's philosophy; but an implicit theory of
concepts must be the central part of a philosopher's philosophizing. For unless doing philosophy is the same as immersing
oneself in the Sea of Ineffability, it must conceptualize by using
language to philosophize at all.

That doing philosophy is conceptualizing in language can also
be seen in the traditional as well as modern questions typical of
philosophy. From Thales to today, and tomorrow too, philosophers ask of the thing x or the word "x": What is the nature of x?
What is the true theory of x? What is the correct (real) definition
of x? What is the correct analysis of x? What is the essence of x?
What are the necessary and sufficient properties of x? What is
the meaning of "x"? What are the necessary and sufficient
criteria of "x"? What is the best contextual definition of "x"?
What is the (nominal) definition of "x"? and, latterly, What is
the correct elucidation of "x"?

However one assesses or ranks these questions or eliminates or
reduces some of them to others or to one, the fact remains that
these questions cannot be asked, nor can any answers be offered,
with only "x" or x or both. For each of these questions and each
of the answers proposed, though not necessarily about an x as a
concept, necessarily involves the concept of x; we cannot even
reduce these questions to What is the role of "x"? without having
the concept of a role. Thus, in its activity, its doctrines, and its
questions, philosophy without concepts is impossible. With
words and things, including words as items in the world, the
philosopher may be able to speak, but he cannot ask his
questions, think (conceptualize), or speak out his answers unless
he employs concepts in the language he uses to talk about the

things he talks about. His concepts, conveyed by his words,
employed to theorize about things, are as basic as they are
indispensable.

A theory of concepts is not the doctrine that there are
concepts, a doctrine that affirms no things but rather denies that
concept talk is reducible to word talk or thing talk. A theory of
concepts is a statement about the nature and role of concepts.
This statement may be explicit; in any case, it must be implicit in
the language of philosophy. An individual philosopher's theory
of concepts is what he says or implies they are or what they do in
what he says or implies about the things he discusses in his
philosophy. What renders his theory of concepts basic in his
philosophy—his specific set of doctrines about knowledge,
reality, truth, morality, or his specific set of techniques for
dissolving traditional philosophical doctrines—is the logic of the
set of properties or criteria that he invests in the concepts he
employs as these are conveyed by the words he uses to make his
doctrinal pronouncements or to demolish those put forth by
others. The assumption or affirmation that all concepts are and
must be closed may not determine his particular ontological,
epistemological, moral, or even skeptical doctrines; the history
of philosophy shows that the univocity of closed concepts is
compatible with a multiplicity of divergent metaphysical, moral,
theological, or epistemological views. What this assumption or
affirmation does is much deeper: it determines that *the* definitive
answer is forthcoming to whatever question, however he formulates it—about essences, meanings, or necessary and sufficient conditions—the individual philosopher has raised in his
philosophy where the criteria of this answer correspond to and
are guaranteed by the definitive criteria of the postulated closed
concept. Indeed, the theory that all concepts are and must be
closed is itself the putatively definitive answer to the putatively
definitive question What is a (closed) concept?

That some concepts may be and are open can also be said to
be a theory of concepts (or part of one). But this theory is not a
definitive statement about the definitive nature and role of
concepts. Rather, it is a statement about the nondefinitive nature
and role of concepts: that concepts need not be entities or
dispositions, that they need not all play the same role, and, most
important, that some concepts may be and are governed by
less-than-definitive sets of criteria.

And this theory of concepts, that some of them are open, is
also basic in the philosophers who subscribe to it—in their sets
of techniques for demolishing traditional philosophy or in their
sets of nontraditional doctrines about the different roles of

24 fundamental concepts—in that it too determines the logic of the questions and answers of philosophy: that it need not be closed, that looking and seeing may disclose certain concepts and their conveying terms that do their respective jobs and can continue to do so only on the condition that they are not, need not be, perhaps in some cases cannot be, governed by definitive sets of properties, conditions, or criteria.

The doctrine that all concepts are and must be closed and the doctrine that some concepts may be and are open are both theories of concepts; and both are basic to two entirely different ways of doing philosophy, to two different conceptions of philosophy. They do not differ in their fundamental role in philosophy. They differ in their different conceptions of theory, which conceptions themselves reflect their different conceptions of what it is to be a concept.

Concepts have been construed as universals, definitions, innate ideas, images, thoughts, conceptions, meanings, predicates and relations, abstract objects, abstracted items, extracted common features, neutral entities, and as habits, skills, or mental capacities. Many philosophers have distinguished radically between concepts and language or between the having of concepts and the ability to wield certain expressions. Some philosophers have identified concepts with uses of language. Others, more recently, reduce talk of concepts to talk about language. Still others reject concepts altogether, regarding them as misleading or misguided projections of certain uses of language or of words by themselves.

Open Concepts

The concept of concept is a family of concepts. Rather than argue for the paternity or the orphanage of one or another of its various usages, I shall begin with the question that I believe Wittgenstein asked, What does any theory of concepts imply about our use of language? For although it is a matter of great and seemingly interminable debate whether concepts are of one ontological sort rather than another and whether philosophical theories of concepts can be transformed into theories about something else, such as words or uses of words or human and animal skills or habits, it is not disputable, I have tried to show, that every theory of concepts implies a corresponding theory about our employment of language and, in particular, about that use which has to do with the terms that convey the concepts.

I start with the major tradition that concepts are entities, the view held in one form or another by philosophers from Aristotle (or, as some view it, from Plato) to Russell and Moore. This doctrine comprises both an ontological thesis that concepts are either simple or complex, where the latter consist of necessary and sufficient—definitive—properties, and a corollary linguistic thesis that the words that name these complex concepts can be correctly employed only if these words are governed by necessary and sufficient—definitive—criteria.

Now, in inquiring whether there are open concepts, all I need ask is whether it is true, as traditional philosophy and its entity theories of concepts imply, that all of our general words or general terms are and must be governed by definitive sets of criteria, and are closed in that crucial sense.

An important theme in recent philosophy is the rejection of the traditional doctrine that all concepts are and must be governed by sets of necessary and sufficient criteria which correspond to the definitive properties of the things named by the concepts. Both the doctrine and its rejection take many

forms. Popper distinguishes methodological essentialism from methodological nominalism; Waismann contrasts closed-texture and open-texture concepts; Wittgenstein distinguishes between concepts buttressed by common properties and those that rest on family resemblances; Gallie compares uncontested and contested concepts with essentially contested concepts; Hart differentiates defeasible from definable concepts; and Sibley contrasts conditioned-governed with nonconditioned-governed concepts.

These recent rejections of the classical doctrine of closed concepts—the doctrine implicit in all the entity, as well as in some of the dispositional, theories of concepts—in both its ontological and linguistic forms, and the accompanying exploration of open concepts, raise many issues—indeed, in my opinion, fundamental issues about the nature of philosophy itself. It is therefore eminently worthwhile to try to arrive at a correct account of the expanding doctrine that at least some of our concepts are not, need not, and perhaps cannot be governed by definitive sets of criteria and are consequently open rather than closed, as the tradition has assumed. To attempt this account is the burden of the present chapter.

Sir Karl Popper launches the contemporary attack on closed concepts in *The Poverty of Historicism* (published in 1945, but first delivered in 1936), chapter 1, section 10, and in *The Open Society and Its Enemies* (1945), volume 1, chapter 3, section 6, and volume 2, chapter 11, section 2. His main target is methodological essentialism; however, because this doctrine implies that universal terms are governed by sets of definitive criteria which correspond to sets of definitive properties, Popper assaults also the claim that all concepts are closed.

Popper distinguishes first between universal terms, such as "whiteness," and singular terms or individual concepts, such as "Alexander the Great," which are proper names. He then defines metaphysical nominalism as the view that there are only individuals and therefore that universal terms are mere labels for particular sets of individuals. This view he contrasts with metaphysical essentialism, which he interprets as the doctrine that these sets of individuals are sets only because of certain intrinsic properties shared by the individuals of the set and that universal terms are therefore the proper names of and denote these properties or essences.

Methodological essentialism, according to Popper, is rooted in historicism. This is the theory, as Popper construes it, that certain social and political terms, such as "society" or "government," must denote unchanging essences if one is to explain change. Historicism leads to metaphysical essentialism, which Popper attributes to Plato and Aristotle as its founders. Metaphysical essentialism is the doctrine that true knowledge or science (*epistēmē*) is the penetration of the essences of things. What is the nature of *x*? is its fundamental question of scientific inquiry. The true definition or the real meaning of "*x*," and thereby of the nature of *x*, constitutes the correct, ultimate, and final answer to its fundamental question. Knowledge proceeds by intellectual intuition of these essences, whose definitions then yield all demonstrative knowledge, the whole of which adds up to an encyclopedia of intuitive definitions of all essences: of their names, together with their defining formulas.

Open Concepts

Methodological nominalism, Popper claims, has been the basic tenet of modern natural science since Galileo. According to it, knowledge is opinion (*doxa*), not *epistēmē*, which is restricted to mathematics. Rather than search for real definitions of essences, it attempts descriptions of the behavior of things and their explanations by means of general laws or regularities. Fundamental is the question how things behave, not what they really are; and putative answers to the question of how things behave are not final, definitive statements of the essences of things but are at best conjectures submitted for refutation.

Methodological essentialism, Popper argues, is totally untenable. Not only is it barren and opposed to the whole spirit and development of modern science, but it is also implausible in itself. Its assumption of the need for and the possibility of real definition, established by intellectual intuition, rests on an erroneous conception of the role of definition itself. Definitions are stipulations, pure and simple. They introduce labels as shorthand terms for longer descriptive phrases about the behavior or properties of things; consequently, they are to be read not from left to right but from right to left, from *definiens* to *definiendum*, where the latter denotes no essence and the former is no proper name of an essence. In short, in science, definition does not answer What is *x*? or What does "*x*" mean? but only How shall we most conveniently abbreviate "*x*"?

Popper's distinctions raise many questions, not least about the historical accuracy of his account of the attributed methodological essentialism of Plato and Aristotle. But, these aside, and given the account as it stands, it is clear, I think, that Popper rejects both the ontological and linguistic theses about concepts, namely, that there are essences and, consequently, that our universal terms are or must be governed by criteria which correspond to these essences. Thus he rejects the traditional doctrine that all concepts are closed: they neither denote necessary and sufficient properties nor are they employed in accordance with necessary and sufficient criteria.

But does he also affirm open concepts? Does he explore the vast range of conflicting criteria for many of our universal terms? It seems to me he does not. However rich his assault on real definitions may be, his inquiries into the vagaries of conceptualization are as barren as the tradition he attacks. His own version of methodological nominalism reduces language and its many uses and criteria of use to mere stipulation, which reduction betrays a contempt for how criteria relate to our concepts. Popper's contention that words are mere instruments, to be defined as we like, serves more as his own impatient stipulation than it does as a painstaking attempt to get clear about the meanings of words: what we do with words and how we do it.

It is C. L. Stevenson, not Popper, who first suggests the possibility of open concepts. Stevenson's "Persuasive Definitions" (1938)[1] is, I think, the first—indeed the most radical—treatment of open concepts in contemporary philosophy. That it is has been completely overlooked, mainly because of Stevenson's emphasis in this paper, as well as in later ones, on persuasive definitions rather than on the logical character of the criteria of the terms that makes the persuasive definitions possible.

Persuasive definitions for Stevenson are one aspect of the general correlation between words and interests. Many words have both a conceptual and an emotive meaning. When a change in the meaning of a word is a cause, not an effect, of a change in interest, and when the change characterizes the conceptual meaning of a word that has a rich, strong emotive meaning, we can speak of a persuasive definition: "A 'persuasive' definition is one which gives a new conceptual meaning to a familiar word without substantially changing its emotive meaning, and which is used with the conscious or unconscious purpose of changing, by this means, the direction of people's interests."[2]

"Persuasive definition," then, as Stevenson introduces it, is a technical term for one kind of definition, to be sharply distinguished from other kinds that classify or simply change our interests, or change the emotive meaning of a word without altering its conceptual meaning. His whole emphasis is on the alteration of the conceptual meaning while the strong laudatory or pejorative emotive meaning remains unaltered.

Stevenson stresses the importance of persuasive definitions both in the history of philosophy, especially ethics, and in philosophical understanding of many nonphilosophical concepts. Their traditional and perennial role has been overlooked or perverted into definition as abbreviation or as analysis of concepts. They are therefore crucial not only to any theory of concepts but also to any adequate conception of disagreement, especially in morals, for they help to explain the distinction between disagreements in belief, which are resolvable by empirical methods, and disagreements in interest, which are not.

Stevenson offers many examples of persuasive definitions: of "real," "true," "poet," "justice," "God." None is more illuminating than his example of the concept and definition of "culture." Consider, he says, a hypothetical community in which "culture" has only a conceptual meaning: "cultured" ("c") means widely read (x) and acquainted with the arts (y). Suppose, further, that eventually these two qualities become so highly valued and acquire so strong an emotive meaning that a person who possesses these qualities is now actually characterized as a man of culture rather than as widely read and acquainted with the arts. "C" now has the same conceptual meaning as "x and y"; but since it has more emotive meaning than "x and y," "c" becomes conceptually vague.

This vagueness can be elucidated by considering a member (B) of the hypothetical community who, let us say, becomes suspicious of the prevailing conceptual criteria of "c." B is enamored of imaginative sensitivity (z). He argues that "x and y" are not criteria of "c" unless x and y lead to z; indeed, he argues that x and y are neither necessary nor sufficient properties of z. Then, by stressing the wooden, mechanical character of x and y, B also rejects "x and y" as necessary or sufficient criteria of "c." "The real meaning of 'culture,' the true meaning of 'culture'," he says, "is *imaginative sensitivity.*" "*C*" is therefore vague in the sense that, whatever its prevailing criteria may be, "*c*" must allow for additional criteria (e.g., "*z*"), or for their emendation (e.g., "*x* or *y* if it leads to *z*"), or for their rejection altogether. "*C*" defined as "*x* and *y*," as "*x* and *y* leading to *z*," or as "*z*" alone are all persuasive definitions of "*c*," provided "*c*" does not alter its emotive meaning.

One may question, as indeed many have questioned, Stevenson's distinction between conceptual and emotive meaning, or his understanding of the correlation between terms and interests, or his reading of traditional definitions in philosophy as persuasive. However, even if Stevenson is inadequate or in error on these issues, they are surely minor blemishes on what is a masterly preliminary drawing of the conceptual life. For what Stevenson primarily illuminates is not one aspect of the correlation of terms and interests but certain neglected features of the relation between terms and their criteria.

Consider again the term "cultured." In insisting on the vagueness of this term, Stevenson in effect distinguishes among three kinds of vagueness. Its prevailing criteria are vague in two different senses. "Imaginative sensitivity" is obscure and unclear in a way that "widely read" and "acquainted with the arts" are not. But the latter two are still vague in the sense that they provide no precise cutoff point or boundary in their application. Individual criteria—"*x*," "*y*," "*z*"—therefore can be vague in meaning or in application.

There is a third kind of vagueness in this example, which Stevenson suggests but does not develop and which is, I think, basic to persuasive definitions as stressed criteria within the set of criteria. This is the vagueness of the inadequacy or incompleteness of the *set* of criteria. "Cultured" is vague in its extant or professed *set* of criteria, but this vagueness differs from the vagueness of the individual criteria. Here vagueness contrasts with completeness, not with clarity or precision.[3]

"*C*" is not only vague; it is open as well. "*C*" has certain criteria of use: "*x*," "*y*" and "*z*." None of these, Stevenson allows, is necessary or sufficient for the correct employment or persuasive definition of "*c*." Fundamental disagreement about what "*c*" means, what *c* is, or whether a particular *a* is *c*—what Stevenson calls "disagreement in interest"—rests on the possibility of the intelligible addition, emendation, or rejection of any of the prevailing criteria of "*c*." "*C*" is open, then, in the sense that it has no definitive set of criteria and, more important, no unchallengeable necessary criterion as well.

That some concepts are open—that, though concepts are governed by criteria, none of these criteria is necessary or sufficient and each is intelligibly rejectable—is Stevenson's greatest discovery. Overshadowed by his powerful theory of persuasive definitions, couched in an intolerable theory of meaning, and unexploited in his later writings, his insight into the perennial debatability of the criteria of certain concepts is the first, and remains the most radical, thesis about conceptualization in contemporary philosophy.

Friedrich Waismann's "Verifiability" (1945)[4] is the acknowledged classic in the contemporary development of open concepts. Waismann introduces his doctrine of open texture (*Porosität*) in order to refute what he takes to be the basic assumption of phenomenalism, namely, that the subjects and predicates of empirical propositions are completely definable. But his net is much wider, for he employs this doctrine to encompass the whole of empirical knowledge in contradistinction to the closed, completely definable character of mathematics and logic.

Terms, Waismann says, may be open or closed; precise or vague; systematically ambiguous or univocal. Most empirical terms are open. (But he gives no example of one that is closed.) All mathematical and logical terms are closed. Some empirical terms, e.g., "gold," are precise; some, e.g., "heap," are vague, since they fluctuate in their use. Some, e.g., "real," are systematically ambiguous in that, though they comprise a family of uses, they are employed on different levels, with different shades of meaning.

Waismann concentrates on open-texture terms or concepts. They are open in the precise sense that no definitive sets of rules or criteria can be laid down for their use. The reason they cannot be is that the use of these concepts must allow for and accommodate the ever present possibility of the new and unforeseen. This possibility is thus a necessary condition for the openness of a term.

Implicit, then, in Waismann's doctrine of open texture is his theory of definition.

A term is defined when the sort of situation is described in which it is to be used. Suppose for the moment that we were able to describe situations completely without omitting anything (as in chess), then we could produce an exhaustive list of all the circumstances in which the term is to be used so that nothing is left to doubt; in other words we could construct a *complete definition*, i.e. a thought model which anticipates and settles once for all every possible question of usage.[5]

Although Waismann in repudiating phenomenalism rejects the verifiability theory of the meaning of empirical statements, his doctrine of open texture, as the above quotation makes clear, is based on a verifiability theory of the meaning of the criteria for empirical terms: to provide a criterion for a particular empirical term, he implies, is to describe a situation in which it is to be used.

Waismann's identification of the meaning with the application of criteria allows him to transform the question Can we state the definitive criteria of any empirical term? into the question Can we describe all the situations in which a term is to be used so that nothing is left to doubt? It is in this context of essentially incompletable descriptions that his doctrine and examples of open-texture concepts become intelligible.

In spite of the importance he attaches to open texture, his examples are few and disappointingly unconvincing. First, "There is a cat next door." We can, Waismann agrees with common sense, go look at the cat; we can touch it, feel its fur, induce it to purr, etc. But suppose it grows enormously, or suppose it dies and is subsequently revived. Do our present rules governing the use of "cat" allow us to say definitively that the creature is an extraordinary cat rather than, perhaps, a new species of animal?

Second, I say: "There is my friend." I approach him and he disappears; I step away and he suddenly reappears. Is my friend or his disappearance a delusion? Again, do we have complete rules for distinguishing the real from the delusory?

Third, I meet someone who looks like and talks like a man but is only one foot tall or is so old that he remembers meeting King Darius. Is our concept of man so fixed that we would unhesitatingly call this being a man, or would we not?

Fourth, if we turn from concepts of natural kinds to scientific ones, these too, Waismann claims, have no exhaustive definitions. Take "gold," for example. It certainly seems to be completely defined by the spectrum of gold, with its characteristic lines. But imagine a newly discovered substance which satisfies all the prevailing tests of gold yet emits a new sort of radiation. Would not this unforeseen situation force us to modify our definition so as to accommodate it by our present concept of gold?

From these examples Waismann argues that neither scientific nor other empirical concepts can be so completely defined as to block all doubts about their application. Although his examples are dubious, since they project fantastic situations, so that we are simply at a loss to know what to say rather than puzzled by

the applicability of prevailing criteria, they nevertheless suggest
that Waismann means by an open-texture concept one that is
perennially flexible. That is, it is a concept whose use, hence
criteria, must be applicable to new situations, with their new
properties, and not necessarily to the fantastic. Given open-
texture concepts, we cannot consider as definitive the prevailing
criteria of most empirical terms because these criteria can be
legitimately augmented to meet a new case with its new property.

Waismann also says: "Definitions of open terms are *always*
corrigible and emendable."[6] Does this mean that no criterion of
open-texture terms is necessary? For Waismann it does: no
criterion of most empirical terms is such that without it we
cannot apply the term. Cats, for example, *can* be six feet long,
nonfurry, and resurrectable.

That a concept is open therefore entails, on Waismann's view,
that none of its criteria is unchallengeable; i.e., every reason for
something's being a cat is rejectable. If I say, "X is a cat because
it is furry," the open texture of "cat" allows someone else to
question not only the necessity of "furry," or the presence of real
fur, but also the relevance of furriness as a criterion of "cat,"
since "cat" is corrigible and emendable. An open concept is,
then, for Waismann, both perennially flexible and perennially
debatable. It must accommodate new criteria which can call for
rejection of the old. Thus, perennial flexibility entails perennial
debatability.

This, it seems to me, is Waismann's central thesis about open
concepts. It is also the most vulnerable. That there are perennially flexible and perennially debatable concepts is an undeniable fact about the logical features of certain concepts. Neither
kind of concept, however, entails the other. Some concepts,
e.g., "tragedy," are both; some, e.g., "drama," are perennially
flexible but not perennially debatable; some, e.g., "ancient
Greek tragedy," are perennially debatable but hardly perennially flexible.[7] In any case, Waismann's implicit claim that the
applicability of a term to a new situation with its new property
entails the corrigibility and emendability, hence rejectability, of
any of the criteria of the term is too wholesale a thesis about
open concepts.

Indeed, Waismann's entire treatment of open concepts is too
wholesale. That the distinction between empirical and formal
knowledge rests on the difference between open and closed
texture; that there are no logical differences among open concepts or even among closed; that open texture is the possibility
of vagueness (rather than, as it must be for Waismann, that

34 vagueness is a species of open texture, since, on his view, his example, "heap," is subject to the same essential incompleteness of definition as an open term)—all these exaggerated claims are suspect.

The basic difference between an open and a closed concept is the absence or presence of sets of necessary and sufficient criteria. The investigation of the logical grammar of certain concepts may reveal concepts with no necessary, no sufficient, and no disjunctive set of sufficient criteria; or concepts with a necessary criterion but no necessary and sufficient set of criteria; or concepts with no definitive set as well as no undebatable necessary criteria. All of these concepts may be said to be open in the sense of having no definitive set of criteria. Yet their differences are as important as their similarity in the functioning and the understanding of concepts. Furthermore, careful eluci-

dation of closed concepts may reveal the same diversity: that, though certain concepts—empirical, scientific, mathematical— function under definitive sets of criteria, these sets differ logically in that, for example, some of them are mere stipulations whereas others serve as putative real definitions of the shared necessary and sufficient properties of all the members of certain classes. Philosophers have scarcely begun to inquire into the logical differences among concepts; and wholesale division into open versus closed concepts can only lead to distortion of the varieties and vagaries of the conceptual life. This criticism, however, in no way detracts from Waismann's greatest con- tribution to our topic: the discovery of perennially flexible concepts and their role in empirical knowledge.

The next important essay in the development of open concepts is H. L. A. Hart's "The Ascription of Responsibility and Rights" (1949).[8] Under attack is the traditional interpretation of a whole group of ordinary and legal concepts that converge on the concept of human action. Distinguishing radically between the meaning or function of certain sentences and their conditions of use, Hart argues that sentences containing these concepts are not employed primarily to describe and that the criteria of these concepts do not constitute a definitive or closed set of necessary and sufficient conditions. The primary use of these sentences— exemplified in judicial decisions or verdicts; recognitions, claims, admissions, and transfers of rights; and admissions or accusations of responsibility, especially in the past tense—is ascriptive. The fundamental feature of the set of criteria or conditions of use of the concepts contained in these ascriptions is its defeasibility.

Of central concern in our present survey of open concepts is Hart's notion of defeasibility. Certain concepts of law, rights, responsibility, and human action, Hart maintains, are defeasible in the sense that, although they have necessary conditions, they have no sufficient conditions because, for every putative sufficient condition or set, there is an indefinite list of mitigating or defeating circumstances, any one of which could rule out the application of the concept.

Thus, for example, the concept of contract is defeasible. It has certain necessary conditions, such as the presence of at least two parties and an offer to one and acceptance by the other. These, however, cannot be said to constitute a sufficient condition, since they could obtain under certain situations of duress, undue influence, fraudulent misrepresentation, and the like, which would nullify the contract. These negating situations or defenses cannot be interpreted as evidence of the absence of the further necessary condition of "true, free, and full consent" because there is no such condition. Indeed, the phrase itself is but a convenient way to refer to the defenses; rather than evidence of the absence of a necessary condition, the defenses are criteria for "no true consent." "Contract," consequently, cannot be defined by necessary and sufficient criteria. All that can be specified for the concept are its necessary criteria plus a list of defenses. "X is a contract if it satisfies the necessary conditions a, b and c, unless there are defenses x, y, and z . . . ."

Defeasible concepts, then, as Hart characterizes them, are open, but they are so only in the minimal sense of having no definitive sets of criteria. They have necessary criteria which cannot be challenged as necessary, even though their presence or absence in a particular situation is disputed. All they lack are sufficient criteria. This lack, however, is enough to rule them out as closed concepts.

That there are defeasible concepts, especially in the law, Hart certainly establishes. That they encompass the concept of human action—which is the major thesis of Hart's essay—he does not show; nor does he now think that he did. In this early paper, Hart contrasts his view of human action as defeasible with traditional views that attempt to state the necessary and sufficient conditions of human action. Whether Hart is right about the defeasible versus the definable character of the concept of human action is not as important as his query itself: What sort of concept is the concept of human action? Is it closed, hence amenable to definition in terms of necessary and sufficient criteria? Or is it open? It need not be defeasible just because it is not definable. Perhaps (as I shall argue in due course) it is open in the more fundamental sense that it has no necessary criterion. In any case, it remains Hart's greatest contribution in this early essay to have raised this latter possibility in his rejection of the concept of human action as closed.

Ludwig Wittgenstein's *Philosophical Investigations* (published in 1953; Part 1, which includes most of the relevant materials on open concepts, was completed in 1945) has become the most important and influential work on open concepts in contemporary philosophy. Anticipated by the *Blue Book* (dictated in 1933–34) and the *Brown Book* (dictated in 1934–35), the *Investigations* contains the most devastating critique of the traditional doctrine of closed concepts—a doctrine that permeates Wittgenstein's *Tractatus Logico-Philosophicus* (1921)—in philosophical literature.

Chapter Two

Thought is surrounded by a halo.—Its essence, logic, presents an order, in fact the a priori order of the world: that is, the order of *possibilities*, which must be common to both world and thought. But this order, it seems, must be *utterly simple.* It is *prior* to all experience, must run through all experience; no empirical cloudiness or uncertainty can be allowed to affect it——It must rather be of the purest crystal. But this crystal does not appear as an abstraction; but as something concrete, indeed, as the most concrete, as it were the *hardest* thing there is (*Tractatus Logico-Philosophicus*, no. 5.5563).

We are under the illusion that what is peculiar, profound, essential, in our investigation, resides in its trying to grasp the incomparable essence of language. That is, the order existing between the concepts of proposition, word, proof, truth, experience, and so on. This order is a *super*-order between—so to speak—*super*-concepts. Whereas, of course, if the words "language," "experience," "world," have a use, it must be as humble a one as that of the words "table," "lamp," "door."[9]

It is this illusion that philosophy is the attempt to grasp the essence of language that Wittgenstein dispels in his famous treatment of "games" and "family resemblances," by now the *locus classicus* of open concepts.

Wittgenstein has been talking about and considering the implications of a number of language-games. He then raises a crucial objection: I talk about language-games without saying what their essence is—what they have in common by virtue of which they are language-games or parts of language. Is not this the easy way out?

We need Wittgenstein's exact reply: "And this is true.——

Instead of producing something common to all that we call language, I am saying that these phenomena have no one thing in common which makes us use the same word for all,—but that they are *related* to one another in many different ways. And it is because of this relationship, or these relationships, that we call them all 'language.'"[10]

Wittgenstein's question and answer, it appears, are not ontological. For he neither asks whether there is an essence of language-games nor denies that there is. His question, rather, is one of logical grammar: whether the assumption is true that there must be an essence of language-games in order to be able to use the word "language-game" correctly. His answer is that it is not true; instead, our correct use of the word is founded on relationships, i.e., family resemblances. So, in effect, he is asking whether, and denying that it is, a necessary condition of our correct, intelligible use of "language-game" that there is or must be a corresponding essence. We need not assume that the criteria for this word correspond to a set of necessary and sufficient properties which is shared by all language-games in order to explain what makes us use the same word for them.

Wittgenstein rejects the linguistic thesis of concepts—that their conveying terms are or must be governed by necessary and sufficient criteria. His commitment to logical grammar precludes his rejection of the ontological thesis that concepts are or must be essences consisting of necessary and sufficient properties. However, because the ontological thesis entails the linguistic, his denial of the latter entails the denial of the former. To deny that "language-game" is or must be governed by necessary and sufficient criteria is to deny an implication of the doctrine that language-games have or must have a set of necessary and sufficient properties and, by *modus tollendo tollens*, to deny the doctrine itself.

What, now, are the criteria or conditions of the correct use of "language-game," according to Wittgenstein? Shifting from "language-game" to "game," Wittgenstein begins by reminding us of our ordinary, everyday use of the term to describe and to classify certain activities: ball games, such as football and baseball; board games, such as chess and checkers; card games, such as poker and solitaire; and track and field games, subsumed under, say, Olympic Games.

These are all paradigms of games. Yet they have nothing in common (no essence) by virtue of which they are called "games" or which makes us use the same word for all. At most they have certain features, such as amusement, winning and losing, competition, skill, luck, rules, etc.; but none of these is necessary or sufficient. Instead these features constitute a family. It is this family—family resemblances—not some essence, that furnishes the criteria of "game." "Game," therefore, can be said to be governed by a disjunctive set of criteria that corresponds to a disjunctive set of properties, where no one of these criteria or properties is necessary or sufficient. The concept of game, then, is open, not closed, for Wittgenstein in the precise sense that it functions under a disjunctive set of criteria which corresponds to a certain family of resemblances, but these criteria are neither necessary nor sufficient.

It is these criteria that make us use the same word for all games, that enable us to explain what a game is, and to justify our claim that we know what a game is without having to provide a definition of "game." The questions, *What* is a game? *Is x* a game? and *Why* is *x* a game? require game-giving reasons,

but these reasons fall back on undisputed examples and family resemblances, not on a disjunctive set of properties shared by all members of the class of games.

"Game," as open in Wittgenstein's sense, is a perennially flexible concept in that its established historical use must accommodate any new example, with its new property. The set of nonnecessary, nonsufficient criteria allows us to extend these criteria to cover a new case, $x + 1$. We decide to call $x + 1$ a "game" because it is sufficiently similar to the accepted examples to allow its dissimilarity to become a new criterion of "game." "$X + 1$ is a game" expresses a decision to enlarge our criteria of "game"; it does not express an inference from a true definition of "game."

Is "game" also perennially debatable? Not for Wittgenstein. None of the criteria—"amusement," "skill," "competition," etc.—is open to challenge or rejection. These criteria furnish good reasons for something's being a game even though they are not necessary or sufficient. "X is a game because it involves competition" hardly invites the query: "But what has competition to do with it?"

In the *Investigations* all the open concepts are perennially flexible ones. The main assault is on the traditional doctrine that they are or must be closed. But how extensive is Wittgenstein's use of open concepts? The openness of "game" serves as a model for "language-game," hence of "language" itself. Is "language" open as Wittgenstein elucidates it? To be sure, he offers no set of definitive criteria; and he interprets it as marking out a family of cases, with their family resemblances. But does he also deny, as he does with "game," that the concept of language has some necessary conditions? Can there be a language without terms that serve to identify items in the world and that serve to reidentify these items—in short, can there be a language without rules? Wittgenstein's powerful arguments against the possibility of a language that only one person could understand—what some call a "private language"—strongly suggest that "rules" is a necessary criterion of "language" in a way that it is not of "game" and that, at least for Wittgenstein, "language" is consequently not open, as "game" is. "Language" is open only in the sense that it has no set of necessary and sufficient criteria, although it has and must have some necessary ones.

Similar difficulties engulf one as one tries to locate other central concepts of the *Investigations* on Wittgenstein's logical map: pain, seeing, understanding, imaging, intending, willing, remembering, and hoping, to mention some of them. Are all of these concepts open? Are all of them modeled on "game"? Are all of them perennially flexible? Does any of them have necessary criteria, or are all of them governed by expandable sets of nonnecessary, nonsufficient criteria? There is an entire unwritten book here on the range of open concepts in the *Investigations*, scarcely begun, yet in my opinion absolutely crucial to the understanding of that work, especially of Wittgenstein's central concern with logical grammar. Yet this much, I think, is clear and indisputable: that Wittgenstein offers no wholesale view about the logic of concepts. Not even his elucidation of "game" and his demolition of the traditional essence doctrine are to serve as a model for all games. For what may be true about the concept of game may not be true about the concept of a particular kind of game. "Major-league baseball," for example, unlike "game," though fluid and flexible enough in its history, can perform its assigned role under the overall condition that it is governed by a set of definitive criteria so fixed as to ensure that no unresolvable doubts and disputes can arise. So, too, with understanding. It is certainly a family of cases, with varying sets of properties. But one kind of understanding, namely, the understanding of a mathematical formula—as Wittgenstein is at great pains to point out—is necessarily a capacity to go on. Here, "being able to apply the mathematical formula" is a necessary criterion of the concept of understanding the formula. So, in this case, the logic of the genus "understanding" differs from the logic of the species "understanding a mathematical formula."

Much of the *Investigations* revolves around the rejection of one purportedly necessary criterion for the correct use of mental concepts, namely, the criterion of an inner, private mental state. Wittgenstein does not so much deny that these states exist as he denies their status as a criterion for our mental concepts. His behaviorism is a logical behaviorism about the role and necessarily outward criteria of mental concepts, not a psychological behaviorism about mental states. His logical behaviorism denies *in toto* one kind of concept, the concept whose necessary and sufficient criteria are privately mental; it denies as well one kind of necessary criterion, the criterion of a private state. But it does not affirm only one kind of open concept, the one which is governed by disjunctive sets of nonnecessary, nonsufficient criteria. As I have tried to show, other kinds are recognized, especially those with some necessary, albeit no definitive, criteria and those that allow for new members of the set. What his logical behaviorism does not affirm but certainly allows for—as it must—are the perennially debatable concepts. It is this omission that confers on the *Investigations* a surprising moderation about the conceptual life, which contrasts sharply with the more radical views of Stevenson in "Persuasive Definitions" and of others who demand a special place for concepts with no unchallengeable criteria.

W. B. Gallie's "Essentially Contested Concepts" (1956)[11] is the first essay entirely devoted to our topic. There are certain uses of certain concepts—best revealed in argument and disagreement, which may remain ultimately unresolvable—that can be explained only by the presence of an essentially contested concept. Such a concept is one whose proper use inevitably involves endless disputes about its proper use on the part of its users. Concepts of this sort are institutional ones that relate to certain highly valued activities, such as art, politics, religion, and morals. Disputes about why or whether x is a work of art, y is a democracy, or z is a Christian life, or what art, democracy, or a Christian life really is, revolve around essentially contested concepts.

Gallie lays down seven necessary conditions of an essentially contested concept which together constitute a set of necessary and sufficient—defining—criteria for such a concept. (1) It must appraise some valued achievement. (2) This achievement must be internally complex, although its worth is attributed to it as a whole. (3) This achievement must initially be variously describable; i.e., its parts or features can be ranked in different orders of importance. (4) This achievement must allow for future modifications which cannot be prescribed or predicted in advance; Gallie calls this feature the "open" character of an essentially contested concept. Condition 3 gives rise to ambiguity, whereas condition 4 engenders persistent vagueness, i.e., "a proper use of it [an essentially contested concept] by P_1 in a situation S_1 affords no sure guide to anyone else as to P_1's next, and perhaps equally proper, use of it in some future situation S_2."[12] (5) The concept must have both an aggressive and a defensive use; i.e., the contending users of the concept recognize that there is a contest and appreciate the different and competing criteria of the concept involved in the dispute. (6) The concept must be derived from an original exemplar, agreed upon by the disputants. (7) Each side of the dispute claims that its use of the concept will best ensure the retention or development of the exemplar's achievement.

Conditions 1–5, Gallie says, are the formally defining conditions of essentially contested concepts. However, without conditions 6 and 7, he adds, these conditions would not guarantee the distinction between radically confused and essentially contested concepts.

It should be clear at once that Gallie confines what I have called "open concepts" and what he calls "essentially contested concepts" to a small group of terms which are employed to praise. Why, on his own criteria, essentially contested concepts do not include certain corresponding pejorative terms, such as "a piece of trash," "a fascist state" (uttered by a liberal), "an evil life," or even "the losers" (to contrast with his model artificial example, "the champions") is obscure.

But, more important, it is difficult to see why Gallie excludes from essentially contested concepts those whose primary use is to describe or to classify. Wittgenstein's "game" seems to satisfy all of Gallie's conditions, revised so as to exclude condition 1, that it must appraise. "Game" is employed to denote an activity that is internally complex yet unified; games are variously describable in terms of rules, skills, competition, fun, goals, etc.; games admit of indefinite modifications that cannot be set down in advance; contending uses of "game" are aggressive and defensive; the concept of game has a history replete with continuing exemplars or paradigms that may figure in any dispute about a contending proper use of "game"; and finally, rival uses, including putative definitions of "game," purport to enhance the tradition of games. The history of the claim and counterclaim— for example, "War is a game," in which neither "war" nor "game" has been used primarily to appraise—illustrates as well as any example the workings of essentially contested concepts.

Gallie's argument that essentially contested concepts must be appraisive—that condition 1 is necessary—rests on his assertion that, without condition 1, preference of one use over another is inexplicable:

Given conditions 2 and 3, we have the sort of situation where a multi-dimensional description or classification of certain facts is possible. But in any such situation ... it would be absurd to prefer one style of possible description or classification to the others. But substitute achievements for facts i.e., an appraisive concept or classification for a purely naturalistic one, and the absurdity disappears, since for the purpose of moral or aesthetic persuasion one style of description or classification may very definitely be preferable to another which is *logically* equipollent with it. Here is a strong reason for thinking that condition 1 is necessary.[13]

However, if, say, A defines "game" in terms of "*a*," "*b*," and "*c*," and B does so in terms of "*a*," "*b*," and "*d*," A's preference of his use of "game" over B's can be explained without resorting to "game" as an appraisive concept. A may simply believe that his criteria of "game" name the defining properties of games whereas B's do not. A's preference—like, indeed, any choice regarding a particular use of an essentially contested concept employed to describe or to classify rather than to evaluate—may be founded on, hence explained by, a metaphysical theory about the nature of games. "Game," therefore, need not be appraisive in order to explain the preference of one use of it over another.

There are many concepts like "game" that satisfy Gallie's conditions 2–7, revised so as to substitute "activity" for "achievement," whose functioning exhibits essential contestedness in spite of the fact that they are not primarily appraisive. For example, "drama" and "novel," in contrast to "tragedy" and "art," have primarily descriptive-classificatory roles. Yet they denote complex, unified wholes; they are ambiguous and open; they are used aggressively and defensively; and they derive from exemplars which serve to sustain and enrich a continuing tradition. I see no reason to refuse these as essentially contested concepts, unless they are legislated out by stipulating condition 1.

Thus, what is essential in Gallie's essentially contested concepts (i.e., conditions 2–7) is a concept whose criteria of application must be expandable so that new cases can be accommodated as continuing examples within a tradition and whose criteria of application must be vague so that competing interpretations of them can be admitted in order to cover the present cases. His whole notion of an essentially contested concept, in short, is simply one kind of openness, that of perennial flexibility. An essentially contested concept is one whose criteria of use must be flexible, hence nondefinitive, in order to be applicable to new cases, with their new properties, or to extant cases with possible new interpretations of their present properties. His insistence on appraisiveness (condition 1) seems an arbitrary addendum to an essentially sound claim about one kind of open concept. What remains in doubt about Gallie's account is whether his sense of "openness"—condition 4—allows for the perennially debatable as well as the perennially flexible.

F. Sibley's "Aesthetic Concepts" (1959)[14] can serve as the final essay and, in its central thesis, as the culmination of our brief survey of the development of open concepts. For Sibley's major claim is that there is a whole group of important concepts that are not governed by conditions at all. It is this logical feature that distinguishes them from closed concepts as well as from Hart's defeasible or Wittgenstein's family concepts. The concepts of this group may be regarded as open, as we have been using the term—though Sibley does not so characterize them—in the sense that, although they ultimately depend on certain conditions or features of the world, the presence of these conditions or features, either singly, disjunctively, or conjunctively, does not logically justify or warrant the application of these concepts. Even so, without conditions that govern their use, these concepts, Sibley adds, have as their primary use the describing of certain objective features of the world; and they are therefore legitimately classifiable as descriptive.

Sibley restricts this whole group of nonconditioned-governed descriptive concepts to the aesthetic, examples of which abound in critical discourse about works of art and in parallel ordinary talk about everyday life. They include adjectives, such as "balanced," "delicate," or "tragic," as well as expressions like "telling contrast" or "sets up a tension." Indeed, they comprise *all* the terms we use in talking about works of art which are not indisputably descriptive, like "red" or "rectangular," or clearly evaluative, like "mediocre" or "great."

No particular aesthetic term has any one condition or set of conditions that determines its use. For example, no amount of true talk about the pale pink color, thin shape, slim line, etc., of a particular vase guarantees its delicacy, even though the vase is delicate. Nevertheless, Sibley insists, a necessary condition for the correct use of any aesthetic term is the exercise of taste. Without taste but with normal eyesight, we can apply nonaesthetic terms, such as "red" or "rectangular," even to works of art. But with normal eyesight and no taste, we cannot apply aesthetic terms, such as "delicate," "balanced," or "tragic." The difference between the aesthetic and the nonaesthetic is marked by the exercise of taste as against its absence.

44 What, now, does Sibley mean by "taste"? It is "an ability to *notice* or *see* or *tell* that things have certain qualities."[15] But once we ask what is to count as having taste—what its criteria are—taste becomes identical with the ability to use certain aesthetic words. There is a circle here: "aesthetic term" is defined in terms of "taste," and "taste" is defined in terms of "aesthetic term."

Let me put this difficulty aside, however, and return to Sibley's central thesis about aesthetic concepts as descriptive and nonconditioned-governed. Whatever our view may be about taste and its relation to the aesthetic, it is certainly true that there is a large group of terms we use in talking about works of art which seem to differ radically in their logical grammar from purely descriptive terms, like "red" or "rectangular," and purely evaluative terms, like "mediocre" or "great."

Chapter Two Is Sibley correct in putting these terms—which he calls the "aesthetic"—into one logical bag? Are all of them employed to describe features of works of art? Are all of them governed by no conditions whatever?

If it is sheer dogmatism, as Sibley contends it is, to hold that none of these terms denotes properties of works of art, it is equally dogmatic to insist that all of them do. Too much blood has been drawn in the age-old debate about expressive properties, or what aestheticians nowadays call regional qualities of works of art, to allow for any wholesale transfusion. If we turn from the expressive properties of works of art to their corresponding locutions, as we must and as Sibley does, we find that utterances containing "aesthetic" expressions, as Sibley classifies them, are, logically, a mixed bag, not a homogeneous one at all. Some of the terms, such as "eerie" or "symmetrical," veer toward the descriptive in their use. Some, such as "trite" or "garish," tend toward the evaluative. Some, maybe even most, of these aesthetic, expressive, regional terms function as interpretive in a straightforwardly explanatory sense. "Cézanne's *Mt. Sainte-Victoire* is monumental" need not describe a quality, either simple or complex, of that painting; the utterance can also serve, as it certainly does in art criticism, as an interpretive hypothesis about what is central in this landscape, that is, what best explains the particular color, drawing, texture, design, composition, representation, etc., of this particular rendition of the mountain. Finally, some of these terms function as interpretive, albeit in an invitational or, to use Stevenson's phrase, "quasi-imperative" way. "*Hamlet* is profound but *King Lear* is profoundly moving"—hardly a descriptive or explanatory remark—is perhaps best heard as an invitation to respond to these

two dramas as expressing primarily the difference between the
intellectual and the emotional understanding of the world. In
any case, it seems more than slightly absurd to couple this
remark with another, also often made: "Neither *Hamlet* nor
King Lear is a unified drama."

Supposing now that Sibley's "aesthetic" is a mixed bag, is his
central thesis about aesthetic terms and expressions—that they
are not governed by any conditions—correct? Sibley distinguishes between conditions and negative conditions and between
features that count for, rather than against, the application of
aesthetic terms. He does not then go on to deny that some
features do count for the application of aesthetic terms. What he
denies is that these features can ever function as logically
justifying or warranting conditions for the application of an
aesthetic term. And this is to affirm that, although there are
criteria for the use of an aesthetic term, these criteria are never Open
Concepts
sufficient: the correct application of the criteria neither entails
the correct application of the term nor precludes the intelligible
withholding of the term.

Formulated in this way, Sibley's aesthetic terms behave logically like Wittgenstein's "pain." It, too, is a term for which there
are criteria of its correct use but no criterion or set of criteria the
satisfying of which in any particular instance logically justifies
or warrants the application of "pain." Furthermore, like "X is
delicate," "X is in pain" can be true and known to be true. And
there are no entailment conditions for the application of either
"delicate" or "pain." Thus, in criteria, truth value, and conditions, "pain" is exactly like Sibley's "delicate" or any other
aesthetic term. It follows that if Wittgenstein is right about
"pain," Sibley is wrong in thinking that nonconditioned-
governed concepts are coextensive with the aesthetic.

Finally, are all aesthetic terms nonconditioned-governed? If
they are logically homogeneous, with "delicate" as a paradigm,
Sibley's affirmative case remains intact. If they are heterogeneous, as I have suggested, some—for example, "eerie,"
"symmetrical," or "violent"—because they are employed in
criticism of art with the same sets of criteria as they are in talk
about everyday objects, may be as condition-governed as they
are in everyday life. But most aesthetic terms, it must be
conceded, are not governed by sets of sufficient conditions. This
observation, unfortunately, comes as no surprise, since many, if
not most, empirical terms have no entailment conditions. Rather
than mark the distinction between the aesthetic and the nonaesthetic, then, Sibley has merely showed that many terms are
open in the sense that they have no sufficient, or sets of

sufficient, criteria. The logical vagaries among these terms—for example, that "tragic" and "delicate," though nonconditioned-governed, differ radically, in that the criteria of the tragic are all open to perennial challenge, whereas the criteria of the delicate are not—Sibley leaves uncharted.

Other contemporary philosophers have clarified and employed open concepts. At least two should be mentioned. Stuart Hampshire, in *Thought and Action* (1959), argues that moral and mental concepts, ultimately reducible to the concept of man and the distinctively human, are essentially disputable. And Renford Bambrough, in "Aristotle on Justice: A Paradigm of Philosophy" (1965),[16] makes the extraordinary claim that all philosophical concepts, including meaning, reason, truth, verification, and proof, are open, in Wittgenstein's sense of family resemblances. He traces this view to Aristotle's implicit doctrine of analogical predication, which he then exemplifies paradigmatically in Aristotle's discussion of justice. Hampshire's "essentially disputable concepts" is a variant of Waismann's open-texture concepts, and Bambrough's "analogical" concepts are an extension of Wittgenstein's family-resemblance concepts. Since both Waismann and Wittgenstein have been discussed, there is no further need to detail the particular version of open concepts offered by Hampshire and Bambrough.

In this chapter I have tried to present an account of the recent development of open concepts. Two final observations on their history are in order. One I have already made: that the first essay on open concepts, Stevenson's "Persuasive Definitions" (1938), remains the most radical, particularly in its implicit doctrines of the perennial debatability and irreducible vagueness of certain concepts.

Second, and even more surprising, is that open concepts play a minor role or no role at all in the work of certain major contemporary philosophers, such as Ryle, Austin, and Strawson, who are not only acknowledged innovators in recent philosophy but, significantly, dedicated practitioners of logical grammar as well. Indeed, along with Wittgenstein, Waismann, and Wisdom, they constitute the recognized leaders of the so-called "revolution in philosophy."

Basic in this revolution is the shift of philosophical concern from ontology and linguistic reconstruction to logical grammar or elucidation of concepts. This shift involves both the rejection of the traditional doctrine that all concepts must be closed and

the exploration of the possibilities for open concepts. In my
opinion, this double (yet related) theme is as important as any in
the development of logical grammar or, for that matter, in
recent philosophy itself. All of the above-mentioned philosophers, along with those others detailed in this chapter, share in
the demolition of the traditional doctrine that all concepts must
be closed. Even so, their attack, at least in the case of Ryle and
Strawson, seems to center on the rejection of putatively necessary criteria for certain concepts rather than on the openness of
these concepts. Austin is a special case: he certainly enjoyed
fielding other philosophers' criteria and theories; but it remains
unclear whether his major concern was with families of concepts
with no common criteria or with families where careful specifi-
cation of their various members could provide defining criteria
for the members.

At any rate, Ryle's *Concept of Mind* is a perfect illustration of
the restricted use of logical grammar. It is of course true that
Ryle in that book converts the philosophy of mind into the
logical mapping of mental concepts, so that the philosophy of
mind is no longer an ontological analysis of the nature of mind
or an ideal reconstruction of the language of psychology (as, for
example, it had been to Russell in *The Analysis of Mind*). This is
revolutionary enough. But instead of exploring the possible
openness of mental concepts, Ryle mainly assaults one kind of
thesis about the closed character of mental concepts, namely,
that a necessary criterion for the correct use of any mental
concept is an inner, uniquely private event or state. He rejects
Cartesianism as one view about mental concepts as closed. But
he does not even hint at the viable possibility of the perennial
flexibility or perennial debatability of at least some mental
concepts. Compared with Wittgenstein's doctrine that most
mental concepts are perennially flexible, or with the intelligible
possibility that some (for example, human action) may be
perennially debatable, Ryle's logical behaviorism, striking as it
is, is still fairly conservative; indeed, it is dangerously close to
Cartesianism in their shared assumption that mental concepts do
have definitive sets of criteria for their correct use—that, as Ryle
once said, these concepts are "hard-edged." On this interpretation, Ryle disagrees with Descartes not so much on the central
issue of the closed character of mental concepts as on one of their
purportedly necessary criteria—the innately private.

If this reading of Ryle is correct, it suggests a further division
in recent philosophy than the acknowledged one between analysis and elucidation, namely, a division between a philosophy

48 that merely rejects closed concepts or certain sorts of closed concepts and a philosophy that takes elucidation all the way in order to explore vast, as yet uncharted, regions of open concepts.

Aesthetics and logic have not been friends. Instead, their relation **Art** historically has been one of indifference, mutual suspicion or contempt, and at times even open warfare. Such hostility is a pity, since logic has as much to learn from aesthetics as aesthetics has from logic. Many, perhaps the most fundamental, problems of aesthetics are conceptual, not empirical; and some of the concepts of aesthetics are especially relevant to logic in its indigenous quest for the limits and scope of valid argument. Thus, if logic requires of aesthetics, as it does of all forms of discourse, adherence to rigorous standards of acceptable inference, aesthetics at least invites logic to consider, if not ultimately to accommodate, certain irreducibly open concepts that do not simply dissolve into the traditional notions of ambiguity and vagueness.

That logic and aesthetics do have much to say to each other I shall illustrate by turning once again to the concept of art. Because I have already argued for the conceptual rather than factual character of the central question of traditional aesthetics, What is art? and for the openness of that concept in "The Role of Theory in Aesthetics" (1956)[1]—an essay that is easily accessible—I shall not reproduce the argument here. Rather, I shall summarize it and shall then state and examine certain major objections to it, including my own. My aim, however, is to strengthen, not repudiate, the open character of the concept of art. The fundamental thesis of that essay remains intact: that all theories of art—past, present, and future—fail and are doomed to fail in their putative real definitions of art because they misconceive the concept of art.

The search for a theory of art, I claimed, has been and remains the preoccupation of aesthetics or the philosophy of the arts.

Theory has been variously construed in the history of aesthetics as real definition of the nature of art or as a statement about the essence, necessary and sufficient properties, or common denominator of art. Every theory of art or of a particular art, such as poetry or tragedy, from Plato and Aristotle to modern aesthetic theories of the fine arts, either states or converges on a statement of the nature of art: what it is and how it differs from what is not art. Without a theory, intelligible talk and thought about art are impossible; thus, a theory of art is a necessary condition for the cogency of criticism and appreciation of the arts. If we generalize to all of the arts Clive Bell's remark about visual art, we have a succinct summative statement of the overriding importance of a theory of art: "For either all works of visual art have some common quality, or when we speak of 'works of art' we gibber" (*Art*, p. 7).

Is there a true theory of art? Can there be such a theory? Need there be such a theory in order to render talk and thought about the arts intelligible? The history of aesthetics or, since this history is recent, the history of philosophy of the arts is in large part a history of successive competing affirmative answers to these three questions. And it was the main burden of my essay to reject these answers, not by offering different affirmative ones, but by giving negative replies to these three questions.

That there is no extant true theory of art is supported by the disagreements among the theories themselves. Each theory purports to enumerate the defining properties of art and to succeed in this endeavor as its competing theories do not. Yet we are as far from unanimity on a true theory as ever we have been. More important, though, is the range and assortment of deficiencies regarding the defining terms which are expressed in the disagreements, for there is not in the entire history of aesthetics a putatively true statement about the nature of art that has not been castigated by its opponents as incomplete, too inclusive, circular, founded on dubious features or principles, vague, or untestable.

These objections to traditional theories, each made by one theorist or another in his efforts to secure a new true theory of art, though they cast serious doubt on an affirmative answer to the question, Is there a true theory of art? do not, so I argued, go far enough, since they allow that further research and probing into the complexities of art can remedy the flaws of extant theories. For them, the difficulties remain factual.

The problem, however, is not factual. It is conceptual. There is no true theory of art, not because no one has yet produced it, but because such a theory forecloses on the concept of art. A theory of art—a true statement of its necessary and sufficient properties, its essence, its nature, its common denominator—is not simply difficult to formulate; it is logically impossible because it states the definitive criteria of a concept whose very use depends upon there being no such set. There is no true theory of art, then, because there cannot be one. The concept of art, as its use reveals, is open; a theory of art presupposes or entails the false claim that the concept of art is closed, governed by necessary and sufficient criteria, corresponding to the definitive properties of art, which criteria can be formulated into a definition of "art" that can then legislate correct talk about art. That the concept of art is open, that it functions under less than definitive conditions, and, consequently, that art can no more be defined in terms of a set of definitive properties than "art" can be defined in terms of a set of definitive criteria: this was the central thesis of my essay.

What is art? entails What is the concept of art? which in turn yields What is the role of "art" in discourse about the arts? Traditional aesthetic theory, I said, gave the wrong answer to What does "art" do? and What are the conditions under which it does it? What, then, did I offer as the right answer? That "art" and its subconcepts, such as "novel," "drama," "music," "tragedy," "painting," and so forth, are employed either to describe or to evaluate certain objects and that, though this description or evaluation is dependent on certain criteria, these criteria are neither necessary nor sufficient. All, therefore, are open in the sense that they perform their descriptive and appraisive jobs on the overall condition that new cases with their new properties can be accommodated by the addition of new criteria for these terms. The history of the arts is in part the history of the creation of new objects with their new properties. The history of the concept of art reflects this origination of the new, which, until it occurs, is unpredictable and unforeseeable, yet must be accommodated by the concept of art. In effect, then, I identified the openness of the concept of art with its open texture, as indeed I assimilated all the subconcepts of art, such as tragedy, to Waismann's notion of open texture. Neither "art" nor any of its subterms, "tragedy," "drama," "music," "painting," etc., could be defined, since their criteria had to allow for the possibility of new ones that render definitive sets of them violations of the concepts they convey.

This wholesale reading of open concepts in aesthetics as open-texture concepts was a mistake. Not that it is a mistake that there are open concepts in aesthetics; the mistake was rather in conflating the open with the open-texture concepts. Some aesthetic concepts are open in the sense that they must allow for the unforeseeably new. But some are also and more radically open in the sense that they must allow for the possibility of the rejection of any of the prevailing criteria as well. Thus, "tragedy," for example, differs from "drama" and even "art" in that it has no unchallengeable criterion; whereas the other two, though also without necessary or sufficient criteria, have some unrejectable criteria, such as "has a plot" or "is made by human skill."

My blunder in not distinguishing in this early essay between the perennially flexible and the perennially debatable—indeed, in assuming that they entail each other—led to another bad mistake, this time about certain concepts that I said were closed, among them "ancient Greek tragedy." This concept is closed, I argued, because the prefix sets boundaries to the concept of tragedy; and within the boundaries and with all the cases in, we

could state the necessary and sufficient properties of all the extant ancient Greek tragedies. Having identified open with open texture, "ancient Greek tragedy" (equated with its extant examples) could hardly be perennially flexible; so I concluded that it is closed. The mistake was in not realizing that "ancient Greek tragedy," though closed in its cases, each of which is indisputable as a Greek tragedy, is nevertheless as open as "tragedy" because each of the reasons given for any of its indisputable examples' being tragic is challengeable and rejectable. That "ancient Greek tragedy" is open in the sense of perennially debatable, as open as "tragedy," can be seen when we shift from the question, absurd as it is, Is *Oedipus Rex* tragic? to the question, intelligible and as alive as it was to Aristotle, Why is *Oedipus Rex* tragic? Even a cursory survey of the reasons that have been given and of the range of disagreement over these reasons points to nothing short of the perennial debatability of the concept of tragedy.

I was wrong about "tragedy" as only a perennially flexible concept. It is that; but it is also a perennially debatable one. But I still think that the concept of art is open in Waismann's sense of open texture: perennially flexible. In my essay, in characterizing the logic of the sets of conditions under which "art" is employed to describe or to evaluate, I said that there are these conditions— which I referred to as "criteria of recognition" and "criteria of evaluation"—but that they do not add up to a definitive set: there are no necessary or sufficient conditions or criteria for the correct use of "art" to describe or to evaluate works of art. "This is a work of art" can be joined with "and it was made by no one," "and it is not an artifact," "and it was created by accident," or with a denial of any statement about a putatively necessary property of a work of art, without misuse of the concept of art, and occasionally to make a true statement about art.

Do we need a theory of art? If there cannot be such a theory and there is not such a theory—whether we deduce the latter from the former or generalize it from the failures of past theories to formulate true definitions of art—then we have no definitive properties to fall back on as we buttress our talk about art. If we require a theory of art to talk about art and there is no such theory, then we cannot talk about art. But we do talk about art. We describe objects as works of art, and we praise certain features of works of art. We also interpret and explain works of art. Is it a necessary condition of our doing these things that we possess a true theory or that we must assume that such a theory is forthcoming? Here—this time with the help of Wittgenstein's talk about games—I argued that we do not need a theory, nor do we have to assume that there is such a theory, in order to talk and argue intelligently about art. My negative answer to this third question of traditional aesthetics—Do we need a theory of art?—was not, however, a negative answer to the ontological question Does art have an essence? Rather, it was a negative answer to the conceptual question Must we assume that art has an essence in order to be able to talk about it? Consequently, to substitute family resemblances for essences or, in the case of art, indisputable examples of works of art and their strands of nonnecessary, nonsufficient properties for sets of definitive properties was to substitute one overall condition of intelligible discourse for another; it was not to supplant one ontological view by an anti-ontological one. Thus, a negative answer to Do we need a theory of art in order to talk cogently about art? is absolutely independent of a negative (or, for that matter, an affirmative) answer to the question Is there a true theory of art? Even if, then, there were a true theory of art or there could be one, it would still not follow that it was required—that this theory is a necessary condition—for being able to say all that we want to say or that needs saying about the arts.

Not all of my observations on classical theories of art were negative. Despite their logically vain attempts to define the indefinable, to state the necessary and sufficient properties of art and, by implication, the definitive criteria of "art," or to construe the openness of the concept of art as closed, I suggested at the end of my essay that each of these classical theories and of those to come could be read as a series of invaluable pedagogic directions for attending to art. I did not intend my suggestion to be a correct reading of classical misreadings of the concept of art; it was instead a recommendation to salvage the illuminating criteria proffered by the theories by converting them from necessary and sufficient into honorific criteria for a stipulated or legislated use of "art."

As everyone knows, it is notoriously difficult and treacherous for an author to expound his early work. I hope my summary of "The Role of Theory in Aesthetics" belies this observation. I think my central thesis was that art is an open concept: that it performs its main jobs of describing and evaluating certain objects under conditions less than definitive and, in particular, under sets of conditions, none of which is necessary or sufficient, but some of which are not rejectable, and others of which must accommodate the unforeseeably new works that are demanded by the development of art. The concept of art and some of its subconcepts, like the novel and drama, music and painting, sculpture and architecture, are open in the precise sense of "perennially flexible." This thesis, especially if it is divorced from the wholly incorrect thesis that perennial flexibility entails perennial debatability, which I built into my essay, remains firm and, if true as well, a contribution to the elucidation of the concept of art and, through that concept, to the elucidation of the major issues of aesthetics.

But is it true that the concept of art is open? The confidence I retain in my affirmative answer is clearly not shared by all. Indeed, if one can judge from the vehemence of the objections that have appeared since the publication of that essay (and expansions of it in *Hamlet and the Philosophy of Literary Criticism*), the openness of the concept of art and of its subconcepts, along with the consequent denial of the possibility of a theory of art or of some of its subconcepts, has been accepted by very few! Perhaps the authors of these objections are right. At any rate, the issues they raise are eminently worth examining, since they embrace the overriding theme of the nature and role of concepts in aesthetics and related humanistic disciplines.

I begin with Maurice Mandelbaum's criticism of my thesis of the openness of the concept of art in his important paper "Family Resemblances and Generalization Concerning the Arts" (1965).[2] Mandelbaum does not affirm a theory of art. Instead he argues against certain contemporary rejections, including mine, of the possibility of a theory of art.

Is it a mistake to offer generalizations concerning the arts? Mandelbaum identifies this question with the entirely different question, Is it a mistake to discuss what art essentially is?— which he regards as only "a more provocative" form of the first question. But surely these questions are different, as their answers show. How, for example, could anyone challenge the making of some generalizations about the arts? There must be literally thousands of these, such as "The arts are enjoyable" or "The arts are more accessible today than they were a hundred years ago." Some of these generalizations are more interesting than others, some are more true than false, some less trivial than others.

So it is not generalizations about the arts that are suspect but only certain kinds of generalizations—those about the essence of art: what all works of art share, by virtue of which they are works of art and without which they would not be works of art. And the mistake that Mandelbaum says opponents of essential-istic generalizations attribute to such generalizations cannot be simply in the "attempt to discuss what art . . . *essentially* is"; it must be in statements about the essence of art, in formulations of the necessary and sufficient properties of art. But why are these statements a mistake? Not because art has no such definitive sets of properties, but because the statements that it does entail that the concept of art and the word "art" in any language are governed by definitive criteria that correspond to the definitive properties where the concept and its conveying words are not so governed. The mistake, when it is a mistake, committed by essen-tialistic generalizations about the arts, is the mistake of imply-ing that there are definitive criteria for a concept when there are no such criteria. It is therefore a mistake about the concept, not the nature, of art.

I emphasize this distinction between ontological and concep-tual affirmation and its truth or falsity (mistake) because it is precisely this distinction that Mandelbaum, I think, conflates in arguing that no one has yet showed that it is a mistake to generalize about the arts. In effect, he construes essentialistic generalization as ontological (which it is) and the contemporary attack on it as anti-ontological (which it is not). For him, the opponent of essentialistic generalization argues as follows: Art has no essence, only family resemblances; so it is a mistake to say it has an essence when it does not. It is because he interprets the issue as ontological rather than conceptual that he quite rightly claims that the contemporary attack rests on the truth of the doctrine of family resemblances.

Mandelbaum's next step is not to refute this doctrine but to tighten it up so that it becomes a version of essentialism. He says that family resemblances are manifest similarities that embody unexhibited genetic connections. Wittgenstein's strands of simi-larities cannot, without the genetic ties, explain what he claimed they explained, that is, why we apply or withhold, in all cases, certain common names, such as "game."

What is Wittgenstein's doctrine of family resemblances? It is a doctrine about the criteria of certain terms, names, or concepts. He holds that these criteria comprise a family, not an essence; or, to express it nonmetaphorically, that many terms, words, or concepts are employed correctly to name certain members of certain classes under disjunctive sets of nonnecessary, nonsufficient conditions rather than under sets of necessary and sufficient conditions. The doctrine, then, is one about the logical grammar of certain words or concepts, not about the less-than-essential ontology of things. It is Wittgenstein's answer to Do we need a theory—a true statement about essences—in order to be able to talk about, name, refer to, certain things, such as games? It is not an answer to Is there such a theory? And his answer is

that, if we look and see instead of impose an overall necessary condition for the intelligibility of discourse, we do find, at least in many cases, that many terms are employed correctly without sets of definitive criteria that can be formulated into essentialistic definitions.

Now, according to Mandelbaum, Wittgenstein's doctrine of family resemblances is inadequate. He offers the example of a man who looks as if he were playing solitaire but who, when asked what he is doing, replies that he is reading his fortune. If we go by ostensible resemblances alone, we cannot, Mandelbaum claims, explain why we withhold "game" and apply "fortune-telling." In order to decide whether this case is a case of one rather than the other, we need to know the man's intention; and the man's intention is a nonmanifest feature of the situation that serves as the decisive criterion in our use of "fortune-telling" rather than "game." Likewise, in all games, all activities, a necessary criterion for correct characterization of them is that of intention or purpose, which is not a criterion of a manifest resemblance. It is rather a criterion of a hidden genetic tie that makes the resemblances a family. Indeed, the tie—in this case, a common ancestry—is what makes the resemblances a family in its literal, not metaphorical, sense.

It is not clear whether Mandelbaum is claiming that there are family resemblances, in his sense of genetic connections among manifest similarities, and that this relationship is what Wittgenstein left out of his account, thereby rendering it inadequate, or whether he is contending instead that it is a necessary condition for the cogent use of certain common names that the criteria for this use must include the necessary criterion of a genetic tie or relationship among the disjunctive sets of nonnecessary, nonsufficient criteria. In any case, it seems to me, the first objection is irrelevant, since Wittgenstein neither affirmed nor denied, or needed to affirm or deny, that there are strands of similarities among members of certain classes but no hidden ties or essences. And the second contention is false: it is not a necessary condition for our correct, intelligible, and cogent employment of common names, such as "game," that all the criteria for this employ-ment—for example, "skill," "amusement," "competition," etc.—be linked together by a necessary criterion of some sort of tie or connection among the criteria. What Mandelbaum must demon-strate but does not and, I believe, cannot is that Wittgenstein's doctrine of family resemblances is incoherent without an overall necessary condition that ties together the disjunctive conditions.

That it is not incoherent can be seen even from Mandelbaum's example of the fortune-teller. For in that example it is not the man's hidden intention that decides whether "solitaire" or "for-tune-telling" applies to what he is doing; it is what he says when asked or provoked by another's utterance. And what he says is decisive only if we believe him or have no reason not to. What he says—"I'm telling my fortune"—is one (and here the most crucial) among manifest criteria, none necessary, none suffi-cient, for applying, withholding, or retracting a common name. Moreover, if he won't tell us what he is doing, we may not be able to decide what the correct term to apply is. Or, suppose he does tell us he is telling his fortune: how does he, or do we, decide to apply or to reject "You have been playing solitaire all this time and didn't even know it"?

Contemporary repudiations of traditional aesthetic theory, Mandelbaum contends, rest on Wittgenstein's doctrine of family resemblances. This doctrine, as Wittgenstein formulated it, is inadequate; so the arguments based on it are also inadequate. Art may yet have an essence; art may yet have manifest strands of similarity united by unexhibited relations that embody its essence while at the same time providing the concept of art and the word "art"—like the concept of game and the word "game" —with a set of necessary and sufficient criteria for their correct use. At any rate, no one has yet showed that such a theory is a mistake or that, in particular, it involves a confusion between essence and strands of similarity.

Is Mandelbaum correct in attributing to contemporary attacks on aesthetic theory the wholesale acceptance of Wittgenstein's doctrine of family resemblances as basic? I cannot speak for the other opponents of aesthetic theory, but I can say that he is not at all accurate in his interpretation of my essay, which he singles out as an argument against aesthetic theory that is rooted in

Wittgenstein's inadequate conception of family resemblances. For my argument against theories of art was (and is) that they attempt to state definitive criteria for a concept whose use has depended on and continues to depend, not on its having such a set, but rather on its being able, for its correct use, to accommodate new criteria that are derived, or derivable, from new art forms whose features demand emendation, rejection, or expansion of extant criteria. However, it is not the history and the future of art but what that history and the unforeseeable possibilities of the future reveal about the functioning or role of the concept of art that are fundamental to my thesis that the concept of art is not amenable to definitive criteria and, therefore, that definitions or theories of art are conceptually, not empirically, impossible.

Mandelbaum is thus in error, at least in my opinion, in thinking that my argument against traditional aesthetic theory rests on Wittgenstein's doctrine of family resemblances or even, as he shifts in his analysis of my essay, on the history and continuing development of art. I hope it is now clear that it rests on neither, but only on what it can be based on: the use and conditions of use of the concept of art. Indeed, Wittgenstein's doctrine of family resemblances is wholly irrelevant to two of the questions I asked: Is there a theory of art? and Can there be such a theory? (I am not even sure that Wittgenstein would have tolerated my negative answers to these two questions.) It is relevant only to the question: Do we need a theory of art? My answer, borrowed from Wittgenstein, was (and is): No; we can get along quite nicely in talking about art—in asking and answering What is art?, Is this a work of art?, and Why is this a work of art?—with reasons that relate to disjunctive sets of nonnecessary, nonsufficient criteria and to their corresponding properties in the works of art that have them.

That there is not and cannot be a true theory of art is not a mistake. It is nothing short of a valid inference from the true description of the logical grammar of "art." The mistake consists in confusing this conceptual truth about "art" with a factual claim about art.

Mandelbaum rejects my rejection of essentialist definitions of art, claiming (mistakenly, I have just argued) that it rests on a mistaken—Wittgensteinian—notion of family resemblances. M. H. Abrams, in "What's the Use of Theorizing about the Arts?" (1972),[3] objects instead to my elucidation—he calls it "analysis" —of the nature and role of theory in aesthetics and literary criticism. With an acumen and a suppleness we have come to

expect from the author of that major work on Romantic critical
theory and the philosophy of criticism, *The Mirror and the
Lamp* (1953), he argues persuasively (almost convincingly) that,
according to my analysis, theory in criticism rests on a mistake,
that it "consists solely, or primarily, in the assertion and
attempted proof of an essential definition and thus is an extended logical mistake" (p. 48). He does not seem to disagree
that such definition is in logical error in trying to lay down
definitive criteria for a concept whose use depends on criteria
that are less than definitive sets of them; nor does he disagree
with me that the concepts of both art and literary criticism are
open. In fact, his whole sustained argument that critical theories
are not amenable to essentialist definitions—not even to the
essentialist definition that he (p. 49), with irony, attributes to me
in my disguised persuasive definition of critical theory as solely
or centrally concerned with essentialist definitions—because of
the inexhaustible, unpredictable diversity of categories and
procedures of critical theory, demands the openness of the
concept of criticism, and in a manner that Abrams does not spell
out in his own elucidation of the nature and role of critical
theory.

Like Mandelbaum's, Abrams' essay is fundamentally a coun-
terattack on what both regard as recent assaults on traditional
aesthetic theory that are directed by linguistic philosophy, with
Wittgenstein forced into its service as the master strategist. And,
like Mandelbaum, Abrams denigrates neither the general nor his
arsenal; indeed, both greatly admire the quality and power of
the weapons. Their quarrel is with Wittgenstein's self-appointed
lieutenants, who, at least so far as Abrams is concerned, employ
the master's methods to repress, not to liberate:

> One of Wittgenstein's liberating insights is that the validity of
> language consists in the way it is in fact used to some pur
> pose, rather than in its accordance with logical models of
> how it should be used; and another is his view that meanings
> do not consist in what expressions name and describe but in
> how they are used [p. 12].

Abrams goes on to say that for Wittgenstein there are many
different uses of language and that to discover the actual use of a
particular language-game, such as criticism or critical theorizing,
we must consider its surroundings—the human purposes, interests, and values (what Wittgenstein calls "the form of life") that a
particular language-game "has evolved to realize" (p. 13).

It is this notion of criticism, including theory and its component of essentialist definitions, as a language-game whose
basic terms are to be given meaning in the uses and purposes

they serve that Abrams both borrows from Wittgenstein and employs him to demolish my and similar repressive attacks on the possibility of a critical theory. Before we consider the details of his use of this notion, it may not be amiss to raise some questions about the notion itself. First, however, it is unfortunately important to point out that at this historical juncture it is as futile to debate who really speaks for Wittgenstein among his exegetes as it has become fatuous to use his obiter dicta—did he ever proclaim it as a doctrine?—on family resemblances as a premise for any argument against essentialism. It may be a mark of his genius or, what is just as likely, an effect of his style; but, in any case, the philosophical writings of Wittgenstein have now attained the dubious logical status of works of art, with the result that all kinds of claims about them can be shown to be conclusively false, but no claim about them or even their

separate parts can be shown to be conclusively true. What we are left with is what we have in regard to *Hamlet*: some readings are more adequate than others; most, because they pervert what is said, are conclusively false. Whether Abrams' notion of criticism—that it is a language-game all of its own—is also Wittgenstein's, I do not know. What I am sure of is that this notion of the self-protective character of this or any other language-game that serves human purposes seems to leave no room at all for those uses of language that serve only "the purpose" of going on holiday. One would have thought that Wittgenstein's strictures on this use of language, especially by traditional metaphysics, force us to distinguish between language-games and language-on-holiday and, with particular reference to Abrams, to show that critical theory, or the essentialist definitions in it, are legitimate language-games and not just language idling—to use another of Wittgenstein's metaphors. If Abrams is correct in his understanding of Wittgenstein, then it follows, it seems to me, that neither he nor Wittgenstein can rule out, as I think at least Wittgenstein wished to, certain uses of language, such as traditional ontology, which, though it satisfies a deep human need and purpose, that of metaphysical solace, nevertheless, condensed in its various drops of grammar, is characterized as no language-game at all but only as language idling, on holiday.

The question, then, that we must put to Abrams is whether his notion of criticism, replete with theory and essentialist definition, as a language-game with a life of its own is his or Wittgenstein's. In particular, are the real definitions of traditional aesthetic and critical theory genuine uses of language, or are they instances of language idling, doing no real work?

My contention, which I thought I got from Wittgenstein, was that the questing for and the proffering of essentialist definitions were more examples of what Wittgenstein castigated as language idling. In the case of criticism, the critic who gives reasons for *x* being what it is in a work of art and who therefore genuinely tries to enhance our understanding of the work is not like the critic who tries to support his reasons by further stating or deducing their necessary and sufficient character and who therefore serves no purpose except to satisfy our obsessive craving for generality, our intellectual greed for final system and order.

I am not saying that critical theory as or with real definition is language idling. Rather, what I am saying is that no one can show that it is not that by legislating some enabling act for all uses of language so long as they realize human purposes and needs. That way lies anarchy, not liberation. Wittgenstein liberated us from our bewitchment by language, not from our repressive fears about accommodating all uses of language as language-games—as genuine, not spurious, forms of life.

What, now, is Abrams' elucidation or understanding of critical theory, which he contrasts sharply with the analysis of it that reduces it to real definition—the analysis he ascribes to me? He begins with an admirable *précis* of my relevant essays, including *Hamlet and the Philosophy of Literary Criticism*, and especially with my claim about the distinctive irreducibility of description, interpretation or explanation, evaluation, and poetics or theory in the practice of criticism. Although in the course of his argument he rejects this claim in favor of the view that all critical discourse, including description, on the one hand, and theory, on the other, is inherently evaluatively interpretive, he allows it to stand in order to call into question my subordinate claims (1) that theory or poetics, unlike description, interpretation or explanation, and evaluation, is not a legitimate procedure in criticism and (2) that theory or poetics—definitional answers to What is art? or What is tragedy?—is invaluable for its pedagogical possibilities despite the fact that it is logically misbegotten in its persistent attempt to state the necessary and sufficient criteria of concepts which, like those of art or tragedy, have no such criteria.

Can it be, Abrams asks, that the great theorizers in the history of aesthetics and criticism "have committed the same grammatico-logical blunders in stubborn pursuit of the same logically impossible goal...?" (p. 12). Are their invaluable recommendations, hidden away in their definitions, "an unintended by-product, a spin-off from an inevitably abortive undertaking?"

(p. 12). Abrams will have none of "this paradox of private errors—public benefits" (p. 12). Instead, following the liberating lead of Wittgenstein, he asks: "What, in fact, have critical and aesthetic theorists been up to?" (p. 13).

"Do all theories of art consist solely or primarily of the attempt to posit and prove an essential definition of art, or of a type of art?" (p. 14). Let us for once, he pleads, turn from Clive Bell's example of how not to theorize to one of his critics—and he cites, in particular, the opening paragraph of my *Hamlet* book. Is not even the very first sentence—"Criticism is a form of studied discourse about works of art"—a definition of the classical "X is *a b c*" form? Yet, Abrams immediately adds, it does not function as an essentialist definition (as I make clear later); it functions rather as "a working definition" that serves, "in a preliminary way, to block out the area of his inquiry, and also to introduce some categories that he will use to organize his inquiry into that area" (p. 16). Without this working definition, Abrams comments, I could not, nor could anyone else, specify and limit what I intend to talk about. What, then, could be more useful or less harmful than such a preliminary formal definition?

Why Abrams chooses to read that first sentence as a definition rather than what it is—a description, a generalization without its universalization—I cannot understand. Surely, not all uses of the verb "to be" express definitions; if my first sentence is a definition of "criticism," then, by the same token, that definition is the definition of "first sentence" in "Weitz's first sentence is ..."—which is absurd. And of course Abrams knows it is absurd, since he himself at the end of his essay characterizes criticism not by defining it but by describing it: by a generalization that he quite rightly does not universalize into an essentialist definition. "One way to describe criticism and related modes of inquiry is to say that they are a language-game—or a family of language-games—designed to cope in a rational way with those aspects of the human predicament in which valid knowledge and understanding are essential, but certainty is impossible" (p. 54). This characterization, much more general than mine, is exactly what Abrams says it is, a description; I would no more call it "a working definition" than I would—or than he should—mine.

Abrams next asks if theorists, whether they define art or define it essentially or not, actually use the definition (presumably when they do define art—otherwise, how could they use it?) as I say they do or as I use my definition of criticism. I do not know what to do with this question, partly because I construe my generalization as no more than an adequate description and mostly because I am not sure what it is that I am supposed to say

theorists use definitions for, especially since I am supposed to
hold the view that critical theory is wholly or primarily the
positing and attempted proof of definitions.

But let us turn from this double difficulty to' the more
interesting question of the role of definition in critical theory as
Abrams elucidates that role. Consider, then, Aristotle's *De
Poetica*, the treatise which "made 'poetics' a standard term for
the theory of art" (p. 18). Abrams points out that Aristotle does
not say that he defines "poetry" and does say that he defines
"tragedy"; but Abrams will grant that Aristotle defines both, as
well as "the arts," in Aristotle's sense of "a phrase signifying a
thing's essence" (*Topics* 1.5) and in our sense of a statement of
necessary and sufficient conditions. "Still, what matters is the
actual role that his definition plays in his over-all inquiry, and
this role, it soon becomes evident, is not legislative but exploratory, and in a very enlightening way" (p. 18).

Abrams then shows with admirable detail and clarity that
Aristotle modified the key predicate of his definition of the arts,
that of *mimēsis*, so that it no longer applied to all human activities or things, as Plato's Ideas did, but restricted the term to the
arts. In this way Aristotle set up a new language-game in which
he distinguished between the objects of human experience imitated, the medium of the imitation, and the manner of rendering
the imitation. These differentia of the genus of mimesis enabled
him to focus on tragedy and to define this species as a genre: as
an imitation of an action that is serious and complete, in
appropriate language and in the dramatic manner, along with its
capacity to arouse pity and fear and their catharsis. With these
"total theoretical tools" (p. 20) Aristotle further discriminates
the plot, characters, diction, and thought, their relative importance, and their interrelations. Aristotle then asks how each
of the elements of tragedy can best serve to maximize the
distinctively tragic fear and pity, and he suggests criteria for the
most effective plots, the need for a unified plot, the fall of the
hero from happiness to misery through his *hamartia*, and so on.

Abrams, having so brilliantly and succinctly expounded the
main ideas and the logical flow of them in the *Poetics*—an
exposition I have baldly summarized—offers a number of crucial
observations on them in order to confirm his hypothesis that the
role of definition among the theorists is exploratory, not legislative, working, not idling. The first of these is that the *Poetics*
counts as theory according to the criteria proposed by the critics
of aesthetic theory. That is, none of it is simply applied criticism,
because all of its basic statements are generalizations about
the arts or about a specific art and its particular elements,

organization, and effects, and all of its references to individual works serve only to exemplify or clarify his general statements. Now, if the *Poetics* is all theory—which it must be in the eyes of Aristotle's anti-essentialist detractors—it is simply not true, Abrams claims, that definition plays a major role in it or that most of the theory is an attempt to prove or to support the definition. Most of the *Poetics*—Aristotle's theory of art and of tragedy—"consists instead of putting to work the terms, distinctions, and categories proposed in the initial definition" (p. 21).

Abrams seems here to agree with the contemporary critics of traditional aesthetic theory that the *Poetics* counts as a theory and that it contains essentialist definitions. (The question, vast as it is, remains, whether Aristotle would concur that the *Poetics* counts as a theory in his or our sense, varied as the latter is. All he says is that the *Poetics* is an inquiry.) However, Abrams

disagrees with the very same critics who claim that definitions are either dominant, supported, or proved in the *Poetics*. He does not merely *differ* from them in taking a stand on one among alternative ways of looking at the *Poetics*, all of which alternatives, like the different but not disagreeing critical theories, should be assessed as fertile or sterile, not as true or false. No, the claim that definitions in the *Poetics* are other than working definitions is not simply a different approach, it is false. Critical theories, Abrams says later, differ from one another; they are not true or false, only more fertile than not. But theories of critical theories disagree, compete, and contradict each other, are true, as Abrams' is about definitions in the *Poetics*, or false, as mine and others are about these definitions. This crucial distinction between difference and disagreement, which Abrams recognizes and employs in refuting erroneous theories of critical theories, evaporates in his own theory of the nature, role, and conflicts among critical theories. It is this conflation of difference and disagreement that wrecks his reading of critical theory in criticism and converts what he describes as a description rather than states as a real definition of criticism, and of theory in it, as "families of language-games" (p. 54) from an elucidation of "critical theory" into yet another recommendation to salvage it.

More immediately relevant to Abrams' first observation is whether his theory of Aristotle's theory is correct: Do definitions play a minor role? What, one wonders, would he say about the interpretation of the *Poetics* that I, among others, would offer: that the *Poetics*, for the most part, is the *explication* of Aristotle's definition of tragedy, which includes the formulation of the definition and the clarification, illustration, enlargement upon, and evaluation of some of its constituents? So far as I can see, this reading of Aristotle's theory fits neither of the alternatives considered by Abrams: that the *Poetics* states a definition which it then goes on to prove or to support; or that the *Poetics* explores the different facets of a definition which is itself more working than real. And, anyhow to me, this third alternative reading seems to explain the lack of overt support or proof in Aristotle's text, as well as the presence of the exploratory sections, better than the two that Abrams mentions. Aristotle writes at the beginning of his discussion of tragedy: "We must now treat of tragedy after first gathering up the definition of its nature— τὸν ὅρον τῆς οὐσίας —which results from what we have said already" (1149b). To be sure, this definition, which results from the gathering-up of what has been said, is not quite the universal or the expression that it is in the *Posterior Analytics* (100a15–100b4; 97b8–14), but the notion of the definition as the result of an inductive process, with or without the leap to νοῦς, is the same: a summative true statement about the essence of a class of things, in this case, of tragedies. In effect, then, the real definition, when it comes, as it does in the *Poetics*, is a finished product, garnered from evidence already in hand and in mind. It is a piece of epistēmē— knowledge *that* something is what it is. And without it, explication is impossible, since the definition is an indispensable condition for its intelligibility. Once stated, the definition needs no further proof, support, or tentative groping for unexplored details. So, definition is central in the *Poetics* in at least two ways: it is a necessary condition for its explication; and it is the answer Aristotle seeks in his inquiry.

Abrams, of course, will have none of this. But the question remains: Is this reading of Aristotle's theory incorrect, or is it merely a sterile alternative among fertile ones? If it is sterile, it is not wrong; it is only different from other, fertile readings. If it is incorrect, what objective textual evidence will decide that it is? I remain unconvinced that Aristotle's definition of tragedy is not central, is not, in its claim to be a true statement about the essence of tragedy, a piece of legislation about what tragedy is, what makes a drama tragic, what a drama must have if it is to be tragic and without which it would cease to be tragic.

Abrams' second observation on the *Poetics* as critical theory is that it makes a valid contribution to knowledge, not to knowledge that art has an essence but to knowledge of how to look at works of art. This contribution is not, as Aristotle's anti-essentialist critics concede, an invaluable by-product of a valueless attempt at real definition; rather, he makes us see art differently because he explores its genus, species, and differentia with us. He also teaches us something about art—for example, how it relates to, yet differs from, history or philosophy.

This observation, that Aristotle's pedagogic insights are integral to his definitions of art and tragedy, not merely bits and pieces that can be dissociated from his definitions, rests ultimately, I think, on the assumption that no criterion for a concept that serves as a necessary or sufficient constituent of a real definition can function instead as a criterion for that concept unless it is construed as necessary or sufficient. And this assumption, I believe, is false. Thus, Aristotle's insights and aperçus are not so much spinoffs or by-products of his definitions as they are his criteria—such as *hamartia*, or reversal and discovery, or even the tragic hero as a relatively good man— converted from necessary to nonnecessary but nevertheless criteria of the tragic, some of which we may find illuminating and others of which—for example, that men but not women should be valorous—we may not. This invitation to look behind the definition to the criteria themselves, without assigning necessary and sufficient status, since it is these criteria, not their assigned status, that teach us what to look for and how to respond to works of art, was what I meant (in "The Role of Theory in Aesthetics") by the invaluable contributions of the logically vain attempts at real definitions in aesthetic or critical theory. I did not intend my admonition to destroy the integrity of the theory and its insights but rather to free those insights from their dubious logical status, which they can live without while they enhance our understanding of art. We need reject none of the components of the definition but only their definitive character; we save the baby by getting it out of the water.

Aristotle's theory is not closed, in spite of the fact that he grounded it on the tragedies of his time and despite the closures imposed upon it by his Renaissance commentators. Employed as the working definition it is, it can be applied to later dramas, both those that resemble Aristotelian forms of tragedy and those that do not. Such is Abrams' third and final observation on the *Poetics*. Both *Macbeth* and *Death of a Salesman* can be accommodated by the criteria of Arisotle's definition; and tragedy in the novel or the cinema can also be covered by some of the criteria of the definition and by some of the criteria for differentiating literary types. Aristotle's theory, then, does not foreclose on its application to new cases with their new properties; his concepts of art and tragedy are open, not closed.

But are they? Abrams allows that they can be employed to cover new cases that Aristotle could not have foreseen; however, all these cases, at least as Abrams construes them, have no new properties that call for the introduction of new criteria that are not included in Aristotle's sets for "art" or "tragedy." It is not enough to be able to say that, for example, *Death of a Salesman* is tragic because it satisfies all or even some of Aristotle's criteria, since this reason is rejected by the counterclaim, perfectly intelligible, that the play is tragic in spite of the fact that it satisfies none of Aristotle's criteria but satisfies other criteria that have to do with low men and their illusions, which, when they burst, puncture bourgeois society, not man. What, now, can the Aristotelian say when, after this move, with all its variations on the tragedy of the absurd, the question arises, as it inevitably does: But is *Death of a Salesman* really tragic? Or, for that matter, when the question arises, as it, too, inevitably does, Is *Oedipus Rex* really tragic because Oedipus is the Aristotelian tragic hero who commits the tragic error? What error? It may be that the Aristotelian definition cannot cover even his paradigm. Aristotle's concept of tragedy is not open in the crucial sense of accommodating new tragedies without his definitive set of criteria and, even more devastating, of accommodating his own examples, the most important of which may intelligibly be called "tragic" without the putatively necessary hamartia. His theory and concept of tragedy can accommodate cases he never foresaw; they cannot accommodate the properties of those cases that are neither extended variations on his criteria nor contradictions of them.

That Aristotle's theories of art and tragedy have been much criticized or repudiated by other critical theorists Abrams recognizes, conceding that this gives an initial plausibility to the contemporary demolition of aesthetic and critical theory, but only because this disagreement between Aristotle and his detractors has been misunderstood. If we look at this conflict of theories in their Wittgensteinian surroundings, they need not be seen as contrary or contradictory ontologies but as the taking of different stands or, as Coleridge said, the employing of different "speculative instruments":

> Whatever analogue we adopt needs to bring out the fact that critical definitions and theories may be discrepant without conflict, and mutually supplementary instead of mutually exclusive, since each delimits and structures its field in its own way. The test of the validity of a theory is what it proves capable of doing when it is put to work [p. 25].

With this, we reach the heart of Abrams' argument, both for his own elucidation of the nature and role of critical theory and for his refutation of mine and similar interpretations of it as an unnecessary logical mistake. And it is absolutely fundamental that his argument does not identify "Critical theories are not conflicting, sometimes mutually exclusive, true-false claims about art or its sub-concepts" with "They need not and, indeed, ought not, be read in this way, but as mutually supplementary alternative, fertile-sterile, working definitions or sets of directions for dealing with works of art." The issue between Abrams and myself must be whether critical theories and their agreements and disagreements as a matter of fact do function as speculative ontologies, not whether they can be salvaged by transforming them into speculative instruments.

Abrams does not identify these two entirely different questions; instead, unless I am badly mistaken, the only argument he gives to support his doctrine that critical theories are *not* mutually exclusive (a doctrine I find entirely unconvincing) is his entirely persuasive recommendation to read critical theories and their conflicts as mutually enlightening different approaches to art.

To support his recommendation to regard critical theory as a speculative instrument—a recommendation that (at least I think) he takes to support, in turn, his elucidation of the nature and role of critical theory and of conflicts among critical theories—Abrams turns from Aristotle to Coleridge, who, for me, is the greatest of the Shakespearean critics, in spite of his metaphysical and critical theories, and is, for Abrams, at least one of the great critics of Shakespeare because of his theories.

> Are we to take it, then, that Coleridge's criticism is a happy escape from his unfortunate metaphysical theory, or achieved in spite of it? If we look and see, all the indications are otherwise. The major insights of Coleridge's critical analyses, interpretations, and evaluations, including the passages on Shakespeare that Weitz most praises, are integral with his metaphysical and critical theory, in that they put to work the terms and categories developed within the theory [p. 28].

Abrams cites as an example of this organic unity of metaphysics, critical theory, and critical practice in Coleridge Coleridge's metaphysical principle of organic unity, which led him to exchange the model of the growing plant for the neoclassic model of the artisan as a cardinal concept of his critical theory, one that he employed throughout his practical criticism, especially of the plays of Shakespeare.

Without entering into any details that would qualify the generalization derived from this one example, that the whole of Coleridge is an organic unity, with no inconsistencies—a thesis I challenged in my discussion of Coleridge that Abrams mentions—I think that Abrams is marvelously right about his

example as a paradigm of the integral character of theory and
practice in criticism. Perhaps we may go even further: Without
the metaphysics and the new model for critical theory, there
would not have been the kind and quality of criticism of
Shakespeare that is Coleridge's.

What follows? For Abrams, it follows that if the principle of
organic unity is derived from a metaphysics of organic unity, we
cannot praise the use of the principle of organic unity in applied
criticism without accepting the metaphysical principle. That this
follows for him can be seen, I think, in his rejection, for
example, of my distinction between Coleridge's happy use of the
principle of organic unity in his criticism of Shakespeare and his
unfortunate pinning of that use to a dubious metaphysical
principle.

What new issue is there here, which differs from our disagreements over the *Poetics?* Both of us agree that Coleridge's
principle of organic unity is integral: it unites his theory with his
practice. Where we disagree, if I may venture to say so, is that
for Abrams the integral is itself an organic unity, so that, for
example, in Coleridge's case, the metaphysical and critical
theory and the critical practice are internally related: one cannot
be taken to be true or be praised or accepted without acclaiming
the others; whereas for me the critical principle and practice of
organic unity, while integral with the metaphysical, is not
organically unified with or internally related to it: one can
accept the one, can praise it and even proclaim as true, without
doing likewise with the other. In other words, for me, Coleridge's theory, like critical or philosophical and scientific theory,
though it is, one hopes, integral, need not be organically unified,
internally related. In Plato's *Meno*, for example, the doctrines of
apriori knowledge, reminiscence, and the preexistence of the
soul, though stated separately, are integral; indeed, for Socrates,
as the dialogue develops, Meno cannot have one without the
others. But surely, in spite of the integral character of these
doctrines, they are not organically related, so that we cannot
accept, praise, or even consider as true the doctrine of apriori
knowledge without doing likewise with the others. If one can
praise Plato's doctrine of apriori knowledge in spite of the
doctrines it rests on or is taken to imply, even though the one is
illuminated by the others, why cannot we do the same with
Coleridge's critical theory and practice? Abrams thinks we
cannot do this, it seems to me, because he, like Coleridge,
substitutes the organic model for the mechanical and so conceives of critical theory as a work of art, having an organic unity
whose parts are internally related, not merely interrelated.

It is this model of criticism and critical theory as an integrated, organically, internally related work of art that leads Abrams to the other integral parts of his theory of critical theories. Critical theories are instruments, not ontologies; hence they are neither true nor false:

> If we accept the view that the meaning and justification of a way of speaking is the purpose it serves in its surroundings, we ought also to accept the difficult conclusion that once a concept or assertion is adopted as the basis of a critical theory, its origin and truth-claim, whether empirical or metaphysical, cease to matter, for its validity in this context is to be determined by its power of illumination when brought to bear in the scrutiny of works of art [p. 29].

Further, critical theories, though they conflict, do not really disagree; they differ, as different instruments differ in what they can or are made to do. Coleridge does not disagree with the French critics on the nature of drama and verisimilitude; rather, he offers a different approach, much as Racine and Shakespeare do not disagree but differ in their conceptions of the tragic.

Now, however original and attractive all this may be—that critical theories are like works of art in their organic unities of theory and practice, in their inexhaustible possibilities for interpretation and approach, in being different from each other but hardly in disagreement, and in being neither true nor false nor amenable to the extraction of items that can be understood independently of their total contexts—it seems to me that, as a description of the nature and role of critical theory in practical criticism, it is false both to the actual functioning of critical theory and to the theorists themselves; for even if it is true that their theories are instruments, speculative or not, they are such instruments to them—including Coleridge—only because they regard them as true; and they are useful because they are (taken to be) true by the theorists. Thus Abrams' pragmatism in regard to the history of critical theory does less than justice to it. And if his pragmatism recommends, as I think it must, that we salvage the central concerns of critical theory with real definitions and their respective ontologies, then it enjoins us to convert mutually exclusive disagreements, some of them irreconcilable, into mutually inclusive differences. Since these disagreements among critical theories are, as data, as indispensable for the elucidation of the concepts and claims of critical theory as the individual theories—indeed, in my opinion, they are much more important, since they reveal certain kinds of openness that the single theories do not—Abrams' recommendation is self-defeating. Abrams, then, I submit, has not correctly elucidated the nature and role of critical theories by describing them as families of language-games. Instead, if I may borrow from his Wittgensteinian analogue, he has invented a new language-game by imposing the old rules for playing the game of art, varied and tractable as these are, on the language-game of criticism—on both its theory and its practice.

There are a number of other points that Abrams makes in his essay, all of them central to issues in the philosophy of criticism but only some of them relevant to our present theme: Is aesthetic and critical theory a logically vain effort to define the indefinable? The first of these points is that critical discourse is fluid in its movement of theory and practice, so that description, interpretation, evaluation, and poetics, when they occur, proceed indistinctly; therefore, any logical models imposed upon this fluid discourse, such as those that I proposed as logically irreducible in my *Hamlet* book, distort rather than elucidate actual criticism. Indeed, Abrams contends, not only does this taxonomy of procedure and utterance pervert the movement of critical discourse; it also, by stressing the logical irreducibility, either exaggerates the independent roles of description and evaluation, neither of which figures much in actual criticism, or misdescribes the omnipresence of evaluative interpretation in all criticism. (I am not sure which of the latter alternatives he attributes to me, since he seems to waver on whether description or evaluation occurs without interpretation.)

Let me answer as best I can this first, rather complex criticism. First of all, I never denied the fluidity of critical discourse. Indeed, I pointed out more than once that sometimes even a single sentence of a piece of criticism contains description, interpretation, evaluation, and poetics, and I cited as one of my examples Coleridge's penetrating critical remark on Horatio's "What, has this thing appeared again to-night?" (*Hamlet*, 1.1.21): "Even the word 'again' has its *credibilizing* effect." But, in any case, even if this example does not convince as to the interdependence of the yet logically irreducible components of description, interpretation, evaluation, and poetics, are my categories any more, or any less, rigid, fixed, or distortive than any other set that philosophers, critical theorists, or linguists employ to clarify the flow of critical discourse—including Abrams' single category for the evaluative-interpretive or, for that matter, Coleridge's taxonomy of educated as against uneducated talk, which he uses with such brilliant effect to illuminate one of the great differences between Hamlet and Mrs. Quickly in his "Method of Thought"? Elucidation, as each of these instances shows, is the study of the logic of discourse, fluid or static, not of its narrative flow.

More important, though, is whether critical discourse is, as Abrams says it is, evaluatively interpretive and, therefore, best categorized—understood, not fixed—by one category rather than by the four that I proposed. Abrams' counterproposal is more a derivative of his recommended reading of critical theory as the taking of a stand—which, for him, is choosing a mode of approach to works of art—than it is a criticism of my view. For I believe that I was at great pains in the *Hamlet* book (chap. 15) to make exactly the same points that Abrams makes about the difficulties both of determining what the *données* of a given work of art that description can truly (or falsely) report on and of deciding where interpretation ends and evaluation begins. These difficulties, however, reflect on the application of the criteria of my categories, not on the criteria themselves, which enable us in certain clear cases to distinguish sharply between a descriptive statement, such as "Horatio asks, 'What, has this thing appeared again to-night?'" and a statement, such as "Horatio asks whether this thing has appeared *again*," where the italics point to a coming interpretation and evaluation and probably would not be uttered without this in mind. Nevertheless, even without the italics, as in the text, the descriptive remark is not only a true report on one item in the play; it is also an illuminating reminder of what is being said, if we read or hear carefully, or of what should not be forgotten when we do read or hear it with care. That Horatio's "again" is, in context, credibilizing is both interpretive and—because for Coleridge it is a criterion of good drama—evaluative. But it is not evaluative and certainly not interpretive in the way that "The judgement of Shakespeare is commensurate with his genius" is Coleridge's uncompromisingly evaluative way of proclaiming the absolute perfection of Shakespeare. He spent half his life trying to justify that claim, which involved interpretation, poetic theory, and description; but, for him, that claim was a (true) pure evaluation, logically miles apart from the good, mostly bad, reasons that could be offered in its support. The question, therefore, is not whether these four critical procedures or utterances are interdependent; of course they are. It is rather whether their interdependence renders them logically reducible, one to the others, so that what counts as a description, for example, always counts for an interpretation and that what counts for an interpretation satisfies the same criteria as those of evaluation, or of poetics, and so on. My doctrine of logical irreducibility constitutes an entirely negative answer to these questions; it is

not an answer, affirmative or negative, to whether critical
discourse is reducible to these four modes, for I of course
heartily agree with Abrams that it is not.

Abrams' next point is that criticism presupposes theory;
consequently, those who, like me, claim that it *need* not do so
are wrong. Of course, he concedes, criticism *does* not presuppose theory in the strict sense of "entailment," although it does
in the looser senses of "generate" or even "control," among
others. Given its historical context, criticism is inevitably influenced by past theories or their criteria. Even Matthew Arnold,
who deliberately eschewed critical theory and set himself "to see
the object as in itself it really is," introduces criteria of evaluation that are tantamount to his presupposing a theory of art or,
at least, of poetic quality.

In Abrams' sense of "presuppose," all criticism, let us grant,
presupposes theory. But what has this to do with the question
Can one criticize a work of art without presupposing—that is,
without assuming as an overall necessary condition of criticism—a theory of art: a real definition of art, or, what is implied
by such a theory or definition, a definitive set of criteria for the
concept of art, or the word "art," or, in the case of Arnold,
"poetic quality"? All Abrams offers as an answer to this, the
third of the three basic questions of traditional aesthetic
theory—Is there, Can there be, Need there be, a true theory of
art?—is that criticism without *some* criteria is impossible. And
this no one denies. But what is left dangling and requires
justification in order to provide the requisite answer to Abrams'
"Does criticism presuppose theory?" is that these criteria add up
to the necessary and sufficient ones of a definitive set.

Abrams' final point is that metacriticism also presupposes
theory. Even anti-theory, a form of metacriticism, presupposes
theory, indeed, is a theory of art. It presupposes theory in the
same sense that criticism does, by assuming and working with
certain terms, categories, and doctrines within a context that
causally presupposes the past and the influences of the past.
Again, all this is true. But why call these presuppositions a
theory if all that is involved is the employment of certain
criteria, or even sets of criteria, for talking about art when these
criteria are not stated or assumed to be members of any
definitive set?

Abrams, however, has another consideration with which to
solidify his ingenious claim that anti-theory is itself a theory.
Anti-theory, in all of its talk about art without real definitions,
nevertheless employs certain terms, such as "art," and certain
presuppositions about the independence of art from other

things, such as religion, politics, and morals. For example, in its insistence on the autonomy of art, Abrams remarks:

> The question arises, why should some analytic philosophers think that just these presuppositions about the nature of art and aesthetic experience are so obviously true as to require no defense, and so free of theory, essential definitions, and aesthetic generalizations that they can serve as the ground of arguments against the validity of all such theory, definitions, and generalizations? [p. 46].

Abrams generously supplies an answer to his question: Only because the anti-theorists, unduly exhilarated by Wittgenstein's attack on essences, do not realize that their presuppositions now serve as commonplaces for them; that is, they will argue from them but not about them. Nevertheless, Abrams insists, these remain presuppositions: theories, essential definitions, aesthetic generalizations. And, as a theory, anti-theory, Abrams allows, is as valid as any other, for it, too, functions as a speculative instrument, "as the great enabling act of modern criticism" (p. 47). It is as valid as any other approach, but it is not, as its exponents claim, the only valid approach to the arts. In any adequate account of the nature and role of theory in criticism, anti-theory must be numbered as only one among many mutually inclusive perspectives on art; it is different from, but not in disagreement with, all the other theories; and, presumably, it, too, is neither true nor false but useful or not useful.

At the risk of being ungracious, I think that Abrams' generosity must be refused and his answer rejected completely. For consider, first, this non sequitur or, perhaps, *reductio:* on Abrams' conception of anti-theory as a form of theory, it follows that his chosen model, Wittgenstein, is also a theorist in the full-blown sense, not only in what he says but also in what he rejects of what others have said. Moreover, Wittgenstein's anti-ontology is itself an ontology; Wittgenstein's shift from ontological theory or even anti-ontological theory to logical grammar is also a theory; and Wittgenstein's rejection of essences for disjunctive sets of nonnecessary, nonsufficient conditions as a condition, though not an overall necessary one, of classification and naming is also a form of essentialism. Each of these statements follows in accordance with Abrams' conception of theory. Now, even though I do not pretend to speak for the master, I still hear these implicative doctrines as monstrous echoes that, by no stretch of the imagination or of Abrams' extreme principle of tolerance, can be traced back to Wittgenstein. Furthermore, if anti-theory is just another theory (as Paul Tillich used to say about atheism, that it is only a variant of

theism), then both prefixes, "anti" and the privative "a," have
been deprived of an indispensable part of their linguistic heritage. Rejection, thus, is not the same as replacement, any more
than disagreement is merely reconcilable diversity. These are
facts, not a stance, of our language-game of the elucidation of
concepts.

Speaking even more directly to Abrams' answer, one can say
that it is simply not true that the presuppositions, whatever they
are or may be, are or need be theories. Such theories include real
definitions, statements about definitive properties of art (or of
an art or of the arts), statements about the definitive criteria of
the concepts of art or any of its subconcepts, or aesthetic
generalizations of a universal sort. The presuppositions of the
anti-theorist can function exactly as they do for the critics he is
trying to understand and elucidate, i.e., as conditions or criteria,
without being members of a definitive set of them. The reason
the presuppositions have become commonplaces is that the
anti-theorist now realizes that the presuppositions of yesterday
no longer require buttressing to achieve definitive status but can
serve as undeniable criteria of "art," or whatever in aesthetics
and criticism, without having to be argued for, as only the
theorist is constrained to do.

Abrams concludes his discussion of critical theory as follows:

> If I am right in asserting that what we account as critical
> theory is diverse in its composition and function and inescap-
> able in extended critical discourse, and also that a diversity of
> theories are valid, in the variety of their usefulness for a
> comprehensive understanding and appreciation of art, then
> we are in a position to judge the assertion by some philosophi-
> cal analysts with which we began. The claim was that all
> critical theory consists solely, or primarily, in the assertion
> and attempted proof of an essential definition of art and thus
> is an extended logical mistake. About this claim we can now
> say that (1) it is itself the attempt to assert and prove an essen-
> tial definition of the term "critical theory," (2) it is a mistake
> which forecloses investigation of what able theorists have in
> fact done, and (3) it actually functions as a persuasive redefini-
> tion of "critical theory," in that it delimits the common uses of
> the term by setting up a preferred criterion for its application
> that serves to discredit what it purports to define [pp. 48–49].

This is a most impressive summary of a most impressive
essay, which I have quoted in its entirety to avoid the heresy of
paraphrase. Since I have already in the course of my present
reply to Abrams made his points (2) and (3) against his account
of the nature and role of critical theories, especially that it
forecloses on the logical differences between disagreement and

diversity and that it recommends rather than describes by inviting us to construe these theories as instruments and not at all as true (or false) statements about the definitive natures of art, tragedy, poetry, or criticism, there is no need to repeat them. Nor can either of us complacently assume that (2) and (3), if true of Abrams' account, are false of mine or that, if they characterize my elucidation of critical theories correctly, they do not apply to Abrams' opposing and (mutually exclusive rather than mutually supplementary) elucidation, since, logical grammar being as elusive as it is, we may both be guilty of (2) and (3)!

What remains, what is of crucial concern to me (since I would not ascribe it to Abrams), and what is still, I think, the main issue is (1): that my reading of the nature and role of critical (and aesthetic) theory is not anywhere near a correct account but is instead an essentialist definition of critical theories—a futile attempt to state and to prove that all critical theories have and must have a definitive set of necessary and sufficient properties and, by implication, to state the definitive criteria for the concept of critical theory and for the phrase "critical theory"; or, more disastrously, it is to lay down definitive conditions for the use of a concept whose very functioning reveals that it has no such set—to misconceive an open for a closed concept.

Abrams derives (1) and its applications to me from his overall attribution to me, along with other analysts, of the claim "that all critical theory consists solely, or primarily, in the assertion and attempted proof of an essential definition of art and thus is an extended logical mistake" (p. 48). Indeed, Abrams deduces (1), (2), and (3) from this attributed premise.

Claim (1), I said, does not apply to Abrams; he is guilty of no essentialist definition of critical theory. Nor, I demur, does it apply to me. Indeed, it is true only of those critics or theoreticians of criticism who have tried or try to define what critical theory really is or must be and who, as it turns out, make up a very small number when contrasted with the many who have tried, still try, and will not stop trying to define what art, poetry, tragedy, or even criticism are or what they must be to be what they are.

Abrams, thus, is in serious error in attributing (1) to me. I do not subscribe to it, nor—more to the point—is it, I believe, implied by anything in the essays Abrams mentions. I never claimed, implied, or presupposed that critical theory is necessarily and sufficiently the attempt to state the definitive properties of art, as Abrams' (1) implies. Nor—even more importantly—did I claim, imply, or presuppose the premise Abrams attributes to me. Without indulging in the futile motions of reproducing

what I said in the writings Abrams quotes and on which he bases
his premise—since Abrams knows these as well as I do—what I
claimed and still maintain is that aesthetics, philosophy of the
arts, and poetics, even when present, usually as first or last
chapters, in books of literary criticism, have been and continue
to be primarily concerned with the definition of art, or of an art,
in the essentialist sense of a statement of its necessary and
sufficient properties, conditions, or criteria. This is not to say or
to imply, as Abrams (and others) seem to think, that aesthetics,
philosophy of the arts, or even critical theory is solely concerned
with real definitions of art or of an art, since aesthetics and
philosophy of the arts have been as much occupied with
definitions of artistic creation, the function of art, or response to art as they have been with the definition of art. It
should also be noted that the nature of the sublime seems to have
supplanted the nature of art as the reigning problem in the
eighteenth century, at least among some of the founders of
aesthetics as an independent philosophical discipline; and—we
must not forget—it was the nature of the beautiful or Beauty
that served as the central problem for philosophers and essay-
ists, from Plato until Tolstoy, of what we have only within the
last two centuries called aesthetics. On the other hand, some
contemporary aesthetics and philosophy of the arts is totally
devoid of the pursuit of definitions of art, essential or otherwise
and is thus contrary to Abrams' (1). Critical theory also need not
and, as Abrams argues convincingly, does not *reduce* to real
definitions of art or of an art even though, like literary theory, it
centers on the definition of art in its presupposition—which both
critical theory and literary theory share with traditional aesthetics and philosophy of the arts—that, without an essential
definition, discourse and thought about art and the arts are
without foundation. Thus, theory *in* aesthetics, philosophy of
the arts, and criticism, where it has traditionally been associated
with poetics, is primarily—sometimes solely—the quest for real
definitions and, because of their overriding importance, for real
definitions of art or an art. It is this quest that is vain because it
entails the determination of definitive criteria for concepts of art
or of the separate arts whose uses reveal that they function under
no such sets.

Now Abrams, in the premise he attributes to me, from which
he derives his devastating conclusions, does not distinguish as
carefully as he should between theory in aesthetics, philosophy
of the arts, and criticism and Aesthetic Theory, Art Theory, and
Critical Theory. His wholesale criticism of my reading of the
nature and role of theory in traditional aesthetics, philosophy of

the arts, or criticism rests on his conflation of the following two
entirely different, legitimate senses of "theory" as (1) "real
definition" or "statement of necessary and sufficient properties,
conditions, or criteria of things or concepts" and (2) as "a framework of ideas," only some of which may be definitions, either
essentialist or working. However, it would be egregious to infer
from this conflation that our disagreement over theory is merely
verbal, since both of us recognize these two different historically
established senses and nevertheless disagree not only on the
nature and role of aesthetic theory and critical theory but on the
nature and role of theory in aesthetics, philosophy of the arts,
and criticism. He thinks that I exaggerate the place of real
definition in both; I think he does less than elucidatory justice to
the differences between disagreement and diversity among aesthetic theories and critical theories and misses entirely the

fundamental essentialist thrust of theory in aesthetics, philosophy of the arts, and criticism. That this thrust is logically futile
follows from the openness of the concept of art and its subconcepts. In rejecting my account of the nature and role of theory in
aesthetics, philosophy of the arts, and criticism, Abrams must
also reject the notion that the concept of art is open, in order to
claim instead that it and its subconcepts are all governed by
definitive sets of criteria and are therefore amenable to the
essentialist definitions he vainly tries to convert into working
ones.

At the very beginning of his essay—to which I have devoted
the inordinate space it deserves—Abrams says:

> In the last two or three decades ... a number of philosophers
> have mounted an attack against critical theory, whether
> applied to a particular genre or to art in general, on grounds
> which, if they can survive scrutiny, are wholly devastating
> [p. 3].

Abrams has fixed the stakes higher than I would. He sees the
collapse of criticism if the contemporary attack is not refuted; I
see only the collapse of those logically unsound and critically
unnecessary first or last chapters of books in literary criticism.
Criticism can survive without poetics, as can critical theory
without theory as real definition; the repudiation of definitive
criteria signifies the abandonment of definition, without which
criticism and critical theory can survive, but it does not require
the rejection of criteria, without which neither can continue.

Mandelbaum rejects my rejection of essentialist definitions of art
and the arts. Abrams rejects my reading of the logical character

of theory in aesthetics, philosophy of the arts, and poetics and
criticism. John M. Ellis, in *The Theory of Literary Criticism: A Logical Analysis* (1974),[4] rejects, among many other doctrines and approaches to literature, my wholesale rejection of all theories of art, including literature—his special concern—since he contends that art and literature can be defined. Thus, he accepts the role that I assign to theory in aesthetics and criticism as the quest for definition, and a definition that is more than stipulatory or conventional. He also subscribes to the doctrine that I have attributed to traditional theories of art, that without a true definition of art and literature, criticism flounders and critical theory remains without secure foundations. Central, then, in critical or literary theory—in the sense that Abrams gives it, as a framework of ideas—is definition or theory of literature—in the sense that I employ it—as a true statement of the nature of literature. Thus, Ellis disagrees with Abrams' conception of critical theory (without mentioning Abrams' essay), that it is not centrally concerned with real, not working, definition; and he disagrees with me (whom he does discuss) that literature is not, cannot be, and need not be truly defined in order to talk about it coherently.

Ellis also begins with the later Wittgenstein, in particular with what he regards as Wittgenstein's demolition of the "reference theory of the meaning of words" and its replacement by the theory that words can be defined by their uses; for, according to Ellis, Wittgenstein's great contribution to literary and critical theory is this substitution of definitions of the uses of words for traditional definitions of the references of words.

However fantastic and (for some) perverse this reading of Wittgenstein may be, Ellis employs it to reject the theory that words mean what they refer to and, consequently, that language has but one meaningful use, which is to talk about things or properties that can be discerned and referred to. It is this theory, which he calls the "reference" theory of meaning, which has generated all past futile attempts to define literature by its inherent properties and the present conception of literary criticism as an amalgam of meaningful description of its inherent properties and meaningless or emotionally charged judgments about the works that possess the descriptive properties.

This whole approach, he says, is wrong, founded, as it is, on an incorrect reference theory of meaning. Meanings are not references of words; definitions are not descriptive statements of common features. Rather: meanings are uses of words, and definitions are of these uses. In the case of literature, we must stop asking what its defining qualities are, for that question leads to the impasse I describe, of trying to define the indefinable; instead we must ask: What circumstances are appropriate to the use of the word "literature"? (p. 31). Ellis' answer is that "literary texts are defined as those that are used by the society in such a way that *the text is not taken as specifically relevant to the immediate context of its origin*" (p. 44; his italics). "Literature" is defined by its use; and literature is also defined by its use—by the society or community that converts certain pieces of language into literature.

Ellis' definition of literature parallels recent attempts to define "art" in terms of the art world or the institution of art. It is left unclear whether such definitions in terms of uses of terms or things rather than properties of things avoids the basic issue, raised by the critics of traditional theory of art, Do the concepts of art and of literature actually function under definitive sets of necessary and sufficient criteria? But, though this question is left unclear or unanswered, it remains that these definitions simply substitute one putative set of definitive criteria—the social or establishmentarian—for another—the artistic or literary. These theorists may not state defining properties of art and literature, but they do imply, in the definitions they offer, defining criteria for "art" and "literature." So the basic question surfaces, not to be hidden away: Does "art" or "literature" perform its roles under this set of definitive conditions, namely, that art or literature is treated as such by some group, including a, or even the, community? In Ellis' definition of "literature," everything turns on what he calls "the community." That this is a criterion of the work of art is dubious, as Ellis admits. But is "the community" an intelligible criterion of the correct use of even "literature"? It is the least explained, yet most important, concept in his book; nevertheless, one is left wondering what, exactly, constitutes a community or the community. The assumption throughout is that it is a univocal presence which, unlike its quarreling members, is in total agreement about what gets treated as literature. Thus, Ellis' definition—nonreferential or not—rests on an assumption so vague that it accounts for nothing. But even worse—at least it seems so to me—it rests on the assumption, implied by the fact that Ellis defines literature in terms of the community, that the concept of literature is a closed concept, governed by a definitive set of criteria. His definition in effect simply replaces one putative set for another, and that he finds the set in society rather than in its art is a minor flaw compared with the fact that he is unable to exorcise the bewitchment of the doctrine that all concepts must be closed; the reference theory of meaning has nothing to do with his definition of literature or, more to the point, with his substitution of his definition for other definitions. The question is not whether literature is definable in terms of its inherent properties or, rather, in terms of the use society invests in it. The question is, as it always has been, whether the concept of literature is amenable to a definition at all—to any statement of its necessary and sufficient criteria. That the community is such a criterion is suspect, not only because it seems preposterous to regard it as either necessary or sufficient, but also because it is impossible to construe it as an intelligible criterion at all. Ellis' project thus fails as an elucidation of the concept of literature; it neither succeeds nor fails to analyze that concept. He has misdescribed the very use of the term he was concerned to define.

This confusion of the elucidation of the concept with the definition of literature in terms of its use rather than its properties vitiates his whole exercise in the logical analysis of literary criticism, since he ties everything to his definition, which he regards as essential for the understanding and justification of literary criticism. Criticism of literature is intrinsically evaluative because it is the same as the exfoliation of the value built into literature by society; stylistic or formalistic approaches to literature are illegitimate because they isolate features in literary texts to serve as the criteria of literature; and a variety of extrinsic approaches, such as biographical, psychological, or historical criticism, are also illegitimate because they too isolate the literary text from its communal context. The only adjunct to literary criticism he allows is biology, enlarged as the study of man as a purposive, functional being in society, since such a study enhances the understanding of literature according to the definition of literature given by Ellis. Thus, his rejections of a variety of critical approaches to literature and his acceptance of one approach, the biological, capricious, and strange as they are, all derive from his definition. His definition and the consequences he draws from it serve as one more example of the implicit and harmful dogmatism of a critical theory that revolves around the need for, and the desperate attempt at, real definition, even at the cost of keeping the concept of literature closed by shifting its definitive criteria from what literature is to what it does.

In many ways, the next and last criticism of the openness of the concept of art, George Dickie's *Art and the Aesthetic: An Institutional Analysis* (1974),[5] is the most challenging of all, for his fundamental claim is that a work of art is an artifact and is institutional, so that artifactuality and institutionality are each a necessary condition and both together are a sufficient condition for all works of art. Consequently, the concept of art is closed, amenable to a definitive set of criteria; and at least one theory—his—is not logically vain but true. He concedes that the subconcepts of art, however, are open, contending that it is as coherent to distinguish between a closed genus and its open species as it is (for me) to allow for the openness of "game" and the closed character of one of its species or members, "major-league baseball." Dickie's concession, though, is puzzling; for there are, to be sure, open concepts that have some closed concepts subsumed under them, and there are also, more provocatively, certain open concepts, such as drama, which, though functioning under disjunctive sets of nonnecessary, nonsufficient, but some undebatable, criteria—the perennially flexible—contain other open concepts, such as tragedy. These last open concepts,

though also perennially flexible, are perennially debatable as well; that is, the criteria of "tragedy" are each of them rejectable by theorists who employ the concept. The genus drama, then, though it shares with its species the logical property of perennial flexibility, not only does not share perennial debatability with its species, tragedy; it contradicts perennial debatability: "What has plot to do with drama?" is not intelligible, but "What has hamartia (or any other putative property) to do with tragedy?" is intelligible. Thus, I agree with Dickie that the subconcepts of art are open; but I cannot understand how he can reconcile this claim with its denial, a denial implied by his insistence that the concept of art is closed. How, for example, can the concept of the novel be open if the novel is among works of art, as it surely is, and the concept of art or work of art is closed?

Dickie distinguishes between the classifying and the evaluative uses of "art" and, within the classifying, between its primary and derivative use. "This is a work of art," he says, is mostly employed to praise, less frequently to classify derivatively (as "This piece of driftwood is a work of art [sculpture]"), and rarely, if at all, as a straightforward descriptive utterance, since it refers to paradigmatic works of art that, though assessed, need no classificatory introduction. Nevertheless, Dickie claims, this primary use is basic.

It is this primary use that he claims is governed by necessary and sufficient conditions; and he points out that I stressed that this use could not be defined. In "The Role of Theory in Aesthetics," I distinguish between the descriptive and the evaluative uses of "art" and argue that, although there are indisputable examples of works of art—Dickie's paradigms—and although these may have many common properties—such as made by human agency, with skill and imagination, and contain all sorts of sensuous qualities and their relations, expressed in public media—the notion that these common properties are necessary and sufficient for all works of art is suspect. So I did not say that these common properties are not necessary or sufficient for the paradigms; but I think that Dickie is correct in claiming that my doctrine of the openness of the concept of art implies that there are none. There are, of course, paradigmatic works of art, just as there are paradigmatic uses of "art." These paradigms, however, do not guarantee the existence of paradigm properties in the requisite sense of definitive properties rather than strands of similarities which add up to no more than disjunctive sets of nonnecessary, nonsufficient properties. It was my point that the criteria for "art" employed in talking about paradigms are not logically different from the criteria employed in talking about the marginal cases. Hence, Dickie is right in saying that I deny definitive criteria for his primary use of "art."

Are the paradigmatic works of art, which are classified, not praised, by "This is a work of art," members of a class whose defining properties can be stated? Does "art," used to classify indisputable examples of works of art, have necessary and sufficient criteria? Dickie's answer to both forms of the question is that there are two necessary properties of all paradigmatic works of art and that these properties in turn serve as the two necessary criteria for the correct use of "art" to classify paradigms of art. These two properties are artifactuality and institutionality. Each is necessary; both together are sufficient. The others—agency, skill, imagination, expression in a public medium of sensuous materials formally related—though omnipresent in the paradigms, are neither necessary nor sufficient.

Artifactuality is the genus of art, institutionality, its differentia. Both are relational properties, nonexhibited in Mandelbaum's sense of the not immediately perceivable. Nothing, then, is or could be a work of art without these two relational features; and with these two, anything is an indisputable example of a work of art. Now, on this, Dickie's, theory, either the necessary and sufficient are analytic of paradigm, in which case all the omnipresent features of paradigmatic works of art are each of them necessary and all of them together sufficient; or the necessary and sufficient hold for all works of art. Nothing is or can be a work of art, including any of the paradigms, unless it satisfies the definitive conditions of being an artifact and an integral constituent of an institution. Moreover, Dickie cannot delimit the paradigms by assuming that the class of paradigms of works of art is fixed by its present members, since this class, however we construe the concept of a paradigm—as open or closed—includes among its most respected members previously disputed examples. In art, as nowhere else, the disputed works of yesterday become the paradigms of today, just as the works of anti-art or non-art of today may become the respected and perhaps revered works of art of tomorrow.

Dickie's primary use, derived from present paradigms or not, must obtain across the board: to *all* works of art, not just the paradigmatic ones. Does it? Are "artifact" and "institutional" necessary criteria for the correct use of "art," and are they, together, its definitive criteria?

A minimum criterion of any criterion, necessary, sufficient, or plain, is that it be intelligible, i.e., reasonably clear. (A maximum criterion of a necessary criterion is that it be itself governed by definitive criteria.) Accordingly, before we can query Dickie's two criteria as definitive for "art," we must ask whether they are themselves intelligible, a not unreasonable request. What, then—to begin with his first criterion—is an artifact? Dickie offers no definition, not even a set of directions for determining or deciding what is to count as an artifact. Instead— and I think quite commendably, since it works so well for art—he provides only examples, with nonuniversalized generalizations based on them. Artifacts, thus, are worked or made objects, to be contrasted with natural objects. A plywood sculpture, for example, is an artifact, though it should be noted that both the plywood and the sculpture are artifacts, while the tree or trees from which the wood originated are natural objects, not artifacts. (Perhaps I should add that this is my example, not Dickie's.) Yet the piece of driftwood on the beach or, later, in the museum, said by me and reluctantly admitted by Dickie (but only in a sense derivative from the paradigm use) to be classifiable as a work of art, can be so classified because it has artifactuality conferred upon it: "Natural objects which become works of art in the classificatory sense are artifactualized without the use of tools—artifactuality is conferred on the object rather than worked on it" (pp. 44–45). This concession makes an artifact a worked or made object or a natural object made into an artifact by having this status conferred upon it. Dickie quite naturally finds "unusual" and "strange" this notion of artifactuality being conferred rather than worked on an object, but he accepts both the example of the piece of driftwood as a work of art and artifactuality in this extended sense as a necessary feature of all works of art. (Presumably he also accepts as an artifact the plywood of my example after it leaves the factory workbench but before it is worked on by the sculptor.)

A piece of driftwood is atrophied wood that was once part of a living tree. It is not strange or unusual to classify it as a work of art and to give, as a reason for doing so, that it has an interesting shape, gnarled texture, and sensuous charm—thus appealing to qualities, praised or described, of works of art but not claiming, implying, or presupposing that these are definitive properties of art or of good art; my reason borrows from no more than disjunctive sets of nonnecessary, nonsufficient qualities of art that I happen to praise as well. How different it is to call this piece of driftwood a work of art and to give as a reason that it has artifactuality conferred upon it; here appeal is made, not to any of its qualities, but to a feature taken to be necessary for all works of art!

If it is a strange and unusual notion that the piece of driftwood is a work of art in part because it is artifactually artifactual, what are we to say of other examples? If dead trees can be classified as works of art, even in a derivative sense because, in part, they have artifactuality conferred on them, not because, in whole, they are regarded as more similar than dissimilar to common (but not definitive) qualities of works of art, what are we to say about skins removed from recently slaughtered humans, not to make lampshades but, for the sake of argument, tapestries, some of high, most of them of low, aesthetic value? If lampshades—which are, after all, artifacts and, for some, are useful, rather than fine, art—why not tapestries—works of art in the classificatory sense? According to the artifactualist, these skins are worked; so they are artifacts in the primary sense, like the worked stone of the sculpture. Is the artifact of the tapestries no different from inanimate and other natural objects? If wood from living trees or wool from living sheep can be worked, why not these skins or, for that matter, decapitated heads that are shrunken or animals and birds that are killed and stuffed? All of these are artifacts, and each is a possible candidate for appreciation within an established practice. But shrunken heads and stuffed animals have not, so far as I know, been displaced from museums of natural history to art museums. One compelling reason for this hesitation, overcome with respect to paintings produced by primates, is that the materials, though worked into artifacts, are (formerly) animate objects. Can it be—to invert Dickie's suggestion—that we withdraw the status of artifactuality from these works and so disqualify them as candidates for appreciation within the established practice of art? The tapestries made of human skins, then, though classified as works of art and as artifacts, are not allowed to satisfy the necessary condition of artifactuality because they are made of (formerly) human objects, not merely natural objects. Quite independently of what is happening to artifactuality as a necessary condition of art in these examples, the criterion of artifactuality becomes more and more complicated as made object, natural object with conferred artifactuality, and made object with artifactuality withheld. Further examples compound this complexity. Consider a sculpture made, not of plywood, marble, or stone, but of a live human person being worked into a piece of sculpture, à la Poe's "Cask of Amontillado," or, like the piece of driftwood, removed from its natural habitat and placed on a pedestal in a museum. Is the exhibited work an artifact or not? Or is it not a work of art (sculpture) because it is made of, or is, a live human being? That my example is not far-fetched can be seen from the real example of 144 Norway-spruce seedlings, planted in bins of peat moss a foot deep in a room whose temperature and humid-

ity were controlled to promote growth; this piece was exhibited by the American artist Robert Morris in the Museum of Modern Art, during its "Space" exhibition. As sculpture or, more likely, as architecture, the seedlings in their setting were offered as works of art or a work of art. Dickie's second necessary condition—conferred status as a candidate for appreciation within an established practice—could not be better met, since the core conferrers were not only peers but absolute dictators in the art world. Is Dickie's first criterion also met in this example of a work of art? If so, we have the queerest possible example of an artifact: live, growing, and nurtured natural objects![6]

Dickie says that artifactuality as a necessary condition—the genus—of the primary sense of art is so obvious and uninteresting that it requires discussion only because some have denied its necessity. The reply to this is that it is not all that obvious that artifactuality is a necessary condition of art, and one of the reasons it is not is that "artifactuality" itself is not only unclear but is perhaps, as these examples show, incoherent. My problem with artifactuality is similar to my problem with imitation: I do not know whether either is a candidate for a necessary condition or a definition of "art," primarily because I do not know what counts and what does not count for either.

There are similar, perhaps greater, difficulties in Dickie's second necessary criterion, institutionality. My doubts are as much about this as a criterion as they are about it as necessary. Dickie derives this criterion from Arthur Danto's notion of the artworld; and with Mandelbaum's concept of a nonexhibited feature, he converts the artworld from an antecedent condition, involving theory and history of art, into a necessary condition of art that, along with artifactuality, becomes sufficient for all art.

Is Dickie's criterion of "institutionality" any more intelligible than Ellis' criterion of "community," which Ellis uses to define "literature"? Here is Dickie's formulation of this second criterion:

> [it is] a set of the aspects . . . which has had conferred upon it the status of candidate for appreciation by some person or persons acting on behalf of a certain social institution (the artworld) [p. 34].

Four interconnected notions are involved in this second condition: "(1) acting on behalf of an institution, (2) conferring of status, (3) being a candidate, and (4) appreciation" (p. 34). The first two, he says, are closely related and can best be understood under their models of conferring status as legal actions; examples are the conferring of knighthood by a king, the indicting of someone by a grand jury, the marrying of a man and a woman by a minister, and so on. Though not as codified or formalized as the legal, the practice that constitutes the artworld includes conferring status on behalf of the artworld's inhabitants by those artists, directors, art-lovers, and critics who are its core. Notions (1) and (2) are satisfied when the inhabitants of the artworld are more than one. This restriction drops out, however, when (3) and (4) are added: "only one person is required to act on behalf of the artworld and to confer the status of candidate for appreciation" (p. 38). Duchamp, for example, did not place his urinal before the public as a plumbing salesman might; he conferred on it the status of candidate for appreciation by entering it in an art show and giving it the title *Fountain*. Dickie's second example is Walter de Maria's *High Energy Bar*, an exhibited stainless-steel bar accompanied by a certificate "bearing the name of the work and stating that the bar is a work of art only when the certificate is present" (p. 39).

Notion (3) requires only the conferring of status of candidacy for appreciation, not for actual appreciation; and not every aspect of the work is included in this conferring, whereas all value properties are excluded, since (3), like the others, characterizes only the primary classificatory use of "art." Notion (4) specifies appreciation, not aesthetic appreciation as a special kind, which Dickie regards as dubious anyway, but the experiencing of the qualities of works of art that are deemed worthy or valuable.

With these four notions built in, the institutional is a necessary condition of art. Together with artifactuality, it provides not only a definition of "art" but a set of necessary and sufficient criteria for "art," therefore for the concept of art as closed;

therefore, "the radical creativity, adventuresomeness, and exuberance of art of which Weitz speaks is possible within the concept of art, even though it is closed by the necessary and sufficient conditions of artifactuality and conferred status" (p. 33). He later adds that neither condition forecloses on creativity; the second, indeed, encourages it: "Since under the definition anything whatever may become art, the definition imposes no restraints on creativity" (p. 49).

Of course, Dickie's second condition of conferral of status of candidacy for appreciation allows for all the craziness as well as the sanity of art. But, with this second condition, who needs the first, since we can confer artifactuality on anything, according to Dickie, and then go on to proclaim it a work of art. I need two moments of conferral, not two separate conditions. Then a work of art is anything you or I say it is, so long as we are, as undoubtedly we are going to insist we are, members of the artworld. Anything is a work of art if one says it is, whether it is an artifact or not (so long as one says it is). How, now, does this version of art as a closed concept enable us to distinguish between art and things that are not art?

But Dickie affirms more than this: he insists that his definition can accommodate all *contending* instances of works of art, that his two criteria banish nothing from the artworld that is art. Beneath all the diversity, excitement, novelty, and insanity there is the protecting condition of conferral of status of candidacy for appreciation. This assumes an overall unanimity in the artworld, a notion that finds a parallel in that univocity of the community's use of texts which Ellis finds defining for literature. But the most revealing feature of the artworld is that, as a concept, it arose or became fashionable only when that world had fallen apart. And fall apart it did, and fallen apart it is. Even the most cursory survey of the present world of art, as reflected in that tiny corner, the New York scene, plus the epigones that have exported it, reveals that, in aesthetically and logically shocking terms, the artworld is no longer a community of differences or even of disagreements over contending works of art. Rather, it is a world of warring factions, including, as one articulate and legitimate though heterogeneous group, composed only of artists (who should know), those who reject the art in their works and others'—works that have been pronounced works of art. These "de-aestheticizers," as Harold Rosenberg aptly calls them, want—as artists—to depose art. He cites Robert Morris, this time as sculptor, not as farmer-architect, who executed before a notary public a document, entitled "Statement of Esthetic Withdrawal," about his metal

construction *Litanies;* in this, Morris, in effect acting on behalf
of the artworld, "hereby withdraws from said construction all
esthetic quality and content and declares that from the date
hereof said construction has no such quality and content."[7]
Other contributing members of the artworld reject not only the
"anxious" object, that previous paradigm of rejected traditional
art, but also all "portable" works of art, in favor of earthworks
of one sort or another. And there are some, like Andy Warhol,
who reject the need of any artist to produce a *work* of art; it is
what the artist does, not what he makes, that is art. This
proclamation—which Rosenberg calls "Set out for Clayton!"—
offers the members of the artworld an enabling act which frees
them from the arduous task of making anything. Saying something's a work of art suffices.

This whole state of affairs depresses Rosenberg very much; for
him, it bespeaks "the profound crisis that has overtaken the arts
in our epoch" (p. 12). How do Dickie's definition of "art" and his
two criteria for "art" illuminate this crisis? His second criterion
does not, as he claims, foreclose on the radical creativity of
modern art. But neither can it accommodate the new property of
some of this creativity: that of the radical rejection of all
previous art, the art of works of art, and traditional—
"portable"—works of art in favor of earthworks as the only true
art. This rejection entails the *withdrawal*, not the conferring, of
status of candidacy for appreciation of an assortment of works,
pronounced to be works of art in favor of only non-art or
anti-art. The criterion of conferral, then, does foreclose on this
condition of the rejection of putative status of candidacy for
appreciation; this is a condition that the concept of art must
accommodate but that no theory of art can. Moreover, if, as
Dickie insists, "a mistake cannot be made *in* conferring the status
of art, [but] a mistake can be made *by* conferring it" (p. 50), he
cannot counter that there is a mistake *in* withdrawing, as well as
by withdrawing, the status of art from works of art. These artists
of non-art and of anti-art may be irresponsible, as Dickie allows,
but (for him) they can hardly be in error in rejecting all claims to
art or to previous art.

Dickie's first criterion also succumbs in the general demise of
modern art. For if art is what anyone says it is, and if what it is is
sometimes what the artist says he does, not only what he makes,
then artifactuality, in Dickie's primary sense of worked object
and even in his derivative sense of conferred artifactuality, has
lost its foothold. "Art is what I do, not what I make"—a boast
that is covered by Dickie's second criterion of conferral of
status—rules in what I do as a candidate for status; and, together

with *what* I do rather than make, it creates a work of art without any semblance of an artifact.

These phenomena of modern art that include non-art and anti-art, whether as art or non-art, are, it may be correctly observed, extreme. But, even if we grant that they are too silly to be taken seriously, I still think that Dickie's two criteria are each of them, taken singly, as inadequate in their claims to be necessary as both are inadequate in their claim to be jointly sufficient. The concept of an artifact remains obscure, and the concept of conferral reduces to "Art is anything that anyone chooses to call 'art'"—a reduction that renders otiose the first criterion. Given artifactuality in the clear sense of "worked object," and institutionality in the sense of "classified (not necessarily praised) as a work of art within an established practice of distinguishing works of art from other things,"

Dickie's two criteria are perhaps jointly sufficient for the paradigms that these two criteria were employed to classify. But these criteria, omnipresent as they are, are no more sufficient and no less necessary than any of the other omnipresent properties of the paradigms. The paradigms of works of art in the history of art reveal, rather, omnipresent properties, which, given its history, preclude any from being sufficient or necessary. Dickie's artifactuality and institutionality, like all the other so-called defining criteria, must take their proper place among the disjunctive set of nonnecessary, nonsufficient criteria for "art." That x is a work of art because it is a worked object or that it is so classified is as good a reason as any other for x's being a work of art; its being a good reason makes it a criterion of "art" but not a necessary or—alone or together with others—a sufficient criterion. The concept of art remains open, with or without an assist from the insanity of modern art.

Philosophers from Aristotle to the present day are almost unanimous in subscribing to the doctrine that the term "tragedy" denotes a class of works of art, distinguishable from all other classes, whose members possess common properties by virtue of which they are tragic and, hence, that these properties are necessary and sufficient, essential or defining, properties of tragedy; that, without a definition of tragedy, critical discourse about particular tragedies cannot be shown to be either intelligible or true; and, consequently, that the major task of a philosophy of tragedy is to provide such a theory. Literary critics and writers of dramatic tragedies, such as Dryden, Corneille, Racine, and Arthur Miller, concur with philosophers in this doctrine.

So we must ask, as we did of art, Is there a theory (a poetics, true statement, or real definition) of tragedy? Can there be such a theory? Need there be such a theory in order to guarantee the cogency of critical talk about why x is tragic or whether x is tragic? Traditional answers have been affirmative. I shall propose the opposite and, in so doing, attempt to establish the openness of the concept of tragedy, which, like the concept of art, is perennially flexible but, unlike the concept of art, is also perennially debatable. It is this logical feature of the concept of tragedy that best illuminates the range of disagreement among the theorists of tragedy—their tragedy-giving reasons—because it enlarges our conception of the varieties of openness among certain concepts.

Aristotle is the first to define the nature of tragedy. Since I have already discussed his definition (or theory, poetics) of tragedy in the preceding chapter, in which I argued that most of the *Poetics* is an explication of his definition—an interpretation vigorously challenged by Professor Abrams—there is little point in entering into details once again. Whether Aristotle provides a working definition, as Abrams persuasively argues, or a real definition of the essence of tragedy, as I contend, and which indeed is the orthodox view, he does offer a definition of tragedy. In fact, it is my conviction that Aristotle actually offers two definitions: of tragedy and of good tragedy. Every tragedy is an imitation of the passage from happiness to misery and contains the requisite pity and fear, hamartia, purgation, thought, melody, representation, and spectacle. Every good tragedy is characterized by all these but has reversal and recognition (together); unity of action; good, appropriate, true, and consistent characters; and a fine use of language, especially metaphor. That Aristotle does offer these two definitions, and hence two different sets of criteria for tragedy, can be seen in the fact that, for him, a certain vehicle may be a tragedy even though it has no reversal, but it cannot be a tragedy if it has no pity and fear.

Is Aristotle's theory true? (I cannot accept Abrams' inference that it is neither true nor false but only fertile or not fertile, since it is a speculative instrument, not an ontology.) Does his theory cover all tragedies, even the Greek ones? Philosophers and critics after Aristotle challenge his description of Greek tragedy and of tragedy altogether. Critics (for example, H. D. F. Kitto, in *Greek Tragedy*) point out that hamartia does not characterize Oedipus or Medea, as it does Creon in *Antigone*, and that awe rather than pity and fear is inspired by *Agamemnon*. Some critics question the priority of plot, the subordination of character to plot, and the denigration of spectacle. They also challenge the contention that hamartia, purgation, and the tragic hero as a relatively good man are necessary properties or even members of a disjunctive set of sufficient properties of tragedy, for there are tragedies without hamartia or purgation and tragedies with a wicked hero or an eminently just one. Many critics and philosophers argue that Aristotle's list of formative elements leaves out the essential property of the hero's *aretē* (excellence), as well as the elements of conflict, doom, regeneration, spiritual waste, and a just punishment, without which there can be no tragedy. Contemporary writers of tragedy, for example, Samuel Beckett and Eugene Ionesco, perhaps echoing the views of Schopenhauer, even go so far as to suggest through their works that tragedy need have no hero, plot, or imitation of a serious action but only the bare presentation of the underlying "absurdity" of life.

Aristotle seems to be on safer ground with his list of evalu-

ative criteria. In the sense in which hamartia, purgation, the
tragic hero, and so forth are challengeable properties of tragedy,
Aristotle's criteria of great tragedy—unity of action, wholeness,
completeness, and magnitude of plot, consistency of character,
and the coincidence of reversal of the situation with recognition—remain intact. "*Oedipus Rex* is a great tragedy because of
(among other reasons) its relentless unity of action and plot and
its messenger scene of reversal and recognition" is an unchallengeable statement in the way that "*Oedipus Rex* is a tragedy
because Oedipus is a relatively good man whose error or frailty
leads to his downfall, which induces pity and fear and their
purgation" is not unchallengeable. Nevertheless, Aristotle's list
of evaluative criteria, brilliant as it is, cannot be said to sum up a
real or true definition of great tragedy; his criteria are neither
necessary nor sufficient for great tragedy.

A. C. Bradley, in his celebrated essay "Hegel's Theory of
Tragedy" (in *Oxford Lectures on Poetry*), writes: "Since Aristotle dealt with tragedy, and, as usual, drew the main features of
his subject with those sure and simple strokes which no later
hand has rivalled, the only philosopher who has treated it in a
manner both original and searching is Hegel." Accurate as this
assessment of Hegel may be, it would be wrong to infer from it
that little or nothing of philosophical interest was written about
tragedy from Aristotle to Hegel; for there are original ideas
about tragedy in the medieval period, as well as ideas derived
from the *Poetics* during the Renaissance and neoclassic periods,
which, because they represent variant uses of the concept of
tragedy, are extremely important for philosophy.

The great medieval contribution to the theory of tragedy is the
tradition reflected in the writings of Boccaccio, Chaucer, and
later medieval authors, according to which tragedies are non-
dramatic narratives like those in *De Casibus Illustrium Vi-
rorum*—stories of the falls of illustrious men. Central in these
tales is a total reverse of fortune that comes upon a man of high
degree who is in apparent prosperity. Chaucer's monk sums up
this medieval notion of the tragic in the *Canterbury Tales*. A
tragedy is a story

> Of him that stood in greet prosperitee
> And is y-fallen out of heigh degree
> Into miserie, and endeth wrecchedly.
> (*Canterbury Tales* B, 3165–67)

Scholarly views differ about the significance of the fall. Lily
Campbell, for instance, argues (in *Shakespeare's Tragic Heroes*)
that these medieval tales function as *exempla* which, by pointing

out man's uncertainty in, and possible fall from, prosperity, warn all men of the fickleness of fortune and, by ascribing the cause of the fall to vice, of divine justice in the world. Consequently, for her, medieval tragedy, like all tragedy, not only presents evil but explains it. English Renaissance tragedy, including that of Shakespeare, incorporates this medieval view but also constitutes a shift from the mere presentation of the fall of princes to the justification of evil in God's retribution against those who bring evil upon themselves in their exercise of passion. Tragedies thus become *exempla* of moral philosophy, admonishing men to attend to the lessons of the consequences of evil in order to avoid ruin and misery. Renaissance theorists of tragedy fused the medieval notion of tragedies as *exempla* with the Aristotelian doctrine of drama as lively imitation, the latter teaching us (delightfully) how not to live.

But Willard Farnham, in *The Medieval Heritage of Elizabethan Tragedy*, interprets the significance of the fall differently. Without acceptance of the world, he claims, there can be no tragedy, only surrender. In spite of their scorn for the world, these medieval tales of the fall of illustrious princes transcend moralizing about man's evil to become absorbed emotionally and sympathetically in the sufferings of these princes. According to Farnham, affirmation of the grandeur of man, not denigration of him, is central to these tales of woe, and it is this affirmation that also characterizes Elizabethan tragedy, as indeed it does all tragedy. Thus, for Farnham, neither medieval nor Renaissance tragedy explains or justifies evil; it is an espousal of life in spite of evil.

Shakespearean and French classical tragedy, along with the ancient Greek, are universally acknowledged as the great moments in the history of dramatic tragedy. Shakespearean tragedy derives in part from the medieval type. The tragedies of Corneille and Racine, however, are partly rooted in Greek drama (and Roman, which was modeled on the Greek) and partly in an extensive interpretation (or misinterpretation) of Aristotle's *Poetics*.

The *Poetics* was not known in the West until the Italian Renaissance. The first critical edition with a commentary was Francisco Robortello's (1548). From the time of Robortello to that of Coleridge (and later, too) certain views about tragedy, either Aristotelian or attributed to Aristotle, were vehemently debated. The most notorious issue, of course, concerned the three unities. But imitation, purgation, probability and necessity, and action also figured prominently in the long discussion.

J. C. Scaliger first formulated the three unities of action, time,

and place. L. Castelvetro and others repeated them as being
necessary for tragedy. But it was the French theorists, and
especially Corneille (after *Le Cid*) and Racine, who codified the
unities and rendered them sacrosanct in their tragedies. The
doctrine that the action of a tragedy must coincide temporally
with the performance itself and that it must occur in one place
they based on an interpretation of Aristotle's notions of probability and necessity as verisimilitude—that is, on the way things
are likely to work in nature. To create and preserve belief in the
action on the stage, strict limitations of time and place must be
preserved. The audience cannot be expected to retain belief in
the action if it covers years or occurs in many different places.

According to French classical theory, however, the three
unities are not the main requirement of tragedy. The stress was
laid on imitation of a serious action, which was conceived of as a
representation of human action during a particular crisis of duty
or honor versus love, or of passion versus will or reason (as in
Racine's masterpiece, *Phèdre*). The tragic hero is not so much
renowned and prosperous as he is noble, in the quite literal sense
of belonging to the nobility. The action is confined to the crisis;
no complicated or double plots are tolerated, and no mixture of
the serious and the comic is allowed. Nor can there be scenes of
violence on the stage. The action also inspires pity and fear and
their purgation, which effects both pleasure and moral instruc-
tion. Finally, insofar as Aristotle's linguistic embellishments are
concerned, only verse, no prose, can be present.

The fact that these characteristics were considered to be
defining properties of all tragedy, and not simply French or
Greek tragedy, can be seen in Voltaire's indictment of the
tragedies of Shakespeare—especially *Hamlet*, which Voltaire
castigated as a "monstrous farce."

Dryden, Johnson, and Coleridge answered the French theorists by challenging, in effect, their restrictive defining criteria in
order to force an enlargement of the concept of tragedy to
include Shakespeare. In his *Essay of Dramatic Poesy* (1668),
Dryden first paid tribute to the three unities, not because they
produce verisimilitude but because they effect an aesthetic unity;
then he rejected the three unities, as well as the French conception of serious action, in favor of Shakespearean tragedy, with
all its irregularities, mixture of the comic and serious, use of
prose, and violation of the rules, on the ground that Shakespearean tragedy possesses a variety whose liveliness pleases as
the French, in all its rigidity, does not. Johnson supplements
Dryden's attack by dismissing credibility as basic to verisimilitude and to the two unities of time and place. He argued that

delusion, not belief, governs our response to the drama; and in order to justify Shakespeare's irregularities, he substituted truth to nature ("just representations of general nature") for truth to conventional rules. Coleridge ended the debate by rejecting both the French insistence upon the rules and Johnson's notion of delusion. Shakespeare's dramas, he argued at length, have their own unity, which is organic, not mechanical, like that of the French tragedies. We respond to these dramas, as we do to all poetry, not with belief or disbelief (delusion) but with the suspension of disbelief that constitutes poetic faith. With Coleridge, the tragedies of Shakespeare enter among the paradigms of tragedy.

Before Hegel, German critics and philosophers theorized about the nature of tragedy. Lessing conceived of tragedy as fundamentally a revelation and justification of the divine order in the universe, whereas Schiller contended that moral resistance to suffering, not suffering by itself, is primary in tragedy. F. Schlegel emphasized the struggle in tragedy between man and fate, which results in man's physical defeat yet also his moral victory; and A. W. Schlegel insisted on the ultimately inexplicable character of the tragic in the world. Goethe's brilliant insight that catharsis is best understood as expiation and reconciliation on the part of the hero rather than purgation on the part of the audience should also be noted.

Hegel, Schopenhauer, and Nietzsche proclaimed metaphysical theories of tragedy. Unlike Aristotle, who did not subscribe to any tragic fact in the world, imitated by dramatic tragedy, but only to the passage in human affairs from happiness to misery, these three philosophers concur in their basic doctrine that dramatic tragedy depicts and rests on some tragic fact in the world. For Aristotle, tragedy existed only in art, but for these philosophers there is tragic art primarily because there is tragedy in life. Hegel makes this explicit in his assessment of the life and trial of Socrates:

> In what is truly tragic there must be valid moral powers on both sides which come into collision; this was so with Socrates.... Two opposed rights come into collision, and the one destroys the other. Thus both suffer loss and yet both are mutually justified.... The one power is divine right, the natural morality ... objective freedom. The other ... is the right ... of subjective freedom.... It is these two principles which we see coming into opposition in the life and philosophy of Socrates.[1]

In his most important work on tragedy, *The Philosophy of Fine Art*, Hegel singles out *Antigone* as the best illustration of the tragic fact of collision and reconciliation. Two great forces are present in the play: public law and order, and familial love and duty. Both are good, both are integral aspects of a moral society (hence of absolute justice), and both are recognized to be such by Creon and Antigone. But both forces are pushed to their extremes by the protagonists, so that they negate each other, thereby violating the absolute nature of justice. And because of this violation, both Creon and Antigone are condemned. Only absolute justice is vindicated.

For Hegel the tragic hero, in drama as in life, is identical with the finite force he represents. Indeed, his tragic flaw consists in this identification, since it renders him one-sided and hence incompatible with the demands of absolute justice. His one-sidedness makes his action and condemnation inevitable.

Dramatic tragedy intensifies, unifes, and embellishes upon the tragic fact through plot, character, language, and scenic representation. It also produces the requisite pity and fear and purgation. But, Hegel argues, dramatic tragedy excites and purifies us by more than the sufferings of the hero, for our pity and fear are directed ultimately toward the might of absolute justice that rules the world, the comprehension of which brings us the feeling of reconciliation; and reconciliation, according to Hegel, is the true tragic effect.

All dramatic tragedies share the basic elements of collision and reconciliation. Ancient dramatic tragedy, however, differs from modern tragedy in regard to the modes of conflict and resolution. Because character is subordinate to ethical forces in ancient dramatic tragedy, the conflict is always between two ethical principles, even in *Oedipus Rex*, in which, Hegel with some strain (and obscurity) suggests, the conflict is between what one consciously wants to do and what one unconsciously has done. Resolution, and with it triumphant vindication of the ethical absolute, is achieved either by the downfall of the hero, as in *Antigone*; the surrender or sacrifice of the hero, as in *Oedipus Rex*; the harmonization of interests, as in *The Eumenides*; or reconciliation in the soul of the hero, as in *Oedipus at Colonus*. In modern dramatic tragedy, in which ethical forces are played down or are not present at all, or other forces than the ethical are at work and the subjectivity of character is paramount, the conflict centers in the hero himself. He is inwardly torn and thereby destroys himself. *Hamlet*, for example, is tragic not because Hamlet violates morality but because his noble nature prevents him from acting, and this, together with external circumstances, brings about his doom. Pure reconciliation is also played down or altogether eliminated in much modern tragedy.

It is present in *Hamlet* but not in *Richard III*, where it is replaced by "criminal justice"; nor is it to be found in many social tragedies, which, since they create only sadness at misfortune, are, for Hegel, not really tragic at all.

For Schopenhauer, the tragic fact in the world that is represented by dramatic tragedy, and without which there could be no such art form, is the terrible side of life—"the unspeakable pain, the wail of humanity, the triumph of evil, the scornful mastery of chance, and the irretrievable fall of the just and the innocent" (*The World as Will and Idea*, book 3, § 51). It is this tragic fact that hints at the nature of the world, at the ceaseless and futile strife of the irrational will; it also hints at the only way to escape from the struggle, namely, by complete renunciation of the will. Man can overcome the tragedy involved in volition not, as Hegel says, by mastering the dialectic of negation but only by totally surrendering the will to live.

Dramatic tragedy mirrors the tragic fact of life and at the same time projects the way out. By centering on the real tragic flaw, which is not the individual sin of the tragic hero but the original sin of being born at all, it demonstrates that "the representation of a great misfortune is alone essential to tragedy."

Great misfortune is represented in three ways: by a character of extraordinary wickedness, such as Richard III, Iago, Shylock, or Creon in *Antigone*, who authors his own misery; by blind fate, such as that which permeates *Oedipus Rex* or *Romeo and Juliet*, dramas in which chance and error dominate man; and by ordinary, decent characters in ordinary circumstances who hurt one another simply through the ways in which they are juxtaposed. This third kind, best exemplified by Goethe's *Clavigo*, is the greatest dramatic tragedy, because it depicts the tragic fact of life as it threatens or is actually experienced by most of us, who are neither monstrous nor placed in extraordinary circumstances. This type of tragedy, Schopenhauer concludes, leaves us shuddering because "we feel ourselves already in the midst of hell."

For Nietzsche, too, human suffering is basic to tragedy; but in his view it yields neither despair nor resignation, as it did for Schopenhauer, nor can it be overcome by reason and knowledge, as Socrates maintained. It can be transcended, but only by an affirmation of the life-force that lies behind it, by the belief that, "despite every phenomenal change, life is at bottom joyful and powerful" (*The Birth of Tragedy*, section vii). It is this affirmation that constitutes the "tragic myth," the fundamental truth about man, without which dramatic tragedy is impossible.

Suffering and affirmation derive from fundamental forces in

the world—the Dionysian and Apollonian; for nature rests upon
the duality between "intoxication" and "dream," between "individuality" and "unification." The world is a constant struggle
between the irrational, absurd, and ecstatic, on the one hand,
and the rational, intelligible, and harmonious, on the other.
Dramatic tragedy joins these two forces, and in this process the
tragic hero, in spite of his terrible suffering and his fall, affirms
his annihilation by accepting his consequent unification with the
Dionysian forces.

Thus, dramatic tragedy is a ritualistic affirmation of life. The
horrors of human experience are rendered palatable by the
principles of artistic order and beauty and triumphant through
the necessary destruction of human individuality. In Greek
tragedy the chorus and the hero represent this fusion of the
Dionysian and the Apollian. Apollo is the artistic victor, but
Dionysus is the metaphysical one. Consequently, the serenity
traditionally attributed to Greek tragedy must give way to the
orgiastic joy of man's identification with nature, which is the
hidden reality of Greek tragedy.

Dramatic tragedy, as myth and ritual, also includes the
spectator. He, too, is part of the pattern of unification with the
Dionysian forces. Like the hero and the chorus, he shares in the
affirmation of life that is presented in the annihilation of the
hero. The tragic effect, therefore, is not purgation, purification,
resignation, or detachment but joyful participation in the tragic
ritual, which alone offers "metaphysical solace" for our existence
in an absurd world.

Theories of tragedy abound in modern thought. Among the
influential (and logically interesting) ones are those of A. C.
Bradley, Joseph Wood Krutch, F. L. Lucas, E. M. W. Tillyard,
Una Ellis-Fermor, and Peter Alexander. For Bradley the essence
of tragedy, both human and dramatic, is the irretrievable
self-waste or destruction of value in the conflict of spiritual
forces in the world. Dramatic tragedy involves the requisite
action or conflict: a hero who need not be morally good but
must be touched by human excellence and who, because of his
one-sidedness (tragic flaw), is partly responsible for his inevitable suffering and fall; and the tragic effect, which includes
awe and admiration as well as pity and fear. But plot, character,
and, of course, dialogue and spectacle are tragic only because
they entail or are entailed by the essential self-waste of good, a
loss that cannot be ultimately justified or explained.

Krutch, in his jeremiad *The Modern Temper*, denies the
possibility of tragedy except in those ages (for example, the
Periclean and Elizabethan) when man accepts as real his own

nobility and importance in the universe. Tragedy, thus, is a representation not of noble actions but of actions considered to be noble. Without this projection—"the tragic fallacy"—there can be no tragedy. Tragedy may contain calamity, but it must show man's greatness in overcoming it. When calamity becomes an end in itself, thereby inducing misery and despair, as it does in modern tragedy (especially in Ibsen), the term "tragedy" loses its correct meaning, for tragedy cannot denigrate man; it must exalt him.

Lucas defines tragedy as "a representation of human unhappiness which pleases us notwithstanding, by the truth with which it is seen and the fineness with which it is communicated.... Tragedy, in fine, is man's answer to the universe that crushes him so pitilessly. Destiny scowls upon him: his answer is to sit down and paint her where she stands" (*Tragedy*, p. 78).

Tillyard distinguishes three types of tragedies: those of suffering, sacrifice, and regeneration. The tragedy of suffering (such as Webster's *The Duchess of Malfi*) involves the suffering of a strong character who is not greatly responsible for his plight and who protests against it as he reflects upon it and its place in the universe. The tragedy of sacrifice, which is rooted in religion, has for its characters a god, a victim, a killer, and an audience and, for its aim, the riddance of a taint on the social organism (as in *Oedipus Rex*). The tragedy of regeneration (such as Aeschylus' *Oresteia*) is one of spiritual renewal after disintegration; it symbolizes the life-cycle from birth to destruction, which leads to re-creation, and it is the "centrally tragic" (*Shakespeare's Problem Plays*, p. 14).

Una Ellis-Fermor, in *The Frontiers of Drama*, describes tragedy as an interim reading of life between religion, on the one hand, and Satanism, or pessimistic materialism, on the other. Basic to tragedy is the equilibrium of the evil that is observed and the good that is guessed at. Dramatic tragedy includes great strength of emotion, revealed through character, action, and thought, directness of presentation, and catastrophe. What is central, however, is the balance between an intense awareness of pain or evil, which is clearly revealed, and an intuitive apprehension of a transcendent realm of values. This balance is achieved by the chorus and outer action, as in *Agamemnon;* by inner and outer action, as in *Hamlet;* or by form and action, as in *Oedipus Rex.* In each case, evil is affirmed; but it is transcended by a higher good, which induces exultation, not despair or faith. The balance is destroyed when evil is denied, as in Milton's *Samson Agonistes;* or is seen as remedial, as in Elmer Rice's *The Adding Machine;* or is affirmed as ultimate, as in

Marlowe's *Dr. Faustus*. These dramas, therefore, are not true
tragedies.

Finally, Peter Alexander, in *Hamlet: Father and Son*, rejects
the traditional conception, according to which tragedy includes
hamartia and purgation, and defines tragedy instead as the
dramatization and celebration of the virtues of men—their
glory, achieved through affliction and calamity. Aretē, not
hamartia, is therefore central. Tragedy includes suffering and
calamity, but these need not be created and sustained by human
frailty or wickedness. Love, honor, or duty can also effect
suffering and catastrophe. Thus, hamartia as the tragic flaw that
justifies the hero's fall and punishment is not basic or even
necessary in tragedy. Nor is catharsis the rational acceptance of
the fall of the hero as a result of his tragic flaw; rather, catharsis
is an active mastery over life's pain, which is intelligible only if
tragedy glorifies human virtues.   Tragedy

Is there, then, a true theory of tragedy? Do any of the critics or
philosophers provide a true statement of the necessary and
sufficient properties of all tragedies, their common, essential
nature, by which all of them are tragic? Does any formula cover
all tragedies—Greek, Elizabethan, French, and modern—without omitting any of their tragic properties?

The fundamental disagreements among the theorists themselves about the nature of tragedy seriously call into question
such a formula; for, as we have seen, the theorists disagree not
only about the essence of tragedy but even about its necessary
properties. Do all tragedies have a hero? Do all tragic heroes
possess the tragic flaw? Are all tragic heroes responsible for their
fate? Do all of them suffer terribly, fall, and die? Are all touched
by greatness? Do all get their just deserts? Do all tragedies
commemorate human excellence? Do all end unhappily? Do all
stir us deeply? Is the action in all of them inevitable? Are there
collision and conflict in all? Do all induce catharsis in any of its
numerous senses—purgation, purification, reconciliation, and
so forth—or do all produce any other uniform reaction in their
spectators? There is much basic disagreement over all these
properties.

Perhaps, as the theorists imply, the disagreements can be
resolved by further examination of dramatic tragedies and of the
human situation. But neither of these yields a true theory of
tragedy. Research into all existing dramatic tragedies and the
probing of their shared properties reveal no essences. What, for
example, do *Oedipus Rex*, *Oedipus at Colonus*, *Medea*, *Hamlet*,
Phèdre, *Hedda Gabler*, *The Weavers*, and *The Three Sisters*, to

mention only a very few, have in common that makes them tragic and distinguishable from other works of art? Perhaps they share some similarities, but no set of necessary and sufficient properties is common to all. Nor will further examination of the human condition furnish us with a theory of tragedy, because there is no tragic fact in the world about which a theory of tragedy could be true or which would corroborate such a theory. There may be spiritual waste, loss of greatness, suffering, struggle, defeat, aretē, regeneration, explicable or inexplicable evil, and catharsis. But whether any of these, or a collection of them, is tragic cannot be determined by any investigation. In spite of the enormous effort expended by the great theorists, one cannot but conclude that there is no established true theory of tragedy.

Can there be a true theory of tragedy? It seems to me that there cannot be, for underlying every theory of tragedy is the assumption that tragedy has a set of necessary and sufficient properties. This assumption is equivalent to the doctrine that the concept of tragedy or the term "tragedy" and its adjectival derivatives have a set of necessary and sufficient conditions for their correct, intelligible use, and this doctrine is false. That it is false is disclosed by the logical behavior of the concept of tragedy, whose use has not and cannot have a set of essential conditions of employment.

It is the disagreements among the theorists about the necessary and sufficient properties of tragedy that provide the clue to the logical character of the concept of tragedy and the consequent impossibility of a theory, for these disagreements are not primarily over the application of accepted criteria for the correct use of the concept but over the very criteria themselves. What is central in the disagreements about the theories of tragedy are the debates over which criteria shall determine the correct use of the concept of tragedy.

The concept of tragedy, thus, is perennially debatable. The employment of the concept, both by the theorists in their attempts to answer What is the nature of the tragic? and by the critics as they proffer definitive reasons for Why is (a particular) x tragic? reveals that "tragedy" is a term whose *every* criterion of use is always open to fundamental question, challenge, rejection, and replacement. There is not a single definition or definitive set of reasons about the tragic in the entire history of tragedy, and of thought and talk about it, that has not been intelligently challenged and rejected, both as a definitive set of properties or conditions and, more important, as a necessary property or condition. Even one theorist's or critic's hamartia as absolutely necessary for tragedy becomes another's irrelevant property, condition, or criterion when he substitutes for it—not supplements it with—aretē, which is the very opposite of a flaw. It is this perennial debatability that best explains the theorists' and critics' employment of the concept of tragedy, and it especially explains their disagreements. Because the concept is subject to this kind of perennial debatability, it cannot (logically, conceptually) have a set of necessary and sufficient conditions of its use. Any putative real definition or any putative definitive reason for the tragic constitutes a violation of the concept of tragedy because it attempts to state or to employ essential criteria for a concept whose employment precludes its being governed by such criteria. The concept of tragedy, then, is open in the precise sense that it has no necessary and sufficient conditions but only a disjunctive set of nonnecessary, nonsufficient conditions and whose every condition is nevertheless intelligently rejectable and supplantable by another. This disjunctive set rules out everything as tragic; the perennial debatability of the concept of tragedy rules out not only any necessary criteria of the tragic but anything as an unchallengeable criterion of it: "What has Φ (whatever Φ may be) to do with x's being tragic?" always makes sense.

Tragedy is not definable (in the theory sense of true, real definition) for another reason, namely, that its use must allow for the ever present possibility of new conditions. It is simply a historical fact that the concept, as we know and use it, has continuously accommodated new cases of tragedy and, more important, the new properties of these new cases. One cannot state the necessary and sufficient conditions for the correct use of a concept whose employment entails the requirement that the concept be applicable to new conditions. Thus, the concept of tragedy is perennially flexible as well as perennially debatable. The concept is both; but neither implies the other. And both the perennial flexibility and the perennial debatability of the concept render a true theory of tragedy conceptually impossible, although either suffices to do so.

What, then, is the saving grace of all theories of tragedy, since they fail in their desideratum of essential definition? As with theories of art, their value lies in their pedagogical possibilities, not in their definitional vacuities. Each theory of tragedy expresses, thus, an honorific redefinition of "tragedy" that restricts the use of the term to a selection from its multiple criteria. It is this selection that gives point and value to all the theories of tragedy, for each serves, through its specific selection, as a recommendation to concentrate upon certain preferred criteria or properties of tragedy that are neglected, distorted, or omitted by other theories. If we attend to these criteria or properties instead of to the unsuccessful attempts at real definitions, we shall have much to learn from the individual theories about what to look for in tragedies as well as how to look at them.

Does criticism need a theory of tragedy in order to give intelligible reasons for any particular drama's being tragic? If it does, then discourse about the tragic is unintelligible, since there is not and cannot be such a theory. But such discourse is intelligible; hence, the reasons for describing something as tragic must depend upon something other than a theory. The critic, for example, says *"Hamlet* is tragic because it has Φ," whatever Φ may be; the words "because it has Φ" are intelligible not because Φ is necessary or sufficient for tragedy but because Φ is a member of an open set of acknowledged, yet debatable, traditional properties or of argued-for new properties of the tragic. The reasons require properties, but none of these properties need be necessary or sufficient; hence, none need depend for its cogency upon a theory of tragedy, although all depend on the openness of the concept of tragedy: that it is perennially flexible, like art and most of its subconcepts, and perennially debatable, unlike art and most of its subconcepts. It is this dissimilarity that makes the concept of tragedy special in the inventory of open concepts.

Genre and style are basic concepts in traditional aesthetics. Particular genre concepts, such as tragedy, have been of philosophical concern at least since Aristotle and are as vigorously discussed today by aestheticians and literary critics as ever they were in the past. Particular style concepts, such as Gothic, High Renaissance, or Baroque, are of relatively recent concern, although there are seminal intimations of them as far back as Vitruvius. Unfortunately, they have been of primary interest not to philosophers but to art historians.

Much has been written on the history of genre concepts; the history of style concepts has hardly been started. In twentieth-century discussions of the arts, genre is still the central concern of aesthetics and literary criticism. At the same time, however, style has become the most important concept of art history.

More striking than this contemporary division is that, historically, style seems to play a minor role in literary criticism and that genre, except in the special sense of a kind of secular painting, plays an even smaller role in art history. For example, it is surprising to discover that, although there are great critical essays on the characters, plot, philosophy, poetry, symbolism, and imagery of Shakespeare's dramas, there is no comparable work on Shakespeare's style.[1] Obviously, other concepts, which may or may not be equivalent to certain uses of style in literature, have been found to be more efficacious and illuminating than style in the analysis of Shakespeare's dramas. And we can accept, it seems to me, the major corpus of criticism of those plays, now annotated by ten generations of critics, as a paradigm of literary criticism. If we substitute for Shakespeare's plays the paintings of Leonardo or Raphael, of Rembrandt or Rubens, we can hardly mention a major critical or historical study that does not focus on the style of these artists. In literary criticism the concept of style seems to be dispensable in a way that it is not in art history. But genre is not dispensable to the literary critic. There is scarcely a book on the tragedies of Shakespeare that does not contain a first or last chapter on the nature of tragedy, a chapter included as an indispensable part of the discussion and judgment. This recurring concern with genre plays no role in art history. There are no first or last chapters on the nature of portraiture, landscape, religious painting, or the nude in which the historian of art tells his particular story. Indeed, when we read Kenneth Clark on *Landscape into Art* or *The Nude*, or Max Friedländer's *Landscape, Portrait, Still-Life*, we realize how ludicrous it would be for these historians to begin, end, or intrude with a definition of these genres, so obvious are they to all.

Chapter Five Whatever vagaries the history of genre and style concepts contains, one assumption about these concepts remains invariant: that they are definable in the Aristotelian sense of real definition, i.e., that necessary and sufficient criteria can be stated for their correct use and that, without such definitions, particular genre and style concepts cannot sustain their assigned roles. Many philosophers, literary critics, and art historians concur in the doctrine that there are such definitions, and, consequently, they direct much effort to formulating theories of genre in literary criticism and of style in art history.

In the two preceding chapters I have argued that the traditional assumption, shared by aestheticians and literary critics, that all genre concepts are or must be definable in order to render critical discussion intelligible, is false. For example, the concept of tragedy, examined in its actual role in poetics or literary criticism, exhibits itself as an open concept rather than a closed one, as has been traditionally assumed. That the concept of tragedy is open in the precise sense of having no undebatable necessary criteria can be seen in the range of disagreement over the nature of the tragic in general and over why or whether a particular work is tragic. The tragedy-giving reasons—that is, reasons given as answers to What is tragedy? Why is x tragic? or Is x tragic?—provide the clue to the perennial debatability of the concept and, in that sense, its openness.

There are, however, different kinds of openness among genre concepts. "Novel," "drama," "satire," "tragedy," and "art" itself are all open, but to consider these all together is to conflate two very different kinds of open concepts, neither of which is governed by sets of necessary and sufficient criteria: those concepts which have no undebatable necessary criteria and those concepts which have some undebatable criteria even though they are neither necessary nor sufficient. "Drama," "novel," and "art," as their uses reveal, have certain criteria that are not definitive yet are undebatable—criteria which "tragedy" does not have. For example, "X is a drama because it has a plot" cannot be challenged in the way that "X is a tragedy because it has hamartia" can be. "Plot" is neither necessary nor sufficient for something to be a drama, but neither can it be intelligibly challenged, as "hamartia" or any other criterion of "tragedy" can be.

Thus, some genre concepts in aesthetics are open in the sense that they have no necessary or sufficient criteria but do have some unchallengeable ones; and some are open in the sense that they have no necessary or sufficient criteria and no unchallengeable ones.

What, now, about the concept of style? Are there definitive sets of criteria for it or for any particular style concept? This is the question to be considered. Instead of beginning with philosophical theories of style, which are, surprisingly, not helpful, I propose to contrast what art historians *say* about style with the way they *use* particular style concepts when they write art history. Although some philosophers pay lip service to the need for detailed examination of style concepts, few have provided it, in spite of the fact that such elucidation is basic in any attempt to determine the nature of style and style concepts.

I shall discuss, in particular, the views of Meyer Schapiro, James Ackerman, Arnold Hauser, and E. H. Gombrich—all art historians—on the nature of style in art history and then test their doctrines in relation to the style concept of Mannerism, especially as it has been explored and developed by Walter Friedlaender, Max Dvořák, Craig Smyth, John Shearman, and Sydney Freedberg—all leading art historians of Mannerism and the *maniera*.

Meyer Schapiro's "Style" is a deservedly acclaimed classic on the nature of style in art history.[2] Its prime achievement, however, is its compendious and brilliant survey of the major theories of style, from Wölfflin to the present day. Schapiro's classification of these theories into cyclical, polar, evolutionary, psychological, and sociological is of singular importance in any philosophical attempt to understand the concept of style in art history. Of special value are his incisive criticisms of the presuppositions and doctrines of Heinrich Wölfflin, Alois Reigl, Paul Frankl, and others. Without making it explicit, he makes us see that theories of style in art history have conflated two distinct problems: What is a particular or period style in art? and How does it arise, mature, and change into a different style? As he abundantly shows, most theorists are concerned with the second—the causal—question rather than with the first—the substantive—question. Much of his critique centers on the deficiencies of the causal theories, especially their implicit determinism, which he rightly attributes to the influence of Hegel.

So far as the substantive question is concerned, Schapiro reminds us of the paucity of explicit definitions of style in art history. Instead of laying down definitive sets of criteria, art historians have applied the criteria they have found to be "the broadest, most stable, and therefore most reliable" (p. 83) for dating and authenticating works of art and for narrating a coherent history of art. These criteria—which Schapiro says are insufficient but which, he implies, are at least necessary in the art historian's use of style concepts—are "form elements or motives, form relationships, and qualities (including an all-over quality which we may call the 'expression')" (p. 83).

Other criteria, advanced by certain theorists, such as technique, subject matter, and material, Schapiro concedes to be important, especially when they are interpreted in formal terms, i.e., as form elements and relations; but he denies that they are necessary features of the concept of style in art history.

Unfortunately, Schapiro, because of the encylopaedic intent of his essay, cannot enlarge upon these formal and expressive criteria. Nevertheless, the terms are clear enough, both in the tradition of aesthetics and in his own use. For unlike, say, Wölfflin's criterion of *malerisch*, Schapiro's criterion of form element, which he clarifies by the example of the pointed as against the round arch, and his criterion of expressive quality, which he clarifies by the example of the cool or warm tertiary qualities of certain colors, are at least semantically unobjectionable as criteria of style in art.

What is most important and provocative in his essay, I think, and what we must later relate to the practice of art history, is Schapiro's own specific view of the concept of style. He writes: "By style is meant the constant form—and sometimes the constant elements, qualities, and expression—in the art of an individual or a group" (p. 81). Does his claim about the *constancy* of certain properties as basic to style or a particular style correspond to, for example, the actual use of the concept of Mannerism by the art historians of Mannerism? I hope to show that testing this claim brings to light the fundamental weakness of Schapiro's elucidation of the concept of style.

In "A Theory of Style," James Ackerman means, by a theory

of style, a definition of style and an explanation of why style changes.[3] For him both are essential to art history. Style for the art historian is not a discovered concept but one created by abstraction from the ensemble of characteristics of works of art found in a particular span of time and place; this concept he then employs as a tool for dating individual works of art and, more important, as a pattern to provide a structure of stability and flexibility in the history of art.

Works of art have many characteristics; consequently, from among them, the art historian must choose those that best satisfy the criteria of stability and flexibility in order to establish a historical order out of the continuum of self-sufficient works of art. On this basis, Ackerman rules out the characteristic of materials (e.g., wood or stone), because it is not sufficiently changeable; he rules out, as well, the characteristic of unique expressiveness, because it is too ephemeral. These are symptoms, not determinants, of style. Rather than these characteristics, or even techniques, which are important to style only when they enhance formal or symbolic elements, Ackerman chooses conventions of form and symbolism because they "yield the richest harvest of traits by which to distinguish style" (p. 56). Conventions include "an accepted vocabulary of elements—a scale of color, an architectural Order, an attribute of God or a saint—and a syntax by which these elements are composed into a still-life, a temple, or a frieze" (p. 56). The assigned meanings of these conventions define the element of symbolism in style.

In explaining why styles change, Ackerman, like Schapiro, among others, rejects the traditional determinist theory that style and changes in style follow a preordained pattern of evolution. In place of the notion of stylistic evolution as a succession of steps toward a solution of a given problem, Ackerman argues—and this, I think, is his most original and radical thesis—that we must explain this evolution "as a succession of steps away from one or more original statements of a problem" (p. 59). The history of style is not a series of solutions of problems but "a succession of complex decisions as numerous as the works of art by which we have defined the style" (p. 60).

This emphasis on the history of style (and hence, of art) as a series of statements away from an original statement rather than as a sequence of attempted solutions culminating in an ideal statement enables Ackerman to lay down his criteria for the cogency of particular style concepts. Any particular style concept is formed on the assumption that a particular ensemble of conventions and symbolism is sufficiently stable, distinct, and relevant to justify hypothesizing it as a style. Each ensemble represents a class of related solutions to a problem which differs from distinguishable previous or later problems. Because of the limited, restrictive nature of a problem in art, the more modest the extension of a particular style concept, the more rewarding it is for study. There is no such defining problem in the Renaissance or Baroque; hence these are too grand for style analysis. Mannerism, on the other hand, is a limited style, with an ensemble of conventional and symbolic characteristics embodied in a clearly distinguishable series of statements away from the original statement of a problem.

Ackerman's article raises many issues, all of which merit scrutiny, but I must confine myself to the one issue that relates most immediately to our problem of theory and practice in art history: Is Ackerman's theory of style consonant with the use of the concept by the art historians of that style? Does "Mannerism" serve to mark out, in a challenging, hypothetical way, an ensemble of conventions and symbolism or a series of related solutions to a clearly statable problem? Here, too, as with Schapiro, I shall try to show that Ackerman overstates his case.

Arnold Hauser writes on the nature of style and changes in style in two books, *The Philosophy of Art History* and *Mannerism: The Crisis of the Renaissance and the Origin of Modern Art.*[4] Both are vigorous defenses of the sociological conception of art, which, in his modified Marxist version, explains art as an expression, rather than a crude reflection, of certain specified economic and social conditions. On his view, Mannerism, for example, is best understood "as an expression of the unrest, anxiety, and bewilderment generated by the process of alienation of the individual from society and the reification of the whole cultural process."[5]

Styles are sociologically conditioned. But to explain them—to do art history—is to understand style itself, without which there can be no history of art. Consequently, much of Hauser's philosophy of art history deals with the substantive question, What is style? In a remarkably eclectic and sometimes penetrating analysis of about 150 pages, in which style is compared to institutions, gestalts, language, musical themes, and ideal types and is contrasted with entelechies, organic wholes, predetermined goals, and platonic ideas, Hauser finally settles on his doctrine of style as "a dynamic relational concept with continually varying content, so that it might almost be said to take on a new sense with each new work."[6]

In his book on Mannerism, Hauser so beautifully articulates the meaning and the implications of this doctrine that I cannot forgo quoting his full statement:

It can rightly be complained that there is no such thing as a clear and exhaustive definition of mannerism, but the same complaint can be made of every other style, for there is and can be no such thing. There is always a centrifugal tendency in the nature of any style, which influences a variety of not strictly adjustable phenomena. Every style manifests itself in varying degrees of clarity in different works, few, if any, of which completely fulfil the stylistic ideal. But the very circumstance that the pattern can be detected only in varying degrees of approximation in individual works makes stylistic concepts essential, because without them there would be no associating of different works with each other, nor should we have any criterion by which to assess their significance in the history of development, which is by no means the same thing as their artistic quality. The historical importance of a work of art lies in its relationship to the stylistic ideal it seems to be striving to achieve, and that provides the standard by which its original or derivative, progressive or retrograde, nature can be judged. Style has no existence other than in the various degrees of approximation towards its realisation. All that exist in fact are individual works of art, different artistic phenomena differing in purpose. Style is always a figment, an image, an ideal type.[7]

As I understand this statement, Hauser's central thesis is that the concept of style, or any particular style concept, is and must be governed by a set of definitive criteria which guarantees its use in the historical ordering of artistic facts. With this as his fundamental premise, he then argues that because these criteria—as a complete set—obtain in no one work of art and yet are essential to art history, they must constitute a fictional ideal. His theory of style as a necessary ideal fiction rests upon his presupposition that style concepts, as they are employed in art history, are logically closed. He shares this doctrine with all the traditional theorists whom he rejects; it is at its most vulnerable, I think, when it is contrasted with the actual procedures of style-giving reasons in art history. Do the historians of Mannerism, for example, talk about its particularity and unity without assuming or needing to assume any set of definitive criteria, ideal or not? Here, again, the contrast between what the art historian says about style and how he uses it becomes glaring.

Our fourth example, E. H. Gombrich, has been much concerned with the many aspects of what he calls "the riddle of style." Among his writings, the two essays "Norm and Form: The Stylistic Categories of Art History and Their Origins in Renaissance Ideals" and "Mannerism: The Historiographic Background" are most pertinent here.[8]

In "Norm and Form" Gombrich's central theme is the derivation of all traditional style terms from an acceptance or rejection of the Classic. The origin of the concepts Romanesque, Gothic, Manneristic, Baroque, Rococo, and Romantic (all initially terms of abuse) as well as the origins of the concepts Classic, Renaissance, and Neoclassic are normative, not descriptive. Beginning with Vasari's castigation of the Gothic or German manner of "Confusion and Disorder," which Vasari bases on Vitruvius' similar denunciation of similar wall decorations of his day, Gombrich contends that traditional concepts of style and particular style concepts in art history blend norm with form, evaluation with description. Every attempt to dissociate these norms from their forms fails, and is bound to fail, because these styles cannot be described without normative criteria. Even Wölfflin's five sets of polarities—linear and painterly, plane and

depth, closed and open form, multiplicity and unity, and clarity and obscurity (which Wölfflin claims are descriptive and which Gombrich reduces to certain principles of composition and representation)—function in his art history as normative, i.e., as the classical versus the less-than-classical.

Traditional style terms are inevitably normative. But, Gombrich suggests, their norms, although historically rooted in the great classic reconciliation of ordered composition and faithful representation, need not be divided neatly into classical and anticlassical. The latter, articulated by the exponents of classicism, tend to be vices or sins to be avoided and hence function according to "the principle of exclusion." But there are movements or styles in the history of art which do not reject the values they oppose, as anticlassical styles do; rather they recognize the multiplicity of artistic values and choose priorities among them. Such styles, Gombrich says, function according to "the principle of sacrifice." Even though it is difficult to draw a line between these styles—which Gombrich calls "unclassical"— and the anticlassical, or between these two and the classical, it can be done by determining which of the two principles is operative. Mannerism has been described as an anticlassical style. But, Gombrich asks, is it so clear that Mannerism aimed at an avoidance of order and harmony rather than at a shift in priorities?

Gombrich poses this question in his essay on "Mannerism." Here he argues, as he has in his Story of Art, that Mannerism is fundamentally a style of experimentation, of virtuosity, of attempts to outdo one's immediate masters in invention and caprice. It has nothing to do with spiritual or personal crisis, occasioned, as some historians claim, by social or religious dislocation.

That Mannerism is unclassical, not anticlassical, that it exemplifies a shift in priorities, not a revolt against classic balance and representation—this, Gombrich insists, is a hypothesis, as indeed are all style concepts. Articulated and defended by Vasari, in the form of *bella maniera* (or *maniera moderna* or *terza e perfetta maniera*), and reformulated by Bellori and later critics who censured it, "Mannerism" as a style concept was created to meet a historiographic need: to secure an artistic ranking for those who emulated and restored the ideal perfection of classical antiquity as against those who merely imitated the great cinquecento masters. Modern historians, such as Dvořák, who praise Mannerism as the sixteenth-century style of spiritualism in its perennial struggle against materialism (or even Gombrich himself, who characterizes Mannerism as a distinct style of virtuosity and experimentation) also hypothesize in their efforts to meet their historiographic needs.

I can hardly do justice here to the subtlety of doctrine and argument of these two essays, let alone to the issues they raise. Gombrich's primary achievement, however, must be noted, namely, his insight that no understanding of the concept of style or of particular style concepts is possible without a delineation of the role these concepts play. His brilliant attempt to establish this role in the historical home base of the concepts—in Vasari and Vitruvius—as essentially normative is of great philosophical importance. But is he correct in his central doctrines, that style concepts are hypotheses and that at least the traditional ones are inevitable blends of norm and form? Do the historians of Mannerism, of which he is a distinguished representative, employ the term as a hypothetical norm? It seems to me that Gombrich's interpretation of the concept is more a stipulation as to how we ought to regard it than a correct elucidation of how it is actually used in art history.

Other historians of art theorize about style and its changes. A full account should include at least the theories of Wölfflin, Reigl, Panofsky, Frankl, and even the metaphysical conception of Malraux that style in art is a transformation of the meaning of the universe. Moreover, certain rejections of style as the crucial concept of art history are relevant to our problem. For example, George Kubler has recently pleaded for the replacement of the concept of style by what he calls the idea of "a linked succession of prime works with replications, all being distributed in time as recognizably early and late versions of the same kind of action."[9]

Then, too, we must not overlook the fact that great histories of art have been written without the concept of style. It is a refreshing shock, for example, to reread Berenson's *Italian Painters of the Renaissance* and discover, unless I have missed it, that he does not even mention "style." To be sure, he refers to "schools," but the categories by which he analyzes them are the aesthetic ones of form, tactile values, and illustration; obviously Berenson thought that these aesthetic concepts were sufficient for coherence in his history of art.

Important as all these considerations are, I reluctantly pass them by and, on the assumption that our four examples constitute a fair sample of theory of style in art history, ask instead whether what they say about style corresponds to what art historians do with it when they turn from theory to practice. What can we now learn from the historians of Mannerism about the concept of style?

I begin with Walter Friedlaender's "The Anticlassical Style."[10] This essay, a historical gem of iridescent argument and flawless organization, helps lay the foundation of our modern conception of Mannerism. Mannerism, Friedlaender contends, begins in Florence around 1520 as a conscious revolt against the ideals of the High Renaissance, especially as these ideals are embodied in the paintings of Andrea del Sarto and Fra Bartolommeo; and it is initiated by two of their pupils, Jacopo da Pontormo and Rosso Fiorentino.

That there is such a break and that it is recognized by their contemporaries, Friedlaender documents from Vasari's condemnation of Pontormo's Certosa frescoes (1522–25). In these frescoes, Vasari says, Pontormo repudiates his former beauty and grace to take over the German manner of Dürer, lock, stock, and barrel. Vasari, Friedlaender points out, correctly perceives in these frescoes a rejection of the ideals of the High Renaissance—the ideals epitomized in the *terza e perfetta maniera* of Leonardo, Raphael, and Michelangelo.

What are these ideals? According to Friedlaender—and this he feels is basic to understanding the origins of the anticlassical style—they are certain aesthetic and ethical norms that govern the representation of the human figure in pictorial space. Central in the classical art of the High Renaissance—which for Friedlaender lasts only twenty years, does not include Michelangelo, and is best exemplified in the mature work of Raphael—is an objectively idealized harmony of figure and space.

Decisive in anticlassical Mannerism is the rejection of this

normative conception of art. "The canon apparently given by
nature and hence generally recognized as law is definitively
given up. It is no longer a question of creating a seen object in an
artistically new way . . . 'as one ought to see it.' . . . Rather . . .
it is to be recreated . . . from purely autonomous motives, [as]
one would have it seen" (p. 6). A new conception of the human
figure in pictorial space, with its attendant new rhythmic
beauty, is central in the new style. Figure and space can be
distorted. Volume can displace space or create a space that is no
longer three-dimensional. Instability rather than harmony becomes the ideal. Friedlaender sums up anticlassical Mannerism
as a spiritually subjective movement, directed primarily against
the canonically objective art of the High Renaissance.

Pontormo is the pioneer of the new style. After a classic and
even transitional period, Pontormo, retreating from the plague
in Florence, composes five scenes from the Passion in the
Certosa of the Valdema near Florence.

> As if impelled by the tragedy of the theme toward another
> and more inward style, Pontormo . . . shed all that was grace-
> ful and shining in the Renaissance atmosphere. All that had
> been established by Andrea del Sarto and his circle, the em-
> phasis on the plastic and the bodily, the material and color-
> istic, the realized space and the all too blooming flesh tones—
> everything outward now disappears. In its place are a formal
> and psychological simplification, a rhythm, a subdued but
> still beautiful coloring . . . and above all an expression rising
> from the depth of the soul and hitherto unknown in this age
> and style [pp. 23–24].

The figures, gothically thin or bodiless, swaying or elongated;
the space, unnatural or unreal; the discordant motifs; and the
intensive religiosity—in part derived from Dürer, in part anticipated in Pontormo's early work but now transmuted—all these
establish Pontormo as the first great artist of Mannerism.

Pontormo's translation of the artistically observed object into
subjectively spiritual terms is paralleled by the work of Rosso
Fiorentino. After his own period of classicism, followed by one
of vacillation, Rosso "takes the decisive step away from the
balanced and classical towards the spiritual and subjective" (p.
29) in his *Deposition from the Cross*, in Volterra (1521).
Intertwinings of vertical ladders and elongated, swaying figures,
unreal space, sharp light and color, even cubistic surfaces and
angularity, together with emotional intensity, contribute "to a
new spirituality, an astonishing soulful expressiveness, which
even Rosso himself rarely reaches again. . . . Everything is

heightened, and everything that would disturb or diminish this heightening—space, perspective, mass, normal proportion—is left out or transformed" (p. 31).

Rosso's *Moses Defending the Daughters of Jethro* (before 1523) goes further in the quest for pure abstraction. Psychic depth is supplanted by an aesthetics of form, color, ornamental overlapping, and spatial layers, which produce an unstable tension betwen picture surface and spatial depth. In construction and color, Friedlaender says, "this painting . . . is the strangest, wildest picture created in the whole period, and stands quite apart from every canonical normative feeling" (p. 34).

The third of the founders of anticlassical Mannerism is the non-Florentine, Francesco Parmigianino. In Parma, under Correggio's tutelage, he inclines toward the bizarre and unnatural. But it is in Rome (1523–27), where he probably encounters Rosso, and after the sack of the city (1527), when he leaves Rome, that his Mannerist style emerges. His famous verticalism, so pronounced in his *Vision of St. Jerome* (before 1527), and notable especially in his *Madonna of the Long Neck* (1535–40), where it becomes elegantly elongated, is probably influenced by Rosso and is certainly anticlassical. The *Madonna of the Long Neck*, not only in its elongations of figure and column but in its astonishing and ambiguous asymmetrical relations and its overall expressive quality of exquisite grace, becomes another of the paradigms of the early Mannerist style of Italian art.

The new style, thus, rests on Pontormo, Rosso, and Parmigianino. It is fully formed between 1520 and 1523. From Florence it proceeds to Rome, whence, after the sack of the city and the consequent scattering of artists, it spreads, mainly through Rosso and his follower, Primaticcio, to the court at Fontainebleau and then to northern Europe. Through Parmigianino it enters the Venetian art of Bassano and Tintoretto, and, through Tintoretto, it influences the greatest of the Mannerists, El Greco. In Florence, Pontormo's pupil, Bronzino, carries on the style that then evolves into the *maniera*—or second generation of Mannerism—which Friedlaender, in a later essay, "The Anti-Mannerist Style," characterizes as a degeneration of "the noble, pure, idealistic, and abstract style" of anticlassical Mannerism.[11]

Friedlaender draws two important conclusions from his account: that Michelangelo is not the founder of Mannerism, and that Mannerism is not a weak imitation of Michelangelo. While it is true that Michelangelo is anticlassical almost from the beginnings of his work, that there are strong Mannerist elements in his treatment of space as far back as 1511, in the spandrels of the Sistine Ceiling, and that his *Last Judgment* (1541) is the "overwhelming paradigm of Mannerism," his characteristic elongations and distortions—so typical of Mannerism—turn up after 1520. Indeed, Friedlaender argues, Michelangelo is a Mannerist only from 1525 to 1530, when he returns to Florence to create the Medici *Madonna* and the *Victor;* and he is Manneristic only in some of his works, since this is the period of his great non-Mannerist *Times of Day* of the Medici Chapel.

Friedlaender's brilliant, revolutionary essay has been much praised and criticized. Few, if any, question what is undoubtedly his greatest achievement: that of bringing us to look at the work of three neglected great artists in a new, historically grounded, and enhancing light. Many, however, object to his chronology, his specific attributions and explanations of influence, his particular examples or criteria of Mannerism, and his interpretation of the work of Pontormo, Rosso, and Parmigianino in relation to the *maniera* proper.

What has not been done and needs doing if we wish to understand the concept of style in art history is to elucidate the role Friedlaender assigns to his basic style term, "anticlassical Mannerism."

What Friedlaender does is to employ a style term which he borrows from the seventeenth-century detractors of the *maniera*, and which he extends to cover the sources of the *maniera* in Pontormo, Rosso, and Parmigianino, in order to distinguish, characterize, relate, and revaluate a whole group of artists and their work. As he employs the term to cover the first generation of painters he is concerned with in his inaugural lecture, "anticlassical Mannerism" functions under certain criteria, but these criteria add up to no definitive set and correspond to no essential set of properties shared by all anticlassical Mannerist works. Friedlaender offers no definition (hence, in one sense of theory, no theory of Mannerism)—no statement of its essence. Nor does he state or imply that, without such a definition, he can give no cogent reasons for particular works' being Manneristic. All Friedlaender suggests is a "decisive" criterion: a new artistic relation to the observed object that, more particularly, is a spiritual or subjective (in a nonoptical sense) conception of figure and space in their asymmetrical relations. It is this criterion that he falls back on both to characterize Mannerism and to contrast that style with the normative, balanced, unambiguous, and stable ideal governing the relations between figure and space in the High Renaissance.

That Friedlaender has no definitive set of criteria for his style term and hence no real definition of "anticlassical Mannerism" can be seen best if we look at the various reasons he gives for particular works' being Manneristic. They comprise a large group. A particular painting, he says, is Manneristic because it has crowding of figures, a narrow layer of space, half-figures seen from the back, bodiless figures, elongated figures, swaying figures, spilling of figures or, again, pictorial elements over the frame, impetuous or harsh color, preciosity, cubistic surfaces, rejection of perspective, overlapping of spatial layers, compression of space, elegant grace, violence, turmoil, the bizarre, or a particular kind of spirituality. And there are others.

Diverse as these reasons are, they function as "Mannerist reasons" for Friedlaender, I submit, only because they derive from or center on the decisive criterion of the subjective relation between figure and space. This criterion, I have already suggested, is not necessary and sufficient—definitive—for Fried-

laender. But is it either necessary or sufficient, as he uses it? It seems to me absolutely clear that this criterion is not sufficient, since he rejects certain works, such as Michelangelo's late frescoes, *Conversion of St. Paul* and *Crucifixion of St. Peter*, and his Rondanini *Pietà*, as Manneristic even though they satisfy this criterion. We must acknowledge, however, that the criterion is necessary for him, because there is no example in his essay of a work that is in the Mannerist style that does not satisfy this criterion.

And now we must ask, Is this criterion clear? If we spell it out, as Friedlaender so beautifully does, as an asymmetrical, uncanonical relation between figure and space, with its consequent artistically subjective, spiritual, expressive quality, or, even more fully, in terms of all the "Mannerist reasons" he presents throughout his essay, we do have a criterion, or rather a related cluster of criteria, regarding unnatural space and figure, asymmetry, violence, elongation, elegance, and the like, that are as empirically grounded as they can be. They have their empirical counterparts in the world outside art. If, for example, "elongation" is vague, its vagueness rests on its ordinary use, not on its use in talking about style. The same is true, it seems to me, for all the criteria surrounding Friedlaender's one decisive criterion. The possible exception is "spirituality." But here again, I think, Friedlaender provides clear, empirically grounded criteria: painting an observed object as you would want it seen as against how it ought to be seen according to an objective canon.

I do not wish to suggest that all of Friedlaender's criteria or reasons, even if they are clear in the sense of being empirically grounded, are descriptive of properties in works of art in the same way. It may well be, as I think it is, that "spiritual," unlike, say, "violent" or "elegant," is more interpretive or explanatory than descriptive. I shall return to this problem later. All that needs saying here is that Friedlaender's criteria are not vague in the way that other criteria of style concepts, such as Wölfflin's "*malerisch*" or even Dvořák's own use of "spiritual," are. The vagueness is not in Friedlaender's decisive criterion or cluster of criteria for "Mannerism" but in the concept itself. This vagueness is the clue to the logic of style concepts, which is not to be found in Friedlaender or any other art historian considered in isolation and which has, as a result, been overlooked by all the art historians writing *about* style concepts. It can be discovered only in the disagreements among the art historians over the criteria—clear or vague—for their style concepts as they employ these concepts in their separate histories.

"El Greco and Mannerism," by Max Dvořák, is another classic in the modern conception of Mannerism.[12] Starting with the climax rather than the beginnings of sixteenth-century Mannerism, Dvořák finds in the Spanish work of El Greco the culmination of three tendencies: the late antinatural form of Michelangelo, the antinatural color and composition of Tintoretto, and the new spirituality of Saint Theresa and the Spanish mystics. All three influence El Greco, all three are embodied in his work, and all three, with minor variations on the new spirituality, characterize the whole of sixteenth-century European Mannerism and show it to be an expression of the perennial conflict between spiritualism and materialism in European culture.

There are great methodological differences between Dvořák and Friedlaender regarding the explanation of the origins of Mannerism. Dvořák concentrates on cultural, Friedlaender on artistic, factors in the development of the new style, but there is little disagreement on the distinguishing features of Mannerism itself as a post–High Renaissance style. Dvořák perhaps emphasizes a particular range of light and color more than Friedlaender, but both stress antinatural figure and space; and both center on the new spirituality. Their great difference is over the content of spirituality. For Friedlaender, we remember, it is purely formal, having to do with an autonomous, subjective mode of observing artistic objects. For Dvořák, it is not formal but iconographical, having to do with artistic embodiments of the doctrine that our knowledge of God and of the Christian mysteries consists in their immediate emotional certainty: "to know what you do not know." This rejection of rationality for mysticism, already present in the late works of Michelangelo and in his disillusionment with the ideals of the Renaissance, and dominant in the visionary style of Tintoretto as well as in the

French artists, Dubois and Bellange, culminates in the works of El Greco in Toledo.

"What I see," said Saint Theresa, "is a white and red that cannot be found anywhere in nature, which give forth a brighter and more radiant light than anything man can see, and pictures such as no painter has yet painted, whose models are nowhere to be found, yet are nature herself and life itself and the most glorious beauty man can conceive."[13] El Greco, Dvořák says, "sought to paint the kind of things the saint beheld in her ecstasy."[14] In the *Burial of Count Orgaz* (1586–88), *Christ in the Garden of Gethsemane* (1608–14), the *Opening of the Fifth Seal* (1610–14), *Resurrection* (1597–1604), and *Toledo in a Storm* (1595–1600), to mention only those Dvořák does, El Greco fuses the formal qualities of antinatural color, figure, and space with the iconographic quality of the vision of the supernatural. These paintings do not represent the supernatural, they reveal it.

Sixteenth-century Mannerism, then, as Dvořák characterizes it, is primarily spiritual in its pictorial manifestation of the mystical knowledge of God and the world. Whether Dvořák regards this spirituality, with or without the formal qualities of antinatural color, space, and figure, as a real definition of "Mannerism" I do not know; that he so regards it is certainly not so obvious as some of his commentators and critics claim. What is obvious—and important to the elucidation of the concept of Mannerism—is that he differs from Friedlaender, not over the definition or criteria of "Mannerism," but primarily over the meaning and criteria of "spirituality." Dvořák's use of "spirituality," unlike Friedlaender's, is, I think, vague precisely because it is obscure: how can immediate, emotional knowledge of the supernatural, whatever that is, become part of a painting? If Friedlaender's "spiritual" is interpretive in an explanatory sense, Dvořák's is at best interpretive in a purely invitational sense. That is, Dvořák's is not a hypothesis that helps to explain a picture; it is a recommendation to see it in a certain way.

I want now to turn to some recent discussions of Mannerism that are radically different from Friedlaender's or Dvořák's. But before I do, I must say something, even if in the baldest way, about one other philosophically important variant on the use of "Mannerism." In *From Leonardo to El Greco*, Lionello Venturi writes on Mannerism as one aspect of European painting in the sixteenth century.[15] On the whole, his account is based on Friedlaender's (and others'), with a stress on anticlassicism—which Venturi traces to the neoplatonism of Ficino—and on the pure formalism of the movement. Classical art's great reconciliation of the ideal with the real is rejected by Mannerism; nature is repudiated, and the ideal is transformed into a cultivation of abstract forms for their own sake, in which imitation of the High Renaissance masters (especially in figures and motifs) and inventions that are purely imaginative supplant imitation of nature. Eventually this imitation and invention lead to mere repetition of forms (in the second generation of Mannerism) and to the consequent debilitation of the movement.

Venturi insists that, whether in its Italian development or as a European International Style, Mannerism is too varied and complex to yield a definition. Rather than an essence or common denominator, Venturi offers "salient characteristics." Hence, what makes his account philosophically significant is that the reasons he gives for particular works' or artists' being Manneristic rest on a family of characteristics, none of them seemingly necessary or sufficient. Pontormo and Rosso, for example, are Mannerists because of their antinatural treatment of figure and space; but Domenico Beccafumi's "sensitive handling of light [e.g., in his *Birth of the Virgin* (1543)] and his *sfumato* implemented by a dexterous use of lights and darks qualify him to rank as a mannerist" (p. 234).

Venturi's most provocative claim, however, has to do with some of the major works of Tintoretto, which most art historians today would count among the paradigms of Mannerism. Venturi argues to the contrary that Tintoretto briefly flirts with Mannerism and then, like Titian and other Venetians, rejects it; consequently, his major works, such as the *Miracle of St. Mark* (1548), the great series in the Scuola di San Rocco (1564–88), or the *Last Supper* (1591–94) in San Giorgio Maggiore, are not Manneristic. They are un-Manneristic, however, not because they fail to meet defining criteria but because their salient characteristics differ from those of Mannerism. These paintings, fundamentally incantatory and religious, stress content, not form. Light and shadow, space and movement, and "one of the richest palettes known to painting" (p. 216) help create a new unity of form and matter, of ideal and real, that transcends Mannerism altogether.

The word "Mannerism" derives from the Italian *maniera.* Linguists and art historians trace *maniera* to Boccaccio's "manner" of doing or behaving (1353), Cennini's "style" of an individual artist or group of artists (1390), Ghiberti's "style" of an age (1450), Raphael's "three styles" of buildings in ancient Rome (1519), and Vasari's "style," used either with a qualifying term, such as "beautiful" or "German," or used absolutely, in the sense that an artist has style. Vasari's conception of *maniera* is regarded as the most important because of its role in sixteenth-century art and criticism. Contemporary art historians debate Vasari's exact meaning of the absolute sense of *maniera,* as well as the relation between this use and his other uses. Whatever the resolution of this issue may be, the term takes on the derogatory meaning of "stereotype" for Dolce (1557) and the even more pejorative sense of "fantastic idea" for Bellori (1672). Baldinucci coins *ammanierato,* "mannered"—again as an abusive term (1681). The substantive "Mannerist" comes from Fréart de Chambray (1662) and is introduced into English by Dryden in his translation of Du Fresnoy's *De Arte Graphica* (1695). "Mannerism" (*der Manierismus, le maniérisme, il manierismo*) as a style term designating a particular period of Italian art comes into general use only in the nineteenth century.[16]

"Mannerism" derives from *maniera.* In the same way, Mannerist art derives from the art of the *maniera.* The *maniera,* hence Mannerism, is a continuation of High Renaissance ideals; consequently it is not anticlassical in form or content. Such is the major thesis of a number of recent art historians. The first of these I wish to consider is C. H. Smyth. In "Mannerism and *Maniera,*"[17] Smyth turns to the sixteenth-century conception of *maniera* as it was articulated by Dolce in his dialogue *The Aretine (Dialogo della pittura, intitolato l'Aretino,* 1557) and by Vasari in his *Lives,* especially in the introduction to part 3 (1550; 2d ed., 1568), the two basic texts. Central in Dolce's dialogue is the contrast he draws between Michelangelo and Raphael. He praises only Raphael, because his paintings have no *maniera,* "namely, bad practice where forms and faces almost always look alike."[18]

This uniformity, which Dolce chastises, is, Smyth claims, the ideal that Vasari praises: "*La maniera* became *la più bella* from the method of copying frequently the most beautiful things, combining them to make from what was most beautiful (whether hands, heads, bodies, or legs) the best figure possible, *and putting it into use in every work for all the figures.*"[19] It is this ideal that reaches perfection in the sixteenth century.

Although Vasari and Dolce agree that *maniera* idealizes uniformity (the one liking it, the other not), neither, Smyth contends, understands what is behind this uniformity, what is fundamental in *maniera* painting, namely, "the more or less consistent application of principles that governed form and movement—principles of posing figures at rest or in motion and of delineating, lighting, and grouping them."[20] It is these principles—conventions, habits, formulas—that characterize *maniera* painting and relate to *maniera* as a sixteenth-century term.

Here is Smyth's list of these conventions: flattening of figures parallel to the picture plane; twisting of poses in two or three directions; flat light that intensifies the forced flatness of figures; juxtaposition of figures; angularity, especially of the arm across the chest or in the air; transformation of live figures into statues; attention to finish and details; and habitual tipping of the ground of the figures. Of these conventions regarding figure, composition, and space, figure is the most important.

What are the sources of these conventions? Primary is antique relief, especially extant Roman sarcophagi of the second to fourth centuries. *Maniera* painting, unlike painting *all'antica*, elaborates upon and modernizes the flatness of light and figure, the uniformity of poses, and so forth, of its models. Other sources are quattrocento neo-Gothic, Michelangelo's *Battle of Cascina* and the Lazarus he contributes to Sebastiano del Piombo's *Raising of Lazarus*, and even Raphael, in *Parnassus*.

After "the gathering of the *maniera*," the *maniera* begins in earnest in Florence, then Rome, then Fontainebleau. Its best practitioners include Bronzino, Vasari, Salviati, Beccafumi, Polidoro, Perino, and Parmigianino, among others, but not Pontormo in the Certosa frescoes. During its heyday, in spite of its emphasis upon uniformity, *maniera* allows for variations and surprise under another Vasarian rubric, that of license within the rules derived from antiquity. These variations range from emotionless distance to high seriousness. Between these extremes, the *maniera* "is in its element as decorative enrichment, encrusting walls, tapestries, and minor objects."[21] It finally disintegrates when uniformity becomes monotony, and invention overelaboration. But in its prime it creates works of art that can no longer be devalued.

Maniera in theory and practice is essentially an art of pose and gesture, modeled on antique relief. In the art and writings of Vasari, for instance, *maniera* represents no revolt against the High Renaissance, no expression of spiritual crisis. How, then, Smyth asks, can the modern conception of Mannerism as a formally anticlassical and expressively spiritual movement be reconciled with its source, the *maniera*? It cannot; consequently, "Mannerism" should apply only to the *maniera* painters and those who anticipated them. Thus, Pontormo's Visdomini altarpiece (1518) is Manneristic but not, for example, his *Christ before Pilate*, "however sensitive, refined, abstract, private, irrational, or eccentrically expressive."[22] This painting and similar ones (which for Friedlaender are among the paradigms of Mannerism) are best regarded, Smyth suggests, following Gombrich, as postclassic experimentations with High Renaissance forms, not as rejections of them. Instead of dividing painting in the period from about 1515 to 1590 into first- and second-generation Mannerism, he concludes, it would be better to retain the old term, "Late Renaissance," as a label for the whole period and restrict "Mannerism" to the *maniera* and its immediate antecedents.

John Shearman, in "*Maniera* as an Aesthetic Ideal" and in *Mannerism*,[23] goes further than Smyth in rejecting Mannerism as an anticlassical style and in identifying Mannerism with the *maniera*. For Shearman, Mannerism has its roots deep in the High Renaissance. "It became something different and individual by taking a part of the High Renaissance and subjecting that part to special development."[24] Among its models are some of Michelangelo's *Ignudi* (1511–12) of the Sistine Ceiling—especially in their elegance, grace, and poise—and the unnatural beauty and harmony of color and form of Raphael's *St. Michael*
(1517). Already anticipated by Leonardo, the refined style—which is the clue to the *maniera*, hence to Mannerism—is as much a theme in the full orchestration of the High Renaissance as the proto-Baroque is. Mannerism begins and develops easily as an art of articulate, sophisticated beauty, not out of spiritual crisis and despair. Its pervasive aesthetics of poise and grace rules out completely the traditionally attributed qualities of strain, brutality, violence, and overt passion. It is neither anticlassical nor a concentration on uniformity of pose and gesture, modeled on antique relief; both Friedlaender and Smyth, therefore, are in error in their conceptions of the Mannerist style.

"Mannerism" must be and can be defined. For without a true definition, Shearman contends, its use remains arbitrary and without controls in the historical account of sixteenth-century art. What is the proper meaning of "Mannerism"? What are the defining qualities of Mannerist works? What group does the term cover? These are the central questions Shearman sets himself. All three answers lie in the sixteenth-century meaning of "*maniera*." For when Lanzi first introduces the term "*manierismo*" (in 1792), which is our direct source of the term "Mannerism," it applies to painters and the qualities of their work that are much talked about, appreciated, and criticized in the sixteenth century.

What, then, is *maniera*? Although there is some variation, the evidence garnered from poetry, from the literature of manners, from certain writings of Dolce and Aretino, but most importantly from Vasari's *Lives*, points to the overwhelmingly absolute use of the term. *Maniera* as "style," which one has or lacks, is Vasari's key term. He uses it to distinguish and to rank periods of Italian art; he singles it out as the only term of his famous five—*regola, ordine, misura, disegno,* and *maniera*—that needs no definition, so well is it understood; and he means by it a certain kind of artistic accomplishment and refinement, with all that these encompass.

Vasari's and the sixteenth-century absolute sense of *"maniera"* descend from the French courtly literature of manners of the thirteenth to fifteenth centuries. Central in this tradition is the notion of *savoir faire*—of comporting oneself with civilized sophistication and manner. To behave with style is to be poised, elegant, refined, and effortless in a perfected performance. From these positive qualities, certain others, perennially regarded as negative, follow: To have style is to be unnatural, affected, self-conscious, and ostentatious. Also involved in this artificial code of behavior is the repudiation of revealed passion, evident effort, and rude naïveté.

The Italian literature of manners, especially Castiglione's *Il Cortegiano* (1528), is basic to Vasari's *"maniera"* as well as to the whole of *maniera* art and criticism. Elegance, refinement, artificiality, effortless overcoming of difficulties (*sprezzatura*), virtuosity, and grace—all construed as positive qualities—are the obvious parallels between style in life and style in art. They are also the defining properties of the *maniera* in sixteenth-century art.

"Mannerism" has its linguistic and historic roots in the *maniera.* It was, and should be once again, a term reserved for an art "drenched in *maniera.*"[25] The alternative, Shearman says, is the chaos of contemporary arbitrary definitions and the consequent distortion of our understanding of sixteenth-century art.

Properly understood, Mannerism, in its overriding concern with the perfection of style, is fundamentally the "stylish style." As it develops, it embraces other aesthetic qualities, all compatible with those invested in *maniera:* variety, abundance, complexity, fantasy, obscurity, finish of detail, even the erotic, grotesque, esoteric, and pornographic. Although it is a style in which constituent parts of a work of art become as important as and sometimes more important than its whole, and in which content or subject is subordinate to form, Mannerism is not anticlassical but merely unclassical in its reversal of the normal relation of form and content. Perhaps, Shearman suggests, it is best understood as a supersophisticated classicism because of its preoccupation with form as style.

Mannerism starts in Rome, not in Florence. Its vital years of growth are 1520–27. "There was then in Rome, by chance, a brilliant group of young men, headed by Perino, Polidoro, Rosso, and Parmigianino, and it was in their hands that Mannerism was shaped into a style of universal significance."[26]

Perino del Vaga introduces it to Florence in 1522–23 with his cartoon, the *Martyrdom of the Ten Thousand*, which in spite of its subject exhibits a rarefied Olympian ballet of *maniera* qualities to serve as a second great model to the young painters (the first model was Michelangelo's *Battle of Cascina*). Perino's cartoon, all refinement and invention, was apparently entered in competition for a commission against Pontormo's design of the same subject, which was "full of passion, dynamic sequences of form, and explosive movements."[27] That Perino's work was chosen instead of the anticlassical contribution of Pontormo constitutes "a turning-point in Florentine art."[28] After his Volterra *Deposition* (1521) and his (newly discovered) *Dead Christ* (1526), done in Rome, Rosso becomes another leader of Mannerism and takes the *maniera* with him to Fontainebleau. The great Florentine period of Mannerism comes in the third through fifth decades of the century, with Bronzino, Vasari, Salviati, Cellini, and Giovanni Bologna. Even Michelangelo, at about the same time, in his architecture, sculpture, and drawing, furthers the *maniera* with his inventions, especially his serpentine line.

Mannerism, with "its self-conscious stylization [as] its common denominator of all Mannerist works of art,"[29] exhibits itself in painting, sculpture, and architecture. It also includes gardens, fountains, and grottoes. Its virtuosity and hedonism accommodate as well the grotesque, the monstrous, and the pornographic—all for the sake of variety and amusement. Its accent on form rather than content, on style for its own sake, is also present in music and poetry. Mannerism, then, for Shearman, is an International Style of the sixteenth century, covering all the arts.

Shearman raises many issues in his spirited account of Mannerism. Central is his definition of *"maniera"* as a sixteenth-century term for style and as a style term. That Mannerism is not anticlassical in form or expression follows from his definition, as do all the reasons he gives for various works' or artists' being or not being Manneristic. Pontormo is never Manneristic, Rosso's *Deposition* is not; nor are El Greco, Tintoretto, Pordenone, or Berruguete, whom he does not mention. Michelangelo is a Mannerist in some of his works—the *Victor*, for example—yet not for Friedlaender's reasons, but because of its "grace, complexity, variety, and difficulty."[30] So, too, with Giulio Romano's Palazzo del Te, whose exterior and interior are both Manneristic, not because of their total rejection of classical principles, but because of their wonderful assortment of variety and caprice, designed to delight rather than depress.

However admirable Shearman's consistency of application of his criteria of *maniera* may be, and however commendable his attempt to force a revaluation of the second-generation Mannerists, we must ask: Is his definition of *"maniera"* correct? And, more important, I think we must ask: Does his account of Mannerism rest on a true definition of "Mannerism"?

I shall come to these questions presently, when all the evidence will be before us. Just here, however, the basic issue between Friedlaender and Shearman can be stated: Is the *maniera*, whatever and whomever it includes, a debilitation of the anticlassicism of Pontormo and Rosso, or is it an entirely separate movement? Friedlaender rests his case on the *maniera* as an outgrowth of anticlassicism; Shearman, on the *maniera* as one flowering of the High Renaissance.

Can this disagreement be resolved by any true definition of *"maniera"*? Shearman thinks it can and must be. He is positive about *maniera* as the refined style. Smyth, we remember, is just as positive that *"maniera"* means ideal uniformity of pose and gesture, modeled on antique relief. Others, even among those who agree that *"maniera"* is predominantly an absolute term of style in the sixteenth century, differ from both Smyth and Shearman in believing that *"maniera"* denotes only "the characteristic and indefinable feature of an artist's expression"[31] and so functions in the same way as the later *"je ne sais quoi"* of the French theorists. That the disagreement over the meaning of *"maniera"* can be resolved by a true definition may be as much a delusion as the assumption that a true definition of "Mannerism" can settle the disagreements over that term.

Our final essay is S. J. Freedberg's "Observations on the Painting of the Maniera."[33] As elusive as the *maniera* is, even in its chronology, Freedberg dates it from about 1540 to 1580 and centers it in Florence and Rome. Its pervasive strain is its artificiality of both form and content, which correctly invites its mannered quality as well as its sixteenth-century name.

In its theoretical aspect, *"maniera"* as sophistication and grace is first attributed by Vasari to the masters of the *maniera moderna*. Leonardo, Raphael, and Michelangelo achieve *bella maniera*, which is to function as the subsequent standard for all art. Thus, *maniera*, as Vasari conceives it, is a special quality which distinguishes the moderns from the quattrocento. Freedberg, however, claims that those masters would not have accepted it as their unique and paramount contribution, for the modern style, which we call the High Renaissance, is one that, like all classical styles, is founded on "a synthetic adjustment between aesthetic preference and actuality" (p. 188). Vasari's *"maniera"* or *"bella maniera,"* because of its emphasis upon achieved perfection in art to the neglect of art in relation to nature, is merely classicistic—an imitation of classical models rather than an acceptance of the classical ideal of reconciliation of the aesthetic with the actual.

That *maniera* is classicistic and hence both an adherence to, and a betrayal of, the High Renaissance, Freedberg continues, can be seen in its practice as well as its theory. In form and content *maniera* painting divorces itself from nature to concentrate upon the aesthetic. Art becomes commentary on appearance instead of description of it. Abstraction and the reworking and transmutation of extant artistic forms replace classical idealization of nature. Plausibility gives way to aesthetic convincingness, achieved by the brilliant technique of hard delineation of line and lucid color, accenting the surfaces of things. Even *maniera*'s emphasis on the plastic, where flesh becomes stone and stone becomes live, is a classicistically borrowed rendition of Michelangelo's sculpture.

In its allegiance to antecedent art as its sole source of inspiration, *maniera* painting is also an art of quotation. Its particular forms, and in many cases its particular subjects, are taken from High Renaissance or antique models. These quotations, severed from their contexts, become distorted and redirected so that their original meanings change in their new *maniera* settings. The inevitable ambiguity and multivalence that result, Freedberg points out, contribute to the over-all elusiveness and artificiality so highly prized by the *maniera*. Even the mask—"the single most pregnant symbol" (p. 187) of the *maniera*—is masked, as in Bronzino's *Allegory*, where it seems to reveal more of life than life's real face.

This penchant for visual quotation often combines with verbal quotation, especially in the *maniera* narrative fresco cycles, which, because of their deliberate obscurity of sources or their transformations of them, constitute some of the most difficult rebuses in the history of art. All that remains clear is the ostensible decorative achievement—the reworking of all the materials into an outsize precious ornament, with total disregard for the preexisting architectural structure surrounding the frescoed wall.

In *maniera* religious art, the apparent contradiction between detached refinement and attached devotion is resolved by the quality of aesthetic exaltation, the *maniera* equivalent of religious devotion, which is generated by the vibrance of the forms

and the tensions of the meanings. This art can best be compared
to the traditional icon: "In both, the subject matter is rigidified, translated from history toward symbol; and the form in which it is presented is made crystalline and tends toward the abstract ... and this form is the object of a precious working and elaboration" (p. 194).

Maniera painting, thus, is an art of disjunction and multivalence. The High Renaissance fuses meanings of form and content. The immediate postclassical painting of some of Raphael's pupils and of Pontormo and Rosso fractures this unity either by emphasizing either form or content to the exclusion of the other or by pitting one against the other. But *maniera* makes "an artistic principle of multiplicity and multivalence" (p. 194). What, then, is the relation between the High Renaissance, the post-Raphaelesque Roman school, the expressionism of Pontormo and Rosso, and the *maniera*? How much of the period 1520–80 is Mannerist?

The pupils of Raphael, especially Perino and Polidoro, are classicistic and become, along with the Roman convert, Parmigianino, the forerunners of the *maniera*. Pontormo and Rosso, "the fractious Florentines," are experimental even to the extreme of being anticlassical; but this is true only from 1520 to 1526, and even then they also strive for the *maniera* qualities of grace, finesse, and ornament. With these two reminders about the limited role of anticlassical revolt and the constant presence of *maniera*, Freedberg returns to the Friedlaender distinction between first-generation or Early Mannerism and the *maniera*. Having characterized the various styles between 1540 and 1580, he proposes a proper use of "Mannerism" rather than a definition of it. Basic to his decision is his affirmative answer to the questions: Are the style or styles of Pontormo, Rosso, and others of the so called first generation of Mannerism "sufficiently close in essential ways to that of the Maniera to be connected with it, rather than distinguished from it by a different name"? and Are the styles of both Early Mannerism and the *maniera* "sufficiently distinguishable in essential ways from that of the classical High Renaissance" (p. 195)?

Mannerism, thus, according to Freedberg, has its linguistic roots in the *maniera* but its artistic roots in the immediate postclassical period of the High Renaissance. The great difference between Early Mannerism and the *maniera* is the restrictive character of the latter. "Its specialized aestheticism is a limit on what we may call the humanity of art" (p. 195). This criterion also serves to relate Tintoretto and El Greco to Mannerism; for both, like Pontormo and Rosso, transcend their *maniera* vocabulary to affirm the "profundity of overt human drama" (p. 195) in art.

Other essays, especially some on the architecture of Mannerism and on Mannerism as an International Style, ought to be considered in any complete discussion.[33] Some reputable historians of sixteenth-century art deny that Mannerism is a separate style, preferring to treat its various manifestations as expressions of the late Renaissance under the general rubrics of Early, High, and Late Renaissance art.[34] The arguments they advance, some for the extension, some for the elimination of the style term, add nothing, I believe, to the logic of the concept of Mannerism, since they revolve around the enlargement or rejection of the same sets of criteria employed by those historians whom we have detailed and who do regard Mannerism as a separate style, "with the same kind of reality (and no more) as the other style periods that are commonly acknowledged."[35]

Proceeding on this assumption, that Mannerism is a style in sixteenth-century art, I want now, in this concluding section, to return to our two central questions: How do the historians of Mannerism use the style concept of Mannerism? and How does their use compare with what art historians say about the concept of style in art history?

Among our six historians, there is much agreement: on the sources, nature, and development of Mannerism and the *maniera* of the sixteenth century, especially in Florence and Rome. But there is as much disagreement over the place and date of the origin of Mannerism and over its specific relation to the High Renaissance, its chronology, its relation to the *maniera*, its paradigms, its range, and its causes.

Fundamental to all these major disagreements, I want to argue, are not the varying purportedly true definitions of "Mannerism," which Shearman claims are the main source of disagreement, but different sets of criteria for the correct use of "Mannerism." If we turn, as we must, from their quarrels about the sources, influences, paradigms, extent, and development of Mannerism to their supporting reasons, we can find the clue to their disagreements as well as to the logic of the concept of Mannerism. Their style-giving reasons are central in the elucidation of the concept of Mannerism. Their answers to What is Mannerism? are to be found in their reasons for particular works' or artists' being Manneristic.

"Mannerism," for each of our six historians, is a style term that functions as a name or label to designate certain sets of certain works of art of the sixteenth century whose similarities

and differences from previous and later works or from some
contemporary works warrant their grouping as an independent
unity or style.

Corresponding to these sets of characteristics—"Manneristic-
making properties"—are certain sets of criteria for the correct
use of "Mannerism." Each historian has his own set, which
differs, sometimes radically, from the others. Only one, Shearman, states that his is a definitive set and therefore a true
definition of Mannerism, although it is possible to attribute such
a set to Dvořák and to Smyth as well. However, if my account
of Friedlaender is correct, he most certainly has no such set of
criteria, only a complex necessary criterion regarding figure in
space. And both Venturi and Freedberg disclaim definitions of
"Mannerism."

Whatever the claims or disclaimers about definitive sets of
criteria or even about the necessary criteria for the correct use of
"Mannerism" as a style term, we must now ask: Is there extant
such a set or a necessary criterion? Can there be, if the concept of
Mannerism is to retain its assigned role? Need there be, in order
to provide a coherent account of Mannerism?

Affirmative answers to these three questions rest on the
assumption that Mannerism and, indeed, all style terms are
logically closed concepts, amenable to true definitions in terms
of their necessary and sufficient criteria, which correspond to
their necessary and sufficient properties.

It is this assumption, I believe, that is false. That it is false can
be seen in the actual functioning of the criteria for "Mannerism"
as these criteria play their role in the style-giving reasons of the
historians of Mannerism. In order to understand the logic of
style concepts, we must turn from the debates about the nature
of Mannerism to the full range of disagreement over why or
whether a particular work or artist is or is not Manneristic.
There we find that Mannerism is not a closed concept; the
concept of Mannerism does its assigned job only on the assumption that there is *no* definitive set of criteria, *no* necessary
criterion for its correct use. For example, Friedlaender, we recall,
says that Michelangelo's *Victor* is Manneristic because of the
figure's "screw-like upward thrust, his long, stretched-out,
athlete's leg, his small Lysippian head, and his regular, large-
scale, somewhat empty features."[36] Shearman agrees that the
work is Manneristic but gives reasons which have nothing to do
with anticlassical figures in space: the *Victor* is Manneristic
because of its "grace, complexity, variety, and difficulty,"[37]
achieved mainly through Michelangelo's serpentine line, which
expresses completed rather than restless or disturbed action.

Again, for Friedlaender, Pontormo's *Christ before Pilate* is a
paradigm of Mannerism; for Smyth, it is a paradigm of sixteenth-century expressionism and is not Manneristic at all,
because it has no ideal uniformity of figure or pose.

And so it goes. Without repeating the evidence, I want to
insist that, unless it recognizes the indigenous vagueness of the
concept, no reading of the vast array of disagreement among the
historians over why or whether a particular work or artist is or is
not an example, let alone a paradigm, of Mannerism can do
justice either to the disagreements or to Mannerism as a historical phenomenon.

As its use in style-giving reasons reveals, "Mannerism" is not
closed but vague, in the sense that the criteria for its correct use
are not complete or completable. To claim that the criteria are
complete or could be—as for example, by stipulation, to render
these criteria as a precise set—is to misunderstand and foreclose
on their assigned role in the history of art.

What is this vagueness that I claim as the basic logical feature
of the concept of Mannerism? Consider as an illuminating model
an example we have already considered from C. L. Stevenson:
the concept of a cultured person. I say of someone that he is a
cultured person; I am asked why he is or why I say he is, and I
reply: "Because he is widely read and acquainted with the arts."
My questioner counters: "Nonsense. To be sure, he reads a lot,
and he knows much about the arts, but he has no imaginative
sensitivity; so he's a boor, not a cultured person at all."

In this exchange, both of us are working toward persuasive
definitions of "a cultured person," definitions that rest on
stressed criteria. These criteria are vague in two different senses:
"Imaginative sensitivity" is unclear and obscure in a way that
"widely read" and "acquainted with the arts" are not. But the
latter two are still vague in the sense that they provide no precise
cutoff point or boundary in their application. Individual criteria,
therefore, can be vague in meaning or application.

There is a third kind of vagueness in this example, one that
Stevenson suggests but does not explore: the inadequacy or
incompleteness of the set of criteria; for "cultured" is vague in its
extant or professed set of criteria, and this vagueness differs
from the vagueness of the individual criteria. Here vagueness
contrasts with completeness, not with clarity or precision.

"Mannerism" is like "cultured." Its individual criteria may be,
although they need not be, vague in their meaning or application. "Spiritual" is obscure in Dvořák's set of criteria. "Elongation" has no exact application in all cases: where, for example,
does "elongation" end and "verticality" begin in Friedlaender's

set of criteria? Friedlaender's "spiritual," on the other hand, is not obscure; nor is his criterion of "spilling over the frame," which is as exact a criterion and no more vague in application than "pregnant: with child" is.

But "Mannerism," like "cultured," is vague in another sense as well: its set of criteria, whether its individual members are clear or not, exactly instanced or not, is incomplete and incompletable.

As we have shown, art historians employ "Mannerism" to label, describe, interpret, and evaluate or revaluate certain works of art with certain specified characteristics in a specified region of space and time. It does its assigned job under certain criteria. For one historian (Friedlaender), it functions under a "decisive" criterion, which comprises a number of others, a, b, and c. For a second historian (Dvořák), it functions under similar criteria, a, b, and c, but, since c has a different interpretation, let us call it d. For a third historian (Venturi), it functions under a cluster of "salient" criteria, a, b, c, e, and f, where no one criterion is necessary and no collection of them is sufficient. For a fourth historian (Smyth), "Mannerism" functions under a general criterion, "*maniera*" (let us call it m), which in turn functions under the criterion of ideal uniformity of pose and gesture, n, and is regarded as definitive for both "Mannerism" and "*maniera*." For a fifth historian (Shearman), it functions under the same general criterion, "*maniera*," which in turn functions under the criteria of refinement, artificiality, difficulty, and grace—o, p, q, and r—which are also claimed to be definitive for both "*maniera*" and "Mannerism." Finally, for a sixth historian (Freedberg), it functions under two sets of criteria: "*maniera*," to which he adds the criterion of multiplicity and multivalence of meanings, s; and experimental or anticlassical expressionism, t.

In every case we can ask whether these criteria are clear and are precisely applicable to the works specified as Manneristic by the historians. If they are not clear or are questionable in their application, they are vague. But they are not vague in the way in which the individual sets of criteria—a, b, and c; a, b, and d; "*maniera*" (as n; as o, p, q, and r; as s); or s and t—are vague or even as all these sets together are vague. For the vagueness of the sets, taken individually or collectively, is a vagueness of the incompleteness and incompletability of the set. Therefore, the fundamental vagueness of "Mannerism" consists in the perennial possibility of intelligibly enlarging or exchanging the criteria for its correct use. Unless we acknowledge this vagueness of the concept of Mannerism, we cannot make sense of the different moves which our historians have successively made and which future historians may make when they choose still different criteria—perhaps even other than formal and iconographical ones—that will enable them to present a new account of Mannerism.

"Mannerism" is not only irreducibly vague; it is also beneficially vague. It is because its criteria, being incompletable, allow for new histories of Mannerism that the concept offers new sources of illumination of the works of art themselves. These new ways of inviting us to look at works of art—explicable only if we assume the possibility of new or enlarged sets of criteria—are as integral a part of art history, and of the role of style concepts in it, as the authentication and dating of works of art. The historian's interpretations of particular works of art or groupings of them are as important as any of his other pro-

cedures. Without the vagueness of "Mannerism," these new interpretations, so rich in their aesthetic implications, would cease to come into being. It is consequently simply not true that without a true or real definition of "Mannerism" its history remains chaotic. Indeed, *with* such a definition—a complete set of necessary and sufficient criteria—there would be no continuing history of Mannerism.

"Mannerism," then, if my argument is correct, has no definition, no set of definitive criteria, or even any necessary criterion. It does not need such criteria in order to support its style-giving reasons. It cannot have such criteria if the historical role of "Mannerism" as an irreducibly and beneficially vague concept is to be preserved.

"Mannerism," we have said, functions under certain criteria, none necessary, none sufficient, none definitive. These individual criteria are sometimes clear and clearly instanced, but they are also often obscure and inexact in their application.

These individual criteria can be classified also as descriptive or interpretive. All are employed by our historians to mark out features of works of art which they label Manneristic. But only some of them are descriptive in their use. I suggested in our discussion of Friedlaender that, as he uses the term "spiritually subjective," it functions as an interpretive term to integrate all the Manneristic elements of a painting. It purports to explain the work rather than to describe one aspect of it. Because it rests on elements in the work—uncanonical space, antinatural figure, asymmetry, unnatural color—that are related under the category of the nonoptically subjective way of observing objects in space, Friedlaender's "spiritually subjective" is a hypothesis about what is central in a Manneristic work. Dvořák's "spirituality" is also in part an interpretation of certain elements in certain works of art, especially the Toledo paintings of El Greco. But because he invests these works with an element that is not clearly present (namely, emotional certainty of religious beliefs), his criterion serves to invite us to see these paintings as spiritual in his sense rather than as an explanation of the elements to be seen in them.

Many criteria of "Mannerism" are interpretive rather than descriptive in their use. All that are claimed to be central, whether definitively or not, are interpretive, serving as explanatory hypotheses about Mannerist works. But there are others, not put forth as central, which are also interpretive: "elusive" as against "violent," "empty features" as against "elongated ones," "menacing" as against "brutal," and so on.

This whole subject of the kinds of criteria, or terms and utterances, to be found in art history deserves thorough investigation. In *Hamlet and the Philosophy of Literary Criticism*, especially in part 2, I have tried to show the fruitfulness of distinguishing among the various kinds of terms and utterances in the clarification of many disputes of literary critics. I have no doubt that similar results could be obtained from a careful consideration of the terms and utterances of art history.

That "Mannerism" is irreducibly vague, it can now be summarily shown, does clarify many of the fundamental disagreements among the historians of Mannerism. Debates about the origins of Mannerism, its place and date of origin, its founders, its paradigms, its range and development, whether or why a particular work or artist or group is or is not Manneristic, whether Mannerism is an International Style, encompassing not only painting and sculpture but architecture, music, and literature as well—all of these, I submit, are not questions that yield true or false answers that ultimately depend upon definitive criteria of "Mannerism." On the contrary, all of them are explicable only in terms of the selected criteria from the inexhaustible, vague set of criteria of "Mannerism." Does Mannerism start in Rome or in Florence? In 1520, or in 1530? With Pontormo or with Perino? Is it inspired by Michelangelo, and by his *Battle of Cascina, Ignudi,* or the *Victor*? Does it include Tintoretto? Does it include Pontormo? Is it anticlassical, unclassical, classicistic, or superclassical? Each of the professed answers revolves systematically around criteria garnered from an inexhaustible class of criteria.

The attempt to pin down the criteria of "Mannerism" to those of the *maniera* rests, I think, on a double illusion: that the *maniera* is clearly definable and that Mannerism is identical with the *maniera*. As we have seen, there is no agreement on the definition of the *maniera*; what is more devastating, even if there were, it would not follow from such a definition that Mannerism as a style phenomenon descends from the linguistic rather than the artistic roots of the *maniera*. On this issue, Friedlaender and Freedberg exploit one range of possibilities among the criteria of "Mannerism," Shearman a different range. Whether Mannerism is to be restricted to its linguistic rather than artistic origins depends on the historian's decision, not on a historical fact.

That the style concept of Mannerism is irreducibly vague contrasts sharply with the various statements about the concept of style in art history by Schapiro, Ackerman, Hauser, and Gombrich. This contrast, therefore, provides the answer to our second question: How does the use of "Mannerism" compare with the art historians' statements about the concept of style in art history? If my account of the role or logical grammar of "Mannerism" is correct, this follows: their doctrines that styles are constancies of form motives, form relations, and expressive qualities; or are stable yet flexible ensembles of characteristics; or are fictional ideals of necessary and sufficient properties; or are hypothetical blends of norms and forms—all these doctrines are inadequate in the same fundamental way. They leave out the irreducible vagueness of at least one style concept, and they do so because they overlook the range and significance of disagreement among art historians in their style-giving reasons.

With the exception of Hauser, whose definition of style as an ideal essence is itself a fiction, invented to satisfy the spurious need for necessary and sufficient criteria as a buttress for style-giving reasons, the various statements about style apply brilliantly to the historians of Mannerism, taken in isolation, independently of their disagreements with one another. Here, especially, constancy and ensemble take root in the particular sets of criteria for the correct use of "Mannerism" offered by the individual historians. Both Schapiro and Ackerman give adequate descriptions of our six historians' different uses of "Mannerism." For each of these historians employs criteria that serve to mark out certain constancies of form elements, form relations, and expressive qualities or certain ensembles of convention of form and symbolism on the assumption that these constancies or ensembles are sufficiently stable and flexible to render Mannerism a separate style. Ackerman's additional claim that these ensembles are hypotheses—which Gombrich generalizes as a universal doctrine about (traditional) style concepts, but which Ackerman restricts to the criteria rather than the style concept—is also sound because the individual sets of criteria for

"Mannerism" do function as interpretive hypotheses about what is central, though not necessarily definitive, in Mannerist works. It is, therefore, not the emphasis upon the hypothetical character of the criteria that is defective in the art historians' account of style; it is their omission of what is implied by this hypothetical character, namely, the perennial possibility, and thus irreducible vagueness, of competing sets of criteria as integral at least to Mannerism as a style concept. Ackerman's reading of Mannerism or any other legitimate style as a series of related statements away from an original statement of a problem is an especially revealing example of this deficiency. Is there, we must ask, a clearly statable problem of Mannerism? What is to count as an original statement of Mannerism, as the historians of Mannerism make abundantly clear, is itself at stake in the intrinsic debatability of the concept.

Gombrich's contention that all (traditional) styles are hypothetical blends of norm and form requires special consideration. As it stands, it is ambiguous. If it means, in the case of Mannerism, that "Mannerism" is used by historians to describe and evaluate, it is certaintly true but hardly exciting. If it means that the extant criteria of "Mannerism" comprise both descriptive and evaluative ones, it is true for some historians, e.g., Shearman's "refinement," but not true for others, e.g., Friedlaender's criteria, which are descriptive or interpretive. If it means, as I think Gombrich intends it, that *every* criterion for "Mannerism" is both normative and descriptive, then we have a thesis that is as exciting as it is false. For example, are all of Friedlaender's criteria reducible to an implicit preference for "the less-than-classical" that parallels Gombrich's reduction of Wölfflin's purportedly descriptive polarities to the normative or preferred classical versus "the less-than-classical"? Does Friedlaender simply exchange one principle of exclusion for another? To be sure, Friedlaender rejects Wölfflin's list of "sins to be avoided," but he does not offer a new set in their place. It may be urged, as Gombrich does, that this is exactly what Dvořák attempts with his criterion of "spirituality." But, as we have seen, Friedlaender's "spiritually subjective" functions as an interpretive, not as an evaluative or even descriptive, criterion. Once it is introduced, he also employs it as a basis for a revaluation of Mannerism. Its introduction, however, blends description of artistic elements with an interpretation of them. Friedlaender offers a hypothesis about form—i.e., antinatural figure in unnatural space—in order to dissociate this form from a traditionally invested norm. This procedure is not to blend norm and form, any more than cleansing our eyes is to exchange one pair of glasses for another. Gombrich, it seems to me, confuses blending norm and form with neutralizing traditional blends in order to procure a new evaluation of form. To neutralize is not necessarily to evaluate or revaluate, although it may be motivated or succeeded by them.

In this chapter, to sum up, I have tried mainly to show that at least one style concept is irreducibly vague; that this vagueness is the fundamental logical feature of the role of this concept, to be discerned best in the range of disagreements among the historians in their style-giving reasons; and, consequently, that it is false that all style concepts or the concept of style in art history are logically closed in the sense that they do have, must have, or require sets of necessary, sufficient, or definitive criteria and their corresponding properties in order to provide a coherent history of art. Whether other style concepts, such as High

Renaissance or Baroque or Gothic, are also irreducibly vague— although I believe that they are—I leave open. Whether all style concepts, including Impressionism, Cubism, and Abstract Expressionism, are irreducibly vague—although I think they are not—I also leave open. Furthermore, there are other issues—for example, the causal use of style—about which I have said little or nothing, even though they may be as important as the substantive use of style. But it seems to me that the substantive use of style is central in the clarification of the other issues of art history, and that is why I have concentrated on it.

One question remains: What is the relation between the openness of at least some genre concepts and the irreducible vagueness of at least one style concept? Is "Mannerism" like "tragedy," which is open in the sense of having no necessary or sufficient criteria and no undebatable criteria, or is it like "drama" or "novel," which are open in the sense of having no necessary or sufficient criteria but at least some undebatable ones, such as "plot" or "character"? "Mannerism," I have argued, has no necessary or sufficient criteria and no unchallengeable criteria; thus it is more like "tragedy" than like "drama" or "novel." But it differs from these genre concepts in at least two important respects. First, its assigned role does not require that it accommodate new cases with their new properties; that is, its perennial flexibility does not extend to future works of art in the way that these genre concepts do. Rather, its flexibility relates to past works of art that are historically bounded by space and time. Second, the disagreements about the correct use of "Mannerism" converge more on the exchange of sets of criteria than on their enlargement to cover new cases or on the rejection of putatively necessary criteria.

Because of these two differences, I am inclined to regard "Mannerism" as distinct from genre concepts and perhaps akin to the explanatory concept of centrality in the criticism of works of art. For the debates and disagreements over what is central or most important in a particular work of art seem to have the same vast array of irreducible vagueness as what is to count as Mannerism.[38] On this interpretation of "Mannerism," we have a striking vindication of Gombrich's hypothesis that style concepts function as hypotheses in art history because they attempt to formulate what is central or most important and distinctive in certain groupings of works of art.

Whether these two differences between "Mannerism" and genre concepts entail a radical distinction between openness and irreducible vagueness, I do not know. But I am confident that all efforts to render open concepts closed and vague concepts complete at once misunderstand those concepts and foreclose entirely their historically established and assigned roles.

The assumption that a necessary condition of our intelligible use of the concept of human action is some set of definitive criteria which governs the correct employment of the concept has been effectively exposed and challenged by Hart, Hampshire, and Wittgenstein, among others. The traditional doctrine, first intimated by Plato in the *Euthyphro*, that in order to know or to state what "human action" means, to have the concept of a human action, to be able to use this term correctly, we must assume that human action has a nature or essence—a definitive set of properties shared by all legitimate members of the class of human actions—is no longer sacrosanct. Nor is it so clear that without a true definition or theory of human action we cannot render meaningful our attribution of moral and legal predicates.

What sort of concept is the concept of human action? This, it seems to me, is the crucial issue in the whole debate now flourishing as a major industry in philosophy, more central than what counts as action as against movement or even Wittgenstein's problem in subtraction. Is the concept closed, i.e., governed by a definitive set of necessary and sufficient criteria which corresponds to a definitive set of necessary and sufficient properties? Or is it open, in Hart's sense of defeasible (necessary but no sufficient conditions), Hampshire's sense of essentially disputable (no undebatable criterion), or Wittgenstein's sense of family resemblance (a disjunctive set of nonnecessary, nonsufficient conditions)? It is my claim, which I shall argue for in this chapter, that the concept of human action is open in the sense that it has no necessary criteria, only sufficient criteria. Thus, "human action" differs radically from "contract," "moral," and "game," the three paradigms offered by Hart, Hampshire, and Wittgenstein. If I am correct in my reading of the logical grammar of the concept of human action, it follows that philosophical theories of human action are, all of them, unsuccessful attempts to lay down putatively necessary criteria for a concept whose use precludes such criteria.

To establish the logic of the concept of human action as open in the sense I have specified, we must, as we do with other concepts, turn from the individual theories to the disagreements among them; for it is here that one finds the clue to the specific kind of openness of the concept of human action. How can we explain, we must ask, the range of disagreement about what is a human action? Why is there disagreement not only, for example, about the nature of intention or agency in human action but about whether intention or agency (or anything else) is necessary for, or even relevant to, human action? Can this disagreement be reduced to true-false claims about what intention or agency is or

about whether nothing is an action without the presence of intention or agency?

Philosophical theories of human action are purportedly true statements about the definitive properties of such action. These theories constitute real definitions and determine the corresponding criteria of our correct use of the concept. Hence, in asking whether human action is a closed concept we are in effect asking: Is there a true theory or real definition of human action? My own view, which I share with Hart, Hampshire, and Wittgenstein, is that there is no such theory; there cannot be; and there need not be. But I wish to go further than they to claim that, though the concept of human action has no necessary condition—hence not even the makings of a theory—it does have sufficient conditions and that these are coterminous with the good reasons for something's being a human action.

Charles Taylor, Richard Taylor, Roderick Chisholm, A. I. Melden, Arthur Danto, and Donald Davidson, among others, have attempted in their various writings to state certain necessary or necessary and sufficient properties of human actions. For them a theory in the philosophical sense of a real definition is forthcoming. Have they succeeded in their attempts?

I begin with Charles Taylor's The Explanation of Human Behaviour (1964),[1] which formulates a complete theory of action and its implications for experimental psychology. In this book Taylor first distinguishes between the inanimate and the animate and, within the animate, between purposive behavior as against mere process or movement. This latter distinction, he claims, is both irreducibly ontological and conceptual. That is, purposive behavior exemplifies a certain category of event and order in the world which is amenable only to a certain kind of teleological

explanation. That there is such an order is a coherent and
empirically testable doctrine; to this he adds that, because of the
available evidence in psychology, it is also a true doctrine.
Mechanistic views, such as behaviorism, that reduce this doctrine to conceptual absurdity and, consequently, the issue of
teleology versus mechanism to the nonempirical, indeed to the
incoherent, for him rest on inadequate causal explanations of
purposive behavior. Instead of teleology's being incoherent,
perhaps it is mechanism (which, as a doctrine of science, is
inherently intentional) that is incoherent. Taylor implies that it
is incoherent without, I think, realizing that, if it is, there cannot
be any empirical issue between mechanism and teleology. In his
searching effort to establish the intelligibility of teleology against
mechanism's attack, he unfortunately, in order to render the
issue between them empirical, reverses the attack, with the result
that, throughout his argument, it is quite unclear whether the
issue between teleology and mechanism is empirical or simply a
conceptual muddle.

At any rate, for Taylor human actions are a type of purposive
behavior. What, then, does he mean by purposive behavior? It is
an event which is observable and whose occurrence depends
upon its being required for some goal. It is therefore a noncontingent, sufficient condition for that goal. Hence, to say of an
event that it is a piece of purposive behavior is to place it in a
system of events with its self-imposed order, which tends toward
a goal. In purposive behavior, then, the behavior is a function,
not of an antecedent event or of a disposition, but of a system of
events, including its environment. That this behavior is such a
function makes it teleological and so requires the formulation of
teleological laws about events noncontingently tending toward
certain ends.

Of immediate concern is Taylor's account of human action.
He begins with what he calls the "strong" sense of human action
and lays down its set of definitive criteria. For anything to be
such an action, it must be goal-directed, in the extended sense of
emitting goal-directedness; it must be intended, hence caused by
an agent or a person who is free and is responsible for what he
does; it must be intentional in the sense that it involves the idea
of the desired goal; and, most important, the intention must be a
noncontingent, sufficient condition for the goal, bringing it
about.

Behavior that is neither goal-directed nor intended, such as
blinking, sneezing, or doodling, may be classified as action, he
allows, but only in a loose sense. However, nothing that is not a
piece of behavior can be an action for him. Nor, he claims, can

behavior that results in a goal but is not intended count as an action. For example, if I kill a man while in a fit, I kill him unintentionally; hence, according to Taylor, I did not act; therefore, I did not perform an action. My intention to kill him must be a noncontingent, sufficient condition, required for the achievement of the goal, before my killing him counts as an action.

This claim seems to me mistaken, supported as it is by only a stipulated, restrictive use of "action"; for in terms of the example, it certainly accords with ordinary usage to say that, because I killed him, I did perform an action—the action of killing—even though I am not responsible, since I was having a fit when I did it.[2] Perhaps I did not act, for I was acted upon; but I did kill him, i.e., perform an action. "Action," at least if we follow ordinary usage, does not entail "act," "intention," or

"responsibility."

Taylor offers another kind of behavior in which there is a goal with no intention, i.e., cases in which one intends goal x but achieves goal z instead. Here we can still talk of actions, though they are qualified by such terms as "inadvertently," "unknowingly," "in ignorance," etc. For example, Socrates, it was said, intended to teach the youth but corrupted them instead. Here, if we do not deny the corruption altogether (and the action of corruption), we can qualify it by some term of excuse, such as "unknowingly." However, in doing so, we qualify the intention, not the goal.

Recognizing and accepting, then, these two exceptions—of nonintentional, nonpurposive behavior (e.g., doodling) and of behavior with a differently intended goal (e.g., Socrates corrupting rather than teaching the youth)—as limited or as qualified actions, Taylor identifies human action with purposive behavior, i.e., behavior intentionally directed toward a goal.

For Taylor, intention, then, is a necessary condition or property of human action. It is also central, in that it is a sufficient condition of the goal. This means that intention is not an antecedent cause of the goal. Rather, it is a noncontingent requirement, amenable only to teleological explanation. Thus, "I did x because I intended to" is not analyzable into "Intending x was contingently followed by doing x." For "part of what we mean by 'intending X' [is] that, in the absence of interfering factors, it is followed by doing X. I could not be said to intend X if, even with no obstacles or other countervailing factors, I still didn't do it. Thus my intention is not a causal antecedent of my behaviour" (p. 33).

Is "'Intending x' entails 'Doing x, unless there are obstacles or other countervailing factors'" a conceptual, necessary, a priori truth? It is not. "Intending to do *x*" does entail "Doing something" (otherwise we have no criteria for "intending"), but it does not entail "Doing *x* unless there are obstacles or other countervailing factors." If I do not do *x* when none of these factors is present, it does not follow that I did not intend to do *x* in the way that it does follow, I think, that, if I do nothing, I did not intend to do *x*. Moreover, if "I did *x* because I intended to" is a conceptual, noncontingent truth, then so is "I did *x* because I had to." For it is conceptually impossible for me to have had to do *x* without doing *x*. Mechanistic determinism can therefore also serve as a paradigm of Taylor's teleological explanation!

For Taylor, then, the concept of a human action is one that characterizes a class of purposive behavior. The concept is governed by a set of necessary criteria: goal-directedness, intention, intention bringing about the goal, agency, responsibility, and intentionality. These reduce to the over-all criterion of an intention, in a noncontingent way, bringing about a goal. Because these criteria are all there are, they function as necessary and sufficient—definitive—for something's being a human action.

Human Action

That human action is necessarily purposive, that it is necessarily intentionally goal-directed, and that intentional behavior is irreducibly teleological—as I have suggested and as others have argued—are challengeable claims. Even our ordinary use of action concepts, hence of the concept of action, covers cases of action which satisfy none of Taylor's criteria. Killing a man in a fit is one example. So, perhaps, is falling in love, which is not a movement, like making love, or a state, like being married, or a condition, like catching or having the measles. Falling in love, even if we have not read Proust, is at least sometimes, to some people, something one does. It is an act that issues in an action which need not be either intended or goal-directed. It may not be a strong case of action, like getting married, but it is not obviously a loose case or no case either. It seems to me to be one of the clear cases, of which killing a man in a fit is another, where intention or goal simply drops out. It may even be a case of a human action where there are no statable criteria of *action*, as there are such criteria for falling in love, and therefore an action for which no good reasons are possible or to be expected.

In his definition of the class of strong actions, I think Taylor provides at best only sufficient criteria for something's being an action. That something is intentional or goal-directed is a good reason for its being, or being called, an action; but that intention and goal-directedness are irreducibly teleological, or that

Taylor's core concept of strong actions is coextensive with the class of clear cases of human actions, or that the class of clear cases coincides with Taylor's strong actions plus the one exception of qualified action he allows, is, if not a stipulation, extremely questionable.

For Richard Taylor, in his book, *Action and Purpose* (1966),[3] the concept of human action is indefinable. It cannot be defined because it cannot be analyzed. That is, no statement about a human action can be shown to be equivalent to a statement about anything other than the action. Human action, however, can be described and in this way be distinguished from everything else. Further, although indefinable, the concept of a human action is absolutely clear and basic, one that all of us possess as we reflect upon human experience. In the spirit of G. E. Moore,

he says that all of us know what human action is—that we act and are not only acted upon—even though we are not able to say what action is or how we know that we act. Philosophical reflection—not introspection, observation, or speculation—reveals action as an ultimate category of human experience.

Richard Taylor's basic dichotomy within the animate is that of action versus process, not (as it is for Charles Taylor) of purposive behavior versus movement. The former dichotomy and not the latter is basic, he argues, because some acts can be purposeless, though no purposive behavior can be without an act. I can, he points out, wiggle my finger with no purpose or goal. What I do may be pointless, but I can and may do it; therefore it is an act.

Action, act, activity (these seem to function as synonyms for R. Taylor) are uniquely human. Process, movement, event characterize man, the animals, and the inanimate. The main philosophical problem of action is to supply "the difference between mere bodily motions and those that represent acts" (p. 89).

What, then, is the difference between an act and a movement? This is Taylor's fundamental question in his attempt to describe, if not to give an analysis of, human action. Both acts and movements are subject to causation, but to causation in a non-Humean sense that ultimately rests on the unanalyzable yet absolutely clearly understood fact of one thing A making another thing B to occur. "A was the cause of B," applied to both acts and movements, cannot reduce to any set of statements which do not repeat the initial statement in another form, such as "A made B to happen by virtue of his power to do so."

Thus the difference between act and movement does not lie in their different kinds of causation, for they are both characterized by necessitation and power—what in traditional terms has been called "efficient causality." The difference between act and movement, then, is that acts are events or movements that are caused—made to happen—by human beings, while movements are events that are caused by other events. The concept of human agency does not derive from that of event causality; rather, Taylor says, it is the other way round.

That human actions involve human agency rather than causation among events, and that it is agency that differentiates act from movement, Taylor purports to prove by the nonreducibility of statements about human agency to statements about events. Can the "can" in "I can move my finger" be interpreted as logically contingent (e.g., "A triangle can be acute"), causally contingent (e.g., "Atoms can swerve from their path"), epistemically contingent (e.g., "This can be the restaurant we ate in last year"), or hypothetically possible (e.g., "This acid can dissolve a piece of zinc")—the four other kinds of possibilities expressed by "can"? It cannot, Taylor claims; for in saying "I can move my finger," I affirm that I have the power to move my finger whether I move it or not. It is up to me, within my power, whether I move it or no. It is this notion, that all of us understand though no one can say what it is, that is *"never embodied in the meaning of 'can' as it is used with reference to physical things; for it never makes sense to say that it is up to a volume of acid whether it dissolves a lump of zinc"* (pp. 55–56; italics in original).

Nor is the analysis of "I can move my finger" in terms of a special kind of causal relationship between events—namely, between an internal event, such as a volition, a desire, a wish, a choice, or an intention, and its external effect—a plausible alternative to the irreducibility of human agency. The reason it is not plausible, Taylor says, is that it postulates a nonexistent entity; that is, there are no such events. Rather, the criterion of the truth of any hypothetical of the form "I can move my finger if I will, want, intend, wish, or choose to" is the effect itself, i.e., the moving of the finger. Indeed, Taylor adds: "Our entire *criterion* for saying what he *wanted* (or tried, or intended, or whatnot) to do, is what he in fact *did*" (p. 52; italics in original). A want is not the cause of a doing; it is conceptually entailed by that doing. "I did *x* because I wanted to" may give a reason for our actions, but it never gives a cause of our actions.

If we turn from human ability to human action, i.e., from "I can move my hand' to "I move my hand," the same radical distinction between action and event can be drawn. For example, when I make a mark with a pencil, it is true (1) that I move my hand; (2) that my hand moves; and (3) that my hand moves a pencil. It is clear that (1) entails (2) but that (2) does not entail (1); (3) entails (2), but (2) does not entail (3); (1) involves the idea of an active being, (2) involves only the idea of an event, change, or motion, and (3) involves a causal relation, without agency, between two things. But, most important, (1), which describes an event as an act, includes an essential, irreducible reference to an active agent who is doing something.

This reference to active agency, rooted in human ability, is, though indefinable, absolutely essential in human action, which is also indefinable. Human acts or actions can be characterized in other ways, e.g., they can be commanded, requested, or forbidden; they may involve change, or absence or cessation of change; they need not be overt. But they must embody agent

causality. Thus, to describe "anything as an act there must be an essential reference to an agent as the performer or author of that act, not merely in order to know whose act it is, but in order even to know that it is an act" (p. 109).

Taylor's next point is that the doctrine of human agency—that I am the cause of my actions and that I am not reducible to any series of events—is entirely different from determinism or its denial, for both entail the distinction between act and event. Consider this schema: (1) e occurs; (2) something makes e occur; (3) A does e; (4) something makes A do e. Determinism and its denial are theses about (4) and, in order to be affirmed or to be true, entail (3). Moreover, this schema, in which entailment proceeds from (4) to (1) but not from (1) to (4), illustrates once again Taylor's central claim about "the absolute difference between bodily motions which are and those which are not acts" (p. 124), since all four statements are about the same finger motion yet are different in their meanings, as their entailments demonstrate. Occurrences (1) and (2) need not refer to acts. But (3) and (4) must, with an essential reference to an agent as the cause of the act.

For Taylor, human action is thus necessarily something done that is produced by an agent. All he allows this to mean is that a human being—not a self, an ego, or a mind—makes something happen because he has the power to do so. Human action is man as efficient cause and not some event or set of events which are correlated with other events.

Human beings act. For Taylor they are the causes of what they do. Sometimes they act in order to do or to get something else: to achieve a certain goal or to realize an aim or a purpose. Here action is purposive. And, for Taylor, all purposive behavior is action, though not all action is purposive behavior. Only human beings, he says, act and are purposive. In their goal-directedness they initiate the direction. Machines that are goal-directed are so merely in the derivative sense that they are designed by humans to aim at certain targets or goals; but machines do not act or initiate anything. Even so, there are no behavioral or observational criteria for distinguishing purposive from nonpurposive behavior. This distinction, as in the case of causal agency versus passive movement, is made by each of us only as we reflect upon actions of ours that are done with some aim or goal in view.

Purpose is therefore, for R. Taylor, another clear, ultimate category of human experience, understood by all, even though no one can say what it is or how we know it. Furthermore, the concept of purpose, which all of us are able to use to characterize purposive behavior, is also indefinable, incapable of further analysis. Along with agency, it is fundamental in any true **Human** philosophy of human nature. Although purpose is an indefin- **Action** able concept, he adds, we can nevertheless attribute purposeful behavior to human beings as acting for the sake of certain goals. Hence it is to be conceived of as a means-end, or teleological, relation. Thus, I act when I do something. I act purposively when I do something in order to get something else.

This purposive behavior, he argues, also cannot be reduced to a causal relation between events, specifically, between internal events or states—such as purposes, aims, or desires, together with certain beliefs about how to realize them—and their effects. For, as he does with wants, choices, wishes, etc., in dealing with agent causality, he denies that there are such internal events.

But he also argues here that the causal explanation of purposive behavior radically confuses reasons with causes. Purposive explanation of purposive behavior—which, he insists, is explanation because it renders intelligible this behavior by citing reasons (goals, aims, purposes)—differs completely from causal explanation. Statements such as "Jones went to the pantry to get some salami" are teleological because they refer to ends and are true or false independently of there being these ends. On the other hand, statements such as "Jones fell because he slipped" are genuinely causal and are true or false depending on there being these causes.

Taylor's schema also implies the irreducibility of reasons to causes. If, for example, I do e in order to get f (Taylor's [3]), it may or may not be true that something made me do e in order to get f (Taylor's [4]). If (4) is true, a causal explanation is forthcoming; if (4) is false, it is not. But, in either case, (4) differs from (3), and (3) does not entail (4). To affirm that (3) is a causal relation between events is to confuse (3) with (4) or, worse, to assume falsely that (3) entails (4). The reasons cited for (3), therefore, are not like the causes given for (4). Taylor thus draws a fundamental, irreducible distinction between reasons and causes in the explanation of human behavior. Causal explanation of movements has its place, but it can accommodate neither the agency nor the purposiveness of uniquely human actions.

Before we consider other theories of human action, a summary of agreements and disagreements between C. and R. Taylor would perhaps be helpful. First, it is important to validate my claim that R. Taylor, in spite of his thesis of the unanalyzable, indefinable character of human action, offers a theory, or at least the beginnings of a theory, when he speaks of a necessary property without which nothing is a human action. It is certainly true that he rejects the analyzability of human action and its corresponding concept. However, the reasons he offers—that causal agency is central to both action and purposive behavior, that purpose also is central to the latter, that neither agency nor purpose can be further analyzed, and that criteria cannot be given for the understanding of agency and purpose—do not show that human action has no distinguishable necessary property or that the concept has no recognizable criteria. Indeed, if they did show this, Taylor would have no human action to describe. What he does show—if his thesis about human action is true—is that it is an absolutely necessary property of all human actions that they are caused by a human being, and he shows that this agent causality is not reducible to event causality. Given his thesis, he cannot deny that agent causality is a necessary feature of all actions, distinguishing them from movements; what he can and does deny is that this causality is definable. Consequently, I take as R. Taylor's basic thesis about human actions his affirmation that they are necessarily caused by an agent and that, when these actions are purposive, they possess two necessary properties, both unanalyzable and indefinable, namely, agency and purpose.

How does his thesis compare with C. Taylor's? For the latter, human action is necessarily more than being caused by an agent. It must also have intention as the factor that brings about a certain goal. Here, then, is one major disagreement: C. Taylor says that intention is a necessary feature of human action; R. Taylor denies that it is, claiming that causal agency alone is necessary, although both are necessary for purposive behavior. For C. Taylor, no action can lack intention and purpose; for R. Taylor, some actions have neither. For him, killing a man unintentionally is still an action, as is wiggling one's finger with no point whatever. For C. Taylor, neither of these is an action, because both lack intention.

What kind of disagreement is this? Is it ontological—about what is a common denominator of all members of the class of human actions? Is it conceptual—about what is a necessary criterion of the concept of a human action? Or is it, as some philosophers maintain, a verbal wrangle about different stipulated uses of the term "human action"? If it is the latter, C. and R. Taylor do not disagree about action; they differ simply in how they wish to use a word, the one choosing to restrict it to purposive behavior, the other, to extend it to all cases of human agency, regardless of purpose. This is a basic question. I shall return to it when we have the full range of disagreement among philosophers about what is necessary in human action. However, the particular disagreement between C. and R. Taylor— whether there are or can be acts without intention or purpose— seems, at least on its face, to be more about the correct criteria of the concept of a human action than it does about mere differences of criteria for two different concepts that are unfortunately conveyed by the same word.

There are other disagreements, as well as agreements, between C. and R. Taylor. Both distinguish sharply between action and movement, though C. Taylor allows that this cleavage applies to some nonhumans as well. For him, dogs and cats can act intentionally; for R. Taylor, they can neither act intentionally nor act at all—only human beings can. Both insist on the irreducible, teleological character of human action, although R. Taylor confines the teleological to one kind of human action— the purposive. Moreover, for C. Taylor, teleological behavior is observable (I see you shake hands, just as I see your hands moving), and it is to be interpreted as a noncontingent requirement for some goal. It is also explicable in terms of teleological laws. For R. Taylor, on the contrary, it is not observable; rather, teleological behavior is imputed to what we do as a means to some end. We can cite reasons to explain what we do, and, in this sense, we explain our actions as purposeful; but we cannot formulate laws about noncontingent events. The two consequently differ on the issue of mechanism versus teleology. For C. Taylor this issue revolves round the reducibility of noncontingent purposive behavior to contingently related movements; for R. Taylor the reduction of acts to events is logically impossible, for, according to his schema, "I did event e" (3) is not equivalent to or entailed by "Event e occurred" or "Some event d made event e to occur" ([1] and [2]). Indeed, he transforms this issue of mechanism versus teleology into the issue of determinism versus libertarianism, both of which latter doctrines entail the cogency of action statements. Of course he also agrees with C. Taylor that a causal account of purposive behavior without agency is impossible; consequently, if the mechanism-teleology issue is conceived of as concerning a competing causal account of "I did *e*" (3), both agree that mechanism is incoherent and that teleology is true, though they give entirely different reasons for their claims.

There is one issue R. Taylor raises which is not discussed by C. Taylor but is debated by other philosophers: that reasons for our purposive actions are never causes of these actions. We shall come to it presently.

Finally, in our initial summary, it should be noted once again that whatever is stated as a necessary condition or criterion for a human action—whether it really is necessary or not—must be

able to serve as a condition or criterion. It is no good saying that intention, goal-directedness, or agency is necessary for human action unless we are told what it is. In this regard, C. Taylor does clarify his notion of intention; and whether we agree with him or not that it is necessary for human action, at least we know what he means by it.

What about R. Taylor's notion of causal agency? He says that all of us know what it is, even though no one can say what it is or we know what it is or how we know what it is; each of us just knows, and that is the end of the matter.

As attractive as the doctrine may be that each of us is in this privileged epistemic situation, it is replete with obvious and enormous difficulties. How, that is, can one learn and teach this concept, which, for Taylor, is both private and has no behavioral, observational criteria? Unlike the concepts of desire, wish, want, choice, decision, and intention, which for Taylor denote external, not internal, occurrences, from which they derive their entire meanings, Taylor's concept of agency seems to function as innately private, with no criteria at all. If this is so, it is notoriously difficult—perhaps, as some philosophers argue, impossible—for agency to be a concept at all. Agency, of course, may still be a property of human action, perhaps even a necessary property; but this property cannot serve as a criterion of the concept of human action if agency remains a concept with no criterion of its own.

In "Freedom and Action,"[4] Chisholm lays bare what he designates the "descriptive" as against the "imputative" element of the concept of act and action. Like C. and R. Taylor, he affirms that human agency is basic. Man is the immanent cause of his

actions, not a transeunt cause, which is an event that makes
another event happen. If, say, I move my hand, I act, I do
something—I move my hand. But in moving my hand I also
make something happen in my brain as well as in the surrounding air. In the way in which I do something when I move my
hand I do not do anything to or with my brain or to or with the
surrounding air. What I do when I move my hand besides move
my hand is to immanently cause a brain event which transeuntly
causes my hand to move, and this in turn transeuntly causes the
air particles to move.

When I move my hand, I am the immanent cause of my hand's
moving—of my action—as well as the immanent cause of a
cerebral event. Chisholm sees no difficulty here in his concept of
an immanent cause that includes both agent-action causality and
agent-event causality. Instead he concentrates on the difficulty
of distinguishing talk of events that simply happen and events
that are caused either by an agent or by another event. Thus, it is
not the distinction between immanent and transeunt causation
that is suspect but that of causation versus mere occurrence.
Once we grant the latter distinction—which of course is not
restricted to the philosophy of human action, and which Chisholm says is unavoidable if we are to persist in talking about
causation in the world—"the only answer that one can give [to
what differentiates these two kinds of causation] is this—that in
the one case the agent was the cause of A's happening, and in the
other case event B was the cause of A's happening" (p. 22).

As unclear as the distinction between causation and mere
occurrence is, Chisholm immediately adds, the concept of
immanent causality is more clear than that of transeunt causality. Indeed, the latter is derived from the former. And the former
is rooted in our experience of causal efficacy. "It is only by
understanding our own causal efficacy, as agents, that we can
grasp the concept of *cause* at all" (p. 22; italics in original). But
now, one may ask of Chisholm, If we are immediately acquainted with causal efficacy, aren't we immediately acquainted
with ourselves as immanent causes, in which case we do know
what causation is? Then we are either acquainted with mere
happenings as distinct from causation, or we are not. If we are,
Chisholm's difficulty about differentiating them vanishes; if we
are not, it still vanishes, for now the difference lies in causation,
which we immediately experience, and occurrence, which we do
not but infer instead. The new difficulty becomes that of
distinguishing between immanent causality, with which we are
acquainted, and transeunt causality as against mere occurrence,
both of which are inferred. If our concept of cause rests on

causal efficacy, we do not need the distinction between causation and mere happening to validate immanent causality, at least in its primary form, namely, when I do *A* rather than when I make *B* (e.g., a cerebral event) to happen. Of course we do need the distinction to validate the concept of transeunt causality, since that concept presupposes it.

Causal agency is one descriptive element of the concept of an act. This, I take it, is Chisholm's claim that a necessary condition for something's being an act or action, or a necessary condition for the concept of a human action, is (exactly what it is to both C. and R. Taylor) an essential reference to an agent or a human being as the cause of what he does. As Chisholm puts it, "at least one of the events that is involved in any act is caused, not by any other event, but by the agent, by the man" (p. 29).

The second descriptive element of the concept of an act is that

it is essentially teleological: "Action involves *endeavor* or *purpose*, one thing occurring *in order that* some other thing may occur" (p. 29; italics in original).

Like C. and R. Taylor, Chisholm rejects the reduction of teleological or purposive action to action as the effect of antecedent desire and relevant belief about realizing that desire. And, like C. Taylor but in major disagreement with R. Taylor, he denies that there can be an action without purpose, since, for him, one cannot act at all without endeavor or purpose. The concept of act or action is necessarily intentional: to act is necessarily to endeavor to make happen. R. Taylor's distinction between "I raise my arm" and "I raise my arm in order to get your attention" remains, but it is no longer that of action as against purposive action; rather, it is of one kind of purposive action, namely, endeavoring to make my arm go up, as against another, namely, endeavoring to make my arm go up for the purpose of getting your attention.

Having stated the two necessary descriptive elements of the concept of an act, Chisholm defines the further descriptive concepts of (1) undertaking or endeavoring to make a certain thing happen, (2) undertaking to make something happen for the purpose of making some other thing happen, and (3) a successful intentional action. Each is defined in terms of the undefined locution indicating that the agent is a cause and that the action is purposive or teleological. This is the locution:

There is a state of affairs *A* and a state of affairs *B*, such that, at time *t*, he makes *B* happen in the endeavor to make *A* happen.

Or, more briefly:

He makes B happen in the endeavor to make A happen.

Or, in symbolic notation:

$$(Ea)\,(Eb)\,M^t\,(b,a).$$

In this locution, "making happen" is a transitive, asymmetrical relation; the states of affairs referred to may be unchanges as well as changes, and they may be complex; and the subject term of "makes happen" may designate a state of affairs or a person.

If I raise my arm, Chisholm says, "make happen" applies to my arm going up, to certain antecedent events inside my body, and to certain subsequent external events, such as the movement of air particles.

"In the endeavor to make A happen" is intentional as well as purposive. That is, one can endeavor to make A happen without thereby actually making A happen. Thus, we cannot infer "He made something happen in the endeavor to make B happen" from "He made something happen in the endeavor to make A happen and he did thereby make A happen" and "A is the same concrete event as B"; and if one makes something B happen in the endeavor to make something A happen, one can know immediately or directly that one is making something happen in the endeavor to make A happen, although one may not know that one is making B happen even if $A = B$.

Action, for Chisholm, is thus describable in terms of making things happen in the endeavor to make other things happen—his undefined locution. When I raise my arm, then, I make something happen in the endeavor to make my arm go up. I do not make something happen in the endeavor to raise my arm. To act is to endeavor to make happen, not to endeavor to act.

What, now, is endeavoring or undertaking to make a certain thing happen? How can this descriptive concept be defined in terms of $(Ea)\,(Eb)\,M^t\,(b,a)$? Let "U^ta" symbolize "He undertakes at t to make A happen." Then we have:

Definition 1: $U^ta = $ Df. $(Eb)\,M^t\,(b,a)$.

From this definition it follows that the agent, in undertaking to make event A happen, does make B happen; he knows that he undertakes to make A happen, though he may not know what B is or whether he is succeeding in making A happen; and it may be that he is not succeeding in making A happen. Moreover, "undertaking," as defined, does not imply contract or commitment, exertion or effort, or trial and error. Like other intentional concepts, such as approval or desire, "undertaking" may take a conjunctive state of affairs as an object without thereby taking each of its conjuncts as objects. Thus, a pianist who undertakes to play a sonata undertakes to play the entire sonata as well as the first measure without then undertaking to play the last measure. The sonata has constituent measures, A, B, C, and ... N; the pianist undertakes to play the whole conjunction, including the first of the conjuncts, A, without thereby undertaking the others.

"Undertaking to make something B happen for the purpose of making something A happen"—Chisholm's second concept involved in describing actions—can now be defined. Let "$Pt\,(b,a)$" symbolize "He undertakes at t to make B happen for the purpose of making A happen" and let "bCa" symbolize "B makes A happen." Then:

$$\text{Definition 2: } P^t(b,a) = \text{Df. } U^t\,(a \,\&\, b \,\&\, bCa).$$

According to this definition, we may describe someone as undertaking to make something B happen for the purpose of making something A happen without thereby implying either that he makes A happen or that he makes B happen. It also rules out, as cases of this second kind of action, situations in which an agent simply undertakes to make B make A happen. Thus, to satisfy the definition, the agent must undertake at t to make B happen, to make A happen, and to make B make A happen.

Chisholm's third concept—"a completely successful undertaking"—can be defined as follows. Let "$I^t a$" symbolize "He made A happen in the way in which, at t, he intended."

$$\text{Definition 3: } I^t a = \text{Df. } M^t(a,a) \,\&\, (c)\,[P^t(c,a) \longrightarrow M^t(c,c)].$$

This definition satisfies the condition that the agent makes happen all of those things which, at t, he undertook for the purpose of making A happen. Consequently, it rules out the extreme cases of inadvertent success or happy failure—symbolizable as "$M^t(a,a)$"—which means that the definition applies to the whole class of cases in which the agent makes, at t, A happen in the endeavor to make A happen, but does not apply to those cases in which the agent makes, at t, all the things he endeavored to make happen for the purpose of making A happen. That is, the definition rules out, for example, the case of an assassin who inadvertently runs over his intended victim—an inadvertent success—as well as the case of an assassin whose escaping victim is killed by an unexpected stroke of lightning—a happy failure; since in both cases the assassin may have undertaken without success to shoot his victim.

Chisholm sets out to define the descriptive element of the concept of an act or action. He does this in terms of his

undefined locution about an agent making one thing happen in
order to make another thing happen. Thus agency and purposiveness, whether themselves undefined or indefinable or
neither, function as necessary conditions of the concept of
action, according to Chisholm. Nothing, therefore, can be a
human action unless it is caused by an agent who endeavors to
make something happen. Actions include an agent as immanent
cause; at least one event, made to happen by the agent; and the
intentional element—that the agent made the event to happen in
order to make another event happen. This means, then, that
nothing can be an action which does not satisfy Chisholm's first
definition: the agent makes B happen by undertaking at t to
make A happen. In the way in which something can be an action
without the agent's undertaking to make something happen for
the purpose of making some other thing happen (Definition 2) or
without the agent's being completely successful in his undertaking (Definition 3), nothing can be an action without undertaking
to make a certain thing happen (Definition 1). If this is correct,
then, for Chisholm, the concept of an act or an action contains
at least one defined element as well as two undefined elements.

Well, now, is it true, as Chisholm claims, that every human
action includes at least one event or state of affairs, B, that is
made to happen by an agent, who makes B happen in order to
make event or state of affairs A happen? If we grant the
intelligibility of his concepts of agency as immanent cause and of
making-happen, Chisholm's thesis I think does cover certain
unexceptionable examples of the class of human actions. There
are indeed many things we do that include as their constituents
things that we make happen in order that other things will
happen. Insofar as there are good reasons for some things being
human actions or being called "human actions," Chisholm provides at least one good reason for, and thereby one sufficient
condition of, the concept of a human action. But has he also
discovered a necessary condition—a common denominator of
all human actions? Are there, can there be, human actions
without agency, causation, or intentionality?

R. Taylor, we remember, claims that some human actions are
not intentional. When I move my hand, I make it happen that
my hand moves, but I do not do something else in the endeavor
to move my hand. Of course, lots of things may happen, or may
be made to happen, but I do not make them happen.

Other philosophers go further. Some acts or actions, they say,
are caused. They are caused by me. But "I am the cause of my
act or action" is not equivalent to nor does it entail "I make B
happen in order to make A happen," since the first may be true

and the second false. If, for example, I unintentionally kill a man, I cause him to die. In Chisholm's terms, I make happen his death. But is my unintentionally killing a man the same as, or does it even entail that, I made happen, say, shooting him in his heart (B) in order to make happen his death (A)? I cannot kill him without making something happen. But what I make happen—either the shooting or his death—need not happen in order that something else happen.

Finally, there are some acts ("deeds," Chisholm calls them) in which the agent, some philosophers point out, does nothing. Or, perhaps more cautiously, the agent neither makes B happen in order to make A happen nor does he make B happen in order to prevent A from happening. If my walk is covered with ice, I do nothing to clear it, and the postman slips and breaks his leg on my walk, I break the law and may even be said to have caused the postman to fall and break his leg. Now, whether I did something or did not, I performed an action—of breaking the law. How odd it sounds to say that I broke the law by making some event B (which event?) happen in order to make another event A (which event?) happen. Whatever actions are, there are in many cases certain redescriptions of events that function as action reports for which the language "making B happen in order to make A happen" is very strained indeed. Chisholm's concept of action consequently plays an important role in the description of some actions, but it has little if any role to play in the redescription of all actions.

In his essay "Freedom and Action," Chisholm says that his third definition—the definition of a successful undertaking—applies to what A. Danto calls "basic actions." This cannot be correct, since, for Danto, if there are actions, there must be basic actions; whereas, for Chisholm, if there are actions, there need not be successful undertakings. In Danto's format, basic action is essential for all actions in exactly the same transitive, asymmetrical way that an agent making B happen in order to make A happen is essential for all actions according to Chisholm. In fact Chisholm, it seems to me, must reject Danto's concept of a basic action, since the latter is defined as an agent simply performing an action, e.g., moving his arm, without any teleological intent. To introduce teleological intent is, for Danto, to move from basic action to action: from Danto's (4) to his (1) in his schema of (1) X Φ's by Ψ-ing; (2) X Φ's because y makes him do so; (3) X Φ's because of a nervous disorder; and (4) X (simply) Φ's. Danto's basic action, thus, is more like R. Taylor's (3), "I move my finger," than it is like Chisholm's "I raise my arm" as entailing "I endeavor to

make my arm go up (A) by making something else (B) happen."
In rejecting R. Taylor's distinction between action and purposive action, Chisholm also denies Danto's notion of a basic action, i.e., an agent-caused, nonteleological action.

Here, then, is another important disagreement: If there are basic actions—and Danto says that there are—are they necessarily teleological as well as agent-caused? Danto and R. Taylor claim that basic actions (Taylor calls them "simple") are not teleological. Chisholm and C. Taylor agree that there are basic actions in Danto's sense of events caused by an agent without the agent's having to do anything else to cause them; but they insist that they are intentional.

This issue, whether there are basic actions and what they are, is of course tied to the whole problem of what a human action is. I shall consider both in their proper place. Just here, however, Danto's essay "Basic Actions"[5] is relevant because it is yet another attempt to secure the concept of human action in agent causality. For Danto, an agent performs an action if he makes something happen, and there are two ways that he can make something happen: by first making something else happen; or by making something happen without first making anything else happen. Both are actions. However, the latter is basic, because the former entails the latter but the latter does not entail the former. "Basic action" thus refers to what we can and do perform without having to perform anything else as the cause of what we do. My moving my foot, but not my foot moving, is a basic action; my kicking a stone or the stone moving is not. Nevertheless, I cannot kick the stone without moving my foot. Kicking the stone (or moving it) is the effect of moving my foot. My moving foot causes the stone to move as an effect of the cause. When I move my foot in order to kick the stone, I do not do anything in order to move my foot. I just move it.

A basic action, then, is not uncaused. Rather, it is caused—by the agent. In Danto's schema, a basic action is an event, e, that is caused by an individual, M, where e is not the effect of an antecedent event as its cause but is the effect of an agent.

Danto supports his claim that there are basic actions by a direct appeal to experience: to our human repertoire of these actions. All of us, for example, if we are normal, know how to move, and how we move, our arms. What we cannot do is to explain how it is done, for there is nothing in the *explanans* which is not already present in the *explicandum*. Basic actions are simply given.

Danto also supports his claim with an argument that certain descriptions of events yield what he calls a full declension of them, while other descriptions do not. Danto separates this argument from the appeal to experience. But it is not clear that the ramifications of this argument do not call into question some of the findings of the appeal to experience. Consider, to begin with, the descriptions, "moving an arm" and "moving a stone." Danto is right in saying that we can decline the first but not the second in the following way:

(1) *M* causes his arm to move, e.g., by hitting it with his other arm.
(2) Someone or something other than *M* causes *M's* arm to move, e.g., by striking it.
(3) *M* suffers from a nervous disorder, so his arm moves spasmodically.
(4) *M* moves his arm without suffering from a nervous disorder, without someone or something causing it to move, or without having to do anything to cause it to move.

This full declension of "moving an arm," Danto says, shows that (1) and (2) are actions (because *M* does *e*, where *e* is the effect of some other antecedent event), that (3) is not an action (because *M* does nothing; he is a patient, not an agent), and that (4) is a basic action (because *M* does *e* without doing anything else to do *e*).

It also shows why "moving a stone" differs from "moving an arm"; for (1) and (2) may decline "moving a stone" but (4) cannot. Hence "moving a stone" cannot denote a basic action. Nor can "laughing" yield a full declension. Assertions (1), (2), and (3) stand, so that when *M* laughs by causing himself to laugh by doing something else in order to laugh or by being caused to laugh by some other person or by some thing, he performs an action. But that he simply laughs (4)—without (1), (2), and of course (3), i.e., because of a nervous disorder—although a possible state of affairs for some abnormal individuals, is not the standard case, like *M's* simply moving his arm. Most of us do not have the true power of laughing as we have the true power of moving our arms. (4) "*M* laughs," therefore, is not a basic action; but it is not nonsense, as is (4) "The stone (simply) moves."

A final example Danto offers is "imaging." "*M* images *I*" (where *I* stands for a mental image) is, like "*M* moves an arm," a locution that does not unambiguously describe an action and, if it does, a basic one. Nevertheless, the full declension works here, too: (1) *M* causes *I*, perhaps by taking a drug; (2) Someone or something causes *M* to have *I*; (3) *M* is obsessed by *I*, where *I* is a symptom of a nervous disorder; and (4) *M* simply produces *I*.

Consequently, (4) is a basic action, (1) and (2) are actions, and (3) is no action at all.

It is not clear in his essay that Danto regards full declension of certain descriptive expressions as a necessary, sufficient, or necessary and sufficient criterion of action and basic action. Moving an arm and imaging, he says, can be actions and basic actions; moving a stone can be an action, but it is not a basic action; laughing can be an action but only an extraordinary basic action. But, now, what about seeing and sitting? If imaging and moving my arm yield the full declension, so do seeing and sitting. Are seeing (or hearing, smelling, tasting, feeling) and sitting (or standing, lying down) actions and basic actions? If full declension is a sufficient condition of a basic action, "I see," "I hear," "I sit," "I stand," etc., where what I do I do (1) without doing anything else to do it, (2) without someone's or something's making me do what I do, and (3) without suffering from a nervous disorder, but where (1), (2), and (3) as well as (4) are intelligible, as they are—then these expressions also describe basic actions. And, if they do, our repertoire of basic actions, which all normal people are acquainted with, becomes an expanding universe whose members are identifiable through full declension of their corresponding descriptive expressions.

Someone may object to my examples. "I see," "I hear," "I sit," "I stand," etc., it might be said, are not descriptive expressions of actions or movements at all. Rather, they are incomplete expressions. One does not simply see, one sees something; one does not simply sit, one sits on something; and so on. "I see y (e.g., a tree)" is the proper expression, like Danto's "I move my arm" or "I image an image" (although the latter sounds fishy). But Danto does allow "M laughs" rather than "M laughs at y (e.g., a joke told by Z)" as a complete description to which he denies (normal) full declension. Consequently, before my examples can be ruled out, we need some criterion for distinguishing expressions which are amenable to declension, full or not, from expressions which are not so amenable. Danto's mixed bag of expressions—"M moves his arm," "M images I," "M laughs," "M moves a stone," "moving an arm," "imaging," "laughing," "moving a stone," etc.—includes no such criterion; so it remains unclear whether "I see," "I am seeing" and "I sit," "I am sitting," etc., are any more illegitimate expressions for declension than "I laugh" or "I image an image," or "laughing" or "imaging."

There is something peculiar about "I see," etc., as a report on an action or a basic action or as a report at all. But the peculiarity, it seems to me, is as much with action and basic action as it is with "I see." Suppose, for example, I say that, when I see, what I do is open my eyes. Now, "I open my eyes" looks analogous to "I move my arm." Is "I open my eyes" fully declinable? Here I cannot make sense of (1) or (3): that I open my eyes by doing something else in order to open my eyes (i.e., what can I do to open my eyes that is like striking my arm to move it?); or that I am suffered to open my eyes (i.e., what nervous disorder could make my eyes open?). Assertion (2) seems all right (e.g., that someone makes me open my eyes, by waking me). Assertion (4), that I simply open my eyes, seems impeccable. Is it, therefore, a basic action? Even if the full declension does not work here with "I open my eyes"?

"I open my eyes" (which is an unexceptionably complete expression) is no clearer a description of a basic action or even of an action (since [1] is suspect) than is "I see" (which, for some, is suspect as a description). To be sure, both are things we do without first doing something else. Therefore, if one is a basic action, so is the other.

The appeal to a repertoire does not help here either. For I know I can see and do see, can open my eyes and do open them, can sit and do sit, can hear and do hear, can stand and do stand, just as I know I can move my arm and do, can conjure up images and do—without knowing how I can and do do these things. Are they all in the repertoire? If they are, full declension is not the clue to the range of the repertoire. If they are not, what, in the appeal to the repertoire, brings them in or rules them out? If the criterion is the givenness of the action in the sense of doing something without doing something else as an antecedent causal event, then seeing, opening one's eyes, sitting, standing, hearing, tasting, lying down, etc., are all basic actions.

I conclude that Danto's concept of a basic action is ill-conceived. He separates his appeal to our repertoire of basic actions from his argument of full declension of certain descriptive expressions. Yet the repertoire enlarges and contracts with the application of the criterion of full declension as necessary, sufficient, or necessary and sufficient. If full declension is necessary, "M opens his eyes" drops out as a description of a basic action in the repertoire. If full declension is sufficient, "M sees, hears, listens, tastes, smells, feels, sits, stands, or lies down" forces us to enlarge the repertoire.

If the criterion of a basic action shifts to what we can and do do without doing anything else as its antecedent causal event, basic actions become coextensive with all of our human abilities or powers and their particular manifestations. Then my seeing, hearing, smelling, tasting, touching, sitting, standing, etc., are as much actions and basic actions as my moving my arm. And if all of these are basic actions, perhaps Verity's yawn, with which Danto opens his essay, is a basic action too. And if yawning, why not all of our bodily functions, including the very basic ones, closer to the belly than the mouth?

A final puzzle: "M hurts his finger." This is fully declinable, and it describes something M can do and sometimes does without necessarily doing anything else as its antecedent causal event. Does it therefore report an action and a basic action? Is it rather a report on what M does not do without first doing something else, hence a report on an action but not on a basic action? Or is it simply a report on a sensation, hence no action report at all? As a description, it is as ambiguous as "M moved a stone"; so, as Danto says, it could describe an action and, if an action, a basic action. Which basic action? M moved his finger? M kept his finger still? Neither or nothing seems appropriate.

A. I. Melden concludes his early essay "Action" (1956)[6] with the following words: "so in the case of the concept of any action the context of practices in which rules are obeyed, criteria employed, policies are observed—a way of thinking and doing—is essential to the understanding of the difference between such bodily movements and actions."

Although Melden argues in this essay that the concept of action is not analyzable or simple and is not nondescriptive, he does lay down, it seems to me, at least one necessary condition for the correct use of the concept: an implicit reference to rule-governed behavior. It is true that he does not identify this condition with a necessary property or constituent—such as agent causality, intentionality, goal-directedness, or teleology—that all actions supposedly share. Rather, this condition functions as an over-all presupposition of there being action terms at all. Actions, thus, for Melden, are coextensive with certain bodily movements that are described under the general rubric of social practices. For example, signaling a left turn while driving a car without mechanical signals is the raising of one's arm in the specific context of the prevailing rules of the road. The difference between "X signaled" (or even "X raised his arm") and "X's arm went up"—between action and bodily movement—is not in the components or the psychological accompaniments of the movement but in the circumstances surrounding the movement.

Actions, Melden reminds us, form a large, extremely varied class, ranging from habitual responses to rational decision. Some involve mere wants, without reasons; others involve motives; still others, deliberation, reasons, choices. All, of course, are done by agents, but not by their unique causal agency. Nor is goal-directedness, intentionality, or teleology always present. Bodily movement is always present but only as an entailed condition and never as a component of action. Thus, it seems, both bodily movement and social practice are necessary for action. Nevertheless, for Melden, only social practice is a necessary condition or criterion of the concept of action. If the social context of practices be regarded as a presupposition of the concept of action, perhaps bodily movement can be construed as a precondition of the concept. Thus, on Melden's view, there cannot be actions or true-false action reports unless there are bodily movements; but these actions and their descriptions involve essential reference to social practices and no reference to bodily movement.

To illustrate the difference between bodily movement and action and to illuminate the essentially rule-governed character of the latter, Melden considers chess moves. (He also implies that playing chess, although it is a highly sophisticated example of action, is subject to moral review. However, that playing chess, in contrast to doing practically nothing else, is a moral activity is extremely dubious and can be argued for only by opting for some extended, persuasive definition of morality.)

Suppose, now, a game of chess in progress. X moves his knight; Y then castles. Here there is bodily movement. But what else? Theories according to which these chess moves are combinations or blends of bodily movements (i.e., finger movements) and psychological processes (e.g., volitions, followed by movements or deliberations, followed by decisions), Melden argues here (as well as more fully in his later book, *Free Action*) are not only indefensible in themselves but, more important, are fatally indifferent to the essentially contextual, social character of action. "To attempt to understand a move in a game of chess in terms of bodily and psychological processes occurring at the time the agent makes his move is to leave out what is essential to the move—the fact that what transpires in the way of such occurrent processes is a case of following the rules" (p. 534). That in their total concern for bodily movements and their psychological causes and accompaniments, these theories in effect fail to elucidate the concept of action is Melden's major criticism of previous analyses or theories of action.

What, then, is the correct elucidation of the concept of action? Following Wittgenstein, Melden reminds us of the varying uses of the concept: the diverse roles of different kinds of action verbs. However—and here he is on his own—essential to all these uses is the condition of following or obeying given rules.

Action concepts, whatever their use, are social in character, "logically connected with the concept of rules" (p. 532).

Rule-governed behavior alone, Melden claims, can explain the distinction between mere movement and action. Thus—to return to our chess game—X cannot move his knight, nor can Y castle, unless they move their fingers. But reports on X's and Y's chess moves are not about their finger movements; they are only about their rule-governed behavior.

Of course, Melden allows, a child could move a knight from one square to another or move the rook and the king in accordance with the castling rule of chess, but the child would not thereby be following or obeying the rules. He might perform an action but not that of moving a knight or of castling. Only one who is versed in the practices of chess can do that.

Is Melden correct in his claim, if I have interpreted him rightly, that rule-governed behavior is at least one necessary condition of the concept of action? It seems to me that, like other putative necessary conditions which at best turn out to be among the sufficient conditions of the concept, rule-governed behavior is also a sufficient condition—a good reason for something's being, or being said to be, an action. "Castling in chess is an action because it involves application of the rules of chess" is as secure a statement about actions as any such statement can be.

But is this condition necessary? R. Taylor, for one, disagrees. "I raise my arm" entails "my arm rises." Action implies movement, and my raising my arm is an action whether it is described in its social context or not. For Melden, Taylor's responsible agent, who simply raises his arm or wiggles his finger and for whom social practices here are irrelevant—that is, who is not signaling, saluting, exercising, etc.—is not acting: "In that case, when the individual raises his arm what happens is that a bodily movement, not an action, occurs" (p. 541). Since Melden admits that it is conceptually possible for an agent to raise his arm independently of a social context, the issue between him and Taylor reduces to whether such an occurrence is an action or not. This issue is analogous to whether there can be and are actions without causal agency, intentionality, goal-directedness, endeavor, or teleology. Consequently, Melden is in basic disagreement about action not only with R. Taylor but with C. Taylor, Chisholm, and Danto as well, for all of whom social practice or rule-governed behavior is not essential or even always relevant to action.

Another difficulty with Melden's necessary condition is that it does not adequately cover those cases where we act or perform actions without following the given rules or even when we act in accordance, not with any rules at all, but only with certain natural regularities or physical laws. The television repairman, for example, fixes the broken set. Like the chess player who castles, he applies the rules and recipes he has learned in his craft. "X fixed the set" as against "X moved a few tools with his fingers" describes an action in Melden's sense of rule-governed behavior. But if a child kicks the set or jiggles it, so that it works, do we want to say that he merely kicked it or jiggled it but fixed nothing, as we might justly want to say that he did not castle by simply moving two chess pieces? Just as an infant can kill a man without murdering him, why can't a child fix the set without following any rules or without even being in accordance with the rules? What are the rules for television repair? Certain recipes derived from physical laws which govern the behavior of the repairman as he fixes the set? But if the child or you or I fixed it by roughing it up, did we perform an action or not? If not, why not? Melden's recourse to doing something in accordance with the rules of repair is an amusing mixup of rules and laws. Of course, if one fixes the set by roughing it up, one must have done something in accordance with the physical laws governing television sets, unless, miraculously, one performed a miracle.

There are thus all kinds of things we do, from breaking things to fixing them, where we follow no rules or where what we do is in accordance with no rules, and all compete for the name of action. In spite of his admonition about generalizing from too few cases and his insistence on the class of actions as a family of cases rather than as a core of strong cases with its characteristic marginal cases, Melden, in denying these nonrule-governed occurrences as action, repudiates the philosophical practice he preaches. Elucidation of the concept of action does not yield Melden's necessary condition any more than traditional analyses do.

In *Free Action* (1961),[7] Melden turns from a primary concern for the elucidation of the concept of action to an investigation of the concepts of volition, intention, and desire as they relate to action. His central thesis is that neither acts of will, motives as intentions, nor desires or wants are occurrences which function as causal antecedents of actions. Rather, they are either non-occurrences, as in the case of acts of will, or occurrences whose descriptions involve concepts, such as intention and desire, that presuppose the concept of action. Intentions and desires cannot cause actions, since they logically imply actions.

Action Melden takes as a primitive concept. It is not thereby indefinable, i.e., unamenable to further analysis; but this is so not because action is simple but rather because analysis is suspect. Action is primitive in the sense that it and its correlative—agent—are the starting point in the whole complicated nexus of human actions. If we turn from the denotation of "action" to its meaning or role, we find that "no account of the concept of action will do that does not attend to the status of a person as a practical being, one who is not only endowed with the primitive ability to move his limbs but who, in his complex dealings with others, acts as he does for the very many sorts of reasons that operate in conduct and out of concern with a variety of envisaged goods" (pp. 80–81).

Human beings who do things for reasons, with proper attention to what they are about: this is where the philosophy of action starts, not with the abstract notion of an action or an agent as such. So the concept of an action is a social one after all. But is the social still essential, as it is in his early essay? Melden denies in this book that it is a necessary condition. For example, one can correctly say of a person that he is raising his arm for no reason at all or for no social or moral reason. It is therefore possible, he concedes, to have a conception of a human action without social and moral conventions and rules. Yet, he adds, "to understand the concept of a human action we need to understand the *possibilities* of descriptions in social and moral terms" (p. 180; italics in original).

Does this mean that the concept of action is essentially social and that some concepts of particular actions describe limiting cases of action, to be understood as actions even without conventions or rules only because we already understand the pervasive social context of action? Such a reading of Melden's view reflects his general observation that, although it is true that people sometimes lie, desire something without doing anything to get it, or do nothing with what they want and already have, it is logically impossible that they should always lie, desire something without doing anything to get it, or do nothing with what they want and already have. Consequently, although it is true that people sometimes act without reasons, it is logically impossible that they always do so. Hence it is conceptually necessary that action is social, even for its limiting cases. Therefore, a necessary condition for saying of anything that it is an action, even of an action without reasons, rules, or conventions, is that it is social, practical, rule-governed. Limiting cases, therefore, are abrogations of rules, not examples of nonrule-governed behavior.

Action, thus, if my reading of Melden is correct, is for him either following or *breaking* the regulations and conventions of social practices. In either case, action is still rule-governed. This must be Melden's final position if it is to be saved from self-contradiction; his counterexamples are counter only because they presuppose examples of action as rule-governed.

That the concept of action is essentially social, involving human beings in transaction with one another, doing things for reasons of course, applies to humans as agents but not to agents as causes, either in the Humean sense of collections of antecedent events in the causal chain or in the metaphysical sense of centers of power or efficacy. This metaphysical sense, shared by traditional philosophers as well as by C. Taylor, R. Taylor, and Chisholm, Melden rejects as an unnecessary appendage to the concept of action, imposed on it by the implausible doctrine of action as psychologically caused bodily movement. Agents can no more cause actions than desires, intentions, or acts of will can cause actions, for, like these latter, they logically imply, hence cannot cause, actions. For Melden, then, agency—the causal power or efficacy of agents—is not only not a necessary ingredient of action, as it is for C. Taylor, R. Taylor, and Chisholm; it is not an ingredient at all. Here, then, is another issue among our theorists: Is agency a necessary constituent of human action? Indeed, is it a constituent at all? What kind of disagreement is this?

In *Free Action* Melden takes as his fundamental problem the explanation of the distinction between movement and action. As noted, his central claim is that the distinction cannot be explicated in terms of the order of causes. Much of his argument is a sustained refutation of certain views about this order: that action is volition followed by bodily movement; that action is intention making movements happen; that action is desire of certain ends, together with beliefs about the means of achieving these ends.

To simplify his argument against the causal theories of action, Melden once again considers the action of signaling while driving a car. In describing what happens, we may distinguish between (1) "A signals," (2) "A raises his arm," and (3) "A's muscles are moving." Statements (1) and (2) are different action reports about different actions, but they are about the same movement or occurrence—A's arm rising; (3) differs from (1) and (2) in that it is not a report on an action at all. Further, (1) and (2) relate in a way that (2) and (3) do not: A signals by raising his arm; however, he does not raise his arm by his muscles' moving, even though his muscles' moving causes his arm to rise. Neither does A move his muscles by raising his arm nor does *A* raise his arm by moving his muscles. So if we introduce (4) "*A* moves his muscles," (2) is not related to (4) as (1) is to (2). *A* does not raise his arm by moving his muscles as *A* signals by raising his arm. The question How does *A* signal? is answered: By raising his arm. How does *A* raise his arm? has a different kind of answer: He just does—it is a primitive ability he comes to possess independently of any acquired, applied knowledge about muscle movements.

Causal theories of action interpret (1), (2), and (4) as bodily movement caused by antecedent psychological events, such as volitions, intentions, and desires. The gap between the physiological happenings of the arm's going up and the muscles' moving is filled by the psychological happenings of acts of will, intention, or desire. Melden's basic argument against this causal bridging of the gap is that it requires the existence of independently identifiable events which cannot be found. However, they cannot be found not because they are empirically undiscoverable but because they are logically impossible. Volitions are logically tied to physical movements; intentions and desires, to actions. Hence the concepts of volition, intention, and desire and their logical implicates of movement and action render impossible any causal account of action in terms of volition, intention, or desire. It is logically impossible, not merely empirically false, that actions are caused by that which implies them.

Having gone this far, it is hard to understand why Melden does not also reject as incoherent the Humean concept of causality. For in the sense in which, say, desire logically implies desire for something, which logically implies doing something to get what one desires, cause logically implies effect; so that the very notion of a cause without its effect, i.e., the possibility of identifying a cause independently of its effect, is logically impossible. If the causal theories of action are incoherent, so too, on Melden's argument that logical implicates cannot be causally related, is the causal theory of events. If cause logically implies effect, nothing can be an antecedent cause of any effect.

Melden's final point is that explanations of actions involve reasons, not causes. Actions are doings and not making things happen: neither implies the other. Doings have reasons; happenings and makings have causes. Motives, intentions, desires, wants—none either necessary or sufficient for actions, nevertheless all action-tied concepts—mark out reasons for what we do, not the causes of our bodily movements that transmute these movements into actions. The introduction of particular motives, intentions, desires, and wants into our description of an action explains the action by giving its reasons and in this manner clarifies the action and the character of the agent. To insist that such clarification is not explanation because it is not causal is to vitiate the entire distinction between action and movement by reducing all actions to sequences of happenings.

In his essay "Actions, Reasons, and Causes,"[8] Donald Davidson shifts from a theory of human action to a theory of the explanation of human action when such explanation involves reasons. Agent A does or did x. Instead of asking what makes x an action, Davidson asks, What is the relation between reason and action when reason explains—"rationalizes"—the action by giving the agent's reason for doing what he did? The relation, he claims, is causal, not logical, as Melden and others say. A does or did x. X is picked out, described or redescribed, and rationalized by naming as its cause A's "pro" attitude toward actions of type x and/or A's belief about such actions. When the reason given why A did x under a certain description of x consists of A's pro attitude toward actions with a certain property and of A's belief that x, so described, has that property, the reason is the primary reason why A performed x. Davidson states two theses about primary reasons: (1) that a primary reason is necessary and sufficient for the rationalization of an action and (2) that it causes the action.

Although Davidson argues for these two theses separately, he does not discuss the relation between them. Nevertheless, if rationalizations are causal explanations, as he contends, then (1) entails (2). That is, there can be no rationalizations of human actions if there are no primary reasons that cause them. Consequently, his theory of explanation of actions—of the causal role of reasons in them—rests upon a theory, or the makings of a theory, of human action. Hence there is no real shift at all in Davidson's discussion of the problem of the nature of human action, for, in stating what he regards as necessary and sufficient conditions of the explanation of human action, Davidson implies that pro attitudes and related beliefs—primary reasons—are at least necessary and causal conditions of human actions. His two theses, therefore, reduce to one thesis about human actions: that they are what we do when what we do is caused by our particular pro attitudes and related beliefs. If there are no such causes, both of his theses collapse. Absolutely central and crucial to his whole doctrine of the explanation of action, then, is his supporting evidence for primary reasons as the causes of action.

In supporting his case for reasons as causes, Davidson distinguishes between "Can reasons be causes of actions?" and "Are reasons causes of actions?"—although he seems to assume that the truth of the first is evidence for the truth of the second, which it is not. He centers on Melden's paradigm: "*A* raised his arm because he wanted to signal." Melden says that the "because" clause gives a reason which explains the action in the social context of driving and the rules of the road. As a reason, it is logically tied to the action; and, since causes must be logically distinct from their effects, "wanted to signal" cannot name a cause. Indeed, for Melden, "raising one's arm"—the action—is a criterion for "wanting to signal"; this relationship (between action and criterion) is the logical tie Melden affirms.

Davidson agrees that the "because" clause gives a reason, but he insists that this reason—"he wanted to signal"—names the cause of the action of the raising of the arm. To me, at any rate, Davidson seems to confuse Melden's point, that the logical tie is between the action and the want, i.e., that the raising of the arm is a criterion of wanting to signal—a logical tie between the effect and the want—with an entirely different point, that there is a logical tie between "wanting to signal" as a cause and "raising one's arm" as an action; by doing this, Davidson correctly dismisses this latter logical tie, but this dismissal does not show that reasons are logically independent of actions; all it shows is that actions are logically independent of causes.

Are reasons causes of action? If they are, Davidson agrees with Melden, they are events that precede their effects. Melden then says that there are no such events: no wants or beliefs that can be isolated and identified as causes of our actions. Davidson replies that there are such events: wants and related beliefs—primary reasons—that can be isolated and identified as the causes of our actions. That there are such events and that they are mental, Davidson suggests, has been denied because philosophers have confused observings and noticings—awareness—with what is observed or noticed. Consider again Melden's driver who raises his arm to signal a turn: "But of course there is a mental event; at some moment the driver noticed (or thought he noticed) his turn coming up, and that is the moment he signaled.... To dignify a driver's awareness that his turn has come by calling it an experience, much less a feeling, is no doubt exaggerated, but whether it deserves a name or not, *it had better be the reason why he raises his arm*" (p. 74; my italics).

If the driver's awareness that his turn has come is "the reason why" he raises his arm, then surely this awareness, because it is not a pro attitude and belief, cannot be a primary reason; and if it is not a primary reason, it cannot be the cause of the driver's raising his arm, according to Davidson's thesis (2). This example, instead of showing that pro attitudes and related beliefs—primary reasons—are antecedent mental events that cause actions, shows only, if it shows anything at all, that some actions, e.g., raising one's arm or signaling, are caused by a mental event: noticing that one's turn has come. This noticing, rather than a reason functioning as a cause, is a cause that functions as a reason in the explanation of why the driver raised his arm to signal.

It is this distinction between reasons as causes and causes as reasons in the explanation of human actions, and not the presence of awareness, that has been overlooked by philosophers in their discussion of this problem of the role of reason in human action. Both Melden and Davidson conflate this distinction. Melden confuses his denial that reasons are causes with his denial that causes are reasons in the explanation of human action, and this is why he restricts causes to bodily movements and reasons to action. Davidson confuses his insight that causes can serve as reasons in an explanation of an action with his claim that reasons are causes of action, and this is why he identifies these causes with the reasons for action. Melden has not shown that among the explanatory reasons for an action may be statements about its causes; nor has Davidson shown that among the causes of an action is its primary reason.

Explanation of human action is indeed a complex problem. The distinction between reasons as causes and causes as reasons must enter into any adequate theory of such explanation. Davidson's theory—that all explanation is causal, hence that rationalization (or justification, or giving reasons for) is a species of causal explanation—does not do justice to the distinction; for even if the cause of an action serves as a reason in its explanation, it does not follow that the reason for the action is its cause, whereas, if the reason for an action is its cause, it does follow that the cause of the action is the reason for the action. No causal theory of explanation can account for this asymmetry between causes as reasons and reasons as causes.

Davidson, thus, has shown neither that reasons can be causes of human action nor that they are *the* causes of human action. Hence he has provided no evidence that a necessary ingredient or condition of a human action is its primary reason—its pro attitude and related belief—which functions as an antecedently identifiable mental event that causes the action. Insofar as his theory of explanation rests upon his partial theory of action, he has therefore not shown that all actions share the common property of primary reason or even that they share some other property. What he has shown is that at least some actions have as their causes certain mental events and that these can properly enter into the explanation of these actions. Perhaps to cite these causes is to tell or to explain why certain actions are performed and why they can serve as reasons for actions or as terms in the "because" clause. But that this procedure is identical with or is convertible into the citation of primary reasons remains mere speculation.

J. L. Austin's "A Plea for Excuses"[9] is universally regarded as a seminal essay in contemporary philosophy of human action. It was the first to raise fundamental questions about the criteria of the identity and individuation of actions "What, indeed, are the rules for the use of 'the' action, 'an' action, 'one' action, a 'part' or 'phase' of an action and the like?" [p. 127]); about the distinction between doing and acting (Is sneezing, breathing, or even simply sitting in my chair an action?); and about the relation between the language of excuses and of action (Are all actions excusable or only those that are wayward in some clearly statable sense?).

What has not been noticed is that Austin's essay does more than challenge a theory of action, in the sense of a statement about the common, definitive properties of all actions. Just as important, it is the first to suggest that, although there are no established necessary conditions of human action, there are sufficient conditions, two of which he states: justification and excuse. For his most fundamental thesis—and his central contribution to the philosophy of action—is that, though there are actions abstractly describable by the dummy expression "A performs an action" and concretely but variously describable by certain verbs, their adverbs, or modifying nouns or prepositions, and though actions form certain subclasses, actions have only sufficient, not necessary, conditions. Thus the concept of action, even as a dummy concept, is governed by sufficient criteria, not necessary ones.

A did or does x. Instead of asking what makes x an action, Austin asks, what does excusing (or justifying) x reveal about x as an action? Not every doing of any x by A is amenable to excuse or justification; x must be (or be said to be) bad, wrong, inept, unwelcome—untoward. This rules out excusability and, what is more surprising, justifiability as a necessary criterion of action. For just as not every act is excusable, so, too, not every act requires justification. Some acts are neither, since they are not untoward; and though excusability or justifiability is not essential to action, doing what is regarded as the untoward is necessary for both excusability and justifiability. Austin thus lays down no set of conditions for all actions but only two sufficient conditions for some actions, when these latter actions satisfy the necessary condition of being (or being said to be) untoward.

Moreover, some actions, given certain standards of acceptable behavior, are inexcusable—for example, stepping on a baby's toes; this is another reason why excusability is not a necessary criterion of action. Nevertheless, a good reason for something's being an action or being called an action is that the specified action—when untoward—is open to excuse or to justification.

If excuse and justification serve as sufficient conditions of actions, what, now, about praise or blame? Austin treats blame like excuse: a necessary condition of both is that what is blamed or excused is the untoward. Will this do for praise? Can we praise any action—untoward or not? If we can, praise differs logically from blame, for the necessary condition of the untoward vanishes. Even if we admit that blame, like the attribution of "voluntary" or "involuntary," is inappropriate to all actions, is it so clear that we applaud actions only when some necessary condition of the unusual or abnormal is satisfied? Of course we do not applaud all actions, but we do praise many which are usual and normal in every way. *A* takes an examination and fails. Here blame, excuse, and even justification can come in. But if *B*—a good student, not just a dubious one—passes, his teacher can praise him without in any way presupposing that *B*'s performance was abnormal.

Praise, therefore, is also a good reason for something's being (or being called) an action. Although it differs from blame in that it has no necessary condition of the wayward, it is like blame in that it too is not a necessary, but rather a sufficient, condition of action. What characterizes excuse, justification, praise, blame, or the voluntary—namely, that though each has its own special conditions of use, none is necessary for human action—applies as well to intention, purpose, and motive. All provide good reasons for something's being or being described as an action; but none is necessary. Each is a sufficient condition, marking out a distinguishing feature of the different subclasses of the class of actions.

Does Austin show that the proffering of an excuse is a sufficient condition or criterion of action? He has certainly shown that it is not necessary. But is it always in any situation a good reason, a sufficient reason, for saying of *x*, when *A* did or does *x*, that *x* is an action? Austin suggests not only that excuses are sufficient conditions of actions but also that different kinds of excuses point to different aspects of actions: their stages (the intelligence, appreciation, planning, decision, and execution involved); their phases (e.g., the difference between putting a dab of paint on a canvas and painting the whole picture); and their stretches (smaller as against larger groups of events). Austin does not claim that all actions are or can be rendered complex in this way; once again, all he argues is that some excuses are sufficient both for something's being (or being described as) an action and for something's being (or being parceled out as) a stage, phase, or stretch of an action. Excuses, consequently, constitute a whole class of different varieties of sufficient conditions. For example, in his famous *Regina* v. *Finney* illustration, Austin points out that Finney's action, whether specified as turning on the wrong tap or as scalding Watkins, is excusable but that the excuse that what he did was inadvertent applies to only one phase of the action because the excuse that what he did was an accident applies to a different phase.

Now, if we grant, as indeed I think we must, that Austin presents a brilliant case for the varieties of excuses, exemplified in certain verbs and especially their adverbs, because these excuses point to different aspects of actions, must we accept excusability as a sufficient condition of action? Austin admits that excuses play a larger role than he describes, so that the excuse of politeness—"Excuse me, please!"—differs from the excuse of accusation. But he also admits that even in the primary situation ("in general," p. 123) in which someone is accused of or is said to have done the untoward, an excuse can be offered which cancels, not merely mitigates, the responsibility. Here excuse does not qualify the action; it denies the action. To deny the action by an excuse that cancels the responsibility, Austin implies, does not entail that responsibility is necessary for action; all this denial entails is that the absence of responsibility is sufficient for no action.

For Austin, then, there are some excuses that do not qualify actions; from this it follows that excusability is not a sufficient condition for action. If A did x and is accused of doing x, where both A and his accuser accept x as bad, and A pleads and proves that he was forced to do x or, like Finney, that he scalded Watkins by mistakenly thinking Watkins was out of the tub, which Watkins was able and supposed to be, A's excuse, in canceling the responsibility, cancels the act. In Finney's case, he was not only acquitted of manslaughter by the judge; he is also relieved, by Austin, of his action of scalding through his cancellation of responsibility. Excuse, therefore, even for Austin, is not a sufficient condition of action. Consequently we must conclude that what Austin shows in "A Plea for Excuses" is not merely that the concept of action has no necessary but only sufficient criteria; he also shows that excuses, unlike justifications, are not members of the class of sufficient criteria. To be able to excuse x when A did or does x may be a reason why we call x an action, but it is not a sufficient reason. Justification, praise, blame, intention, purpose, and responsibility, among others, he also allows us to infer, are both good reasons and sufficient criteria for something's being or being described as an action. At any rate, this thesis—that the concept of a human action is governed by criteria, some of which are sufficient but none of which is necessary—first suggested (at least to me) by Austin's essay, is, I wish to contend, the thesis that best illumines the logical grammar of that concept. That x is a human action because it is goal-directed, agent-caused, basic or caused by a

Chapter Six basic action, intentional, governed by conventions, or done for a reason, each of which functions as a necessary condition in the individual contemporary theories of action already considered, is at best—and then only if it can first be rendered intelligible as a criterion—a sufficient condition of such action.

What is a human action? Is the class of human actions distinct from the class of human (and other) movements, processes, events? How do we decide whether a particular x is a human action? What counts as a good reason for an x's being a human action? What answers why x is a human action?

These are the main questions our contemporary theories try to answer. Each of these theories, whether it takes human action or its concept to be definable or not, offers, I have tried to show, at least a necessary property, feature, condition, or criterion; some proffer necessary and sufficient properties. An ideal theory—*the* theory of human action—would presumably be the one that formulated the definitive set of properties shared by all human actions.

Among these putatively necessary properties, either affirmed or implied by the various theories, are agency, responsibility, intention, intentionality or goal-directedness (purpose), an agent making one thing happen in the endeavor to make another thing happen, an agent causing things to happen without first causing other things to happen, reason that functions as cause, and convention.

These properties serve as necessary or as definitive criteria of the identity and individuation of a human action in the various theories. They function as basic in answering not only what a human action is but also why x is, or whether x is, a

human action. It is also these properties and criteria that
determine the nature and range of good reasons for anything's
being a human action.

Are there such properties? Are they necessary for human
action? The theorists disagree among themselves; for each of
them, some of these properties are nonexistent, or, if it is
allowed that they do exist, they are not necessary, sufficient, or
even relevant to human action. The theorists also disagree about
the nature of these properties, about what constitutes agency,
intention, purpose, or reason in human action. All they agree on
is that some of their opponents' claims about necessary properties are false and that at least one of the claims—for each, his
own—is true.

Is any claim true that there is a necessary property of human
action? I have argued that none stated by our theorists is true.
Thus, C. Taylor says that human action is intentional behavior.
But he does not show that the class of human actions is
coextensive with the class of intentional behavior, nor does he
show that the latter class is coextensive with the class of clear
cases of human action. What he does is to mark out a class of
"strong" cases of human action—those that are intentional—and
give an account of these in terms of noncontingent, irreducibly
teleological laws. The concept of human action, consequently
for him, becomes a core concept, one that gets its definitive
criteria from the shared properties of the "strong" cases. That
there are these "strong" cases—of intentional behavior—seems
indisputable, however debatable his account or his interpretation of them as the core of human action. For his core concept
does not cover equally indisputable, clear cases of human
action. All that remains intact in his theory is that some
indisputable examples of human action are undeniable cases of
intentional behavior. "X is a human action because A intended
x" gives a (tautologically) necessary reason for x's being intentional but only a sufficient reason for x-as-intentional's being a
human action.

R. Taylor implies that agency—the human being as causally
efficacious—is a necessary property of all human actions. This,
too, is questionable, both as a property and, if a property, as
necessary for all action. My argument is this: if agency is a
property, it can be identified; to be identified, its corresponding
name must have some criterion for determining its correct
identification; but on Taylor's reading of the term, it has no such
criterion. "Agency," for Taylor, becomes a word or concept that
each of us supposedly learns for himself and teaches others to
use with the sole putative criterion of the individual's experience

of agency. Such an inner criterion, however, is no criterion at all, because it serves to identify nothing. And if it identifies nothing, it is no word or concept either; it plays no role in any language of human action. Taylor's argument against the privacy of "desire" applies equally to his private "agency."

Chisholm also maintains that agency—the agent as immanent cause—is necessary (and, if necessary, certainly intelligible). Like R. Taylor, he rests his claim that there is agency, and that it is necessary for all human action, on our experience of causal efficacy: "It is only by understanding our own causal efficacy, as agents, that we can grasp the concept of *cause* at all" ("Freedom and Action," p. 22; italics in original). This ultimate appeal to individual inner experience also entails, as it does for R. Taylor, an incoherent doctrine of causality, namely, that causality is ultimately private, consequently that the concept of cause is governed by the necessary and sufficient criterion of one's own experience of causal efficacy.

However irreducible statements about human ability and human action may be to other statements about events and their Humean causal regularities, it does not follow from this irreducibility alone that there are centers of power—causal efficacy— or that agents are immanent, not transeunt, causes of events. All that follows is that there are no intensional or extensional equivalents of statements about human abilities and actions. Thus, R. Taylor and Chisholm (and others, too, including Austin) are correct in contending that "I can move my finger" and "I am moving my finger" are not reducible to conditional statements or to statements about events. But that "I" or "can" or "move" in these statements refers to a center of causal efficacy—agency—does not follow from this irreducibility. That these statements do refer to such agency requires a further argument or evidence that there is this unique center which distinguishes action from movement. Neither Taylor nor Chisholm provides this argument or evidence; nor, it seems to me, can they provide it without rendering the concept of agency incoherent. Our talk about human ability and action, it can be argued, presupposes that there are agents or persons—the authors of actions; otherwise we cannot make intelligible an essential part of our ordinary referring use of language. It is also cogent to hypothesize agency as a necessary presupposition of the intelligibility of such talk, in which case agency is conceived of in transcendental, nonempirical terms, perhaps like agents as substances. But that our talk of human ability and action refers to, names, or describes inner agency—man's unique causal

efficacy—is no condition, either necessary, sufficient, or even
intelligible, of that talk.

Chisholm also affirms that an agent making one thing happen
in the endeavor to make another thing happen is a necessary,
albeit indefinable, property of all human actions. As we have
seen, this criterion also has its difficulties; for example, some of
our actions involve making things happen but not in the
endeavor to make other things happen. Even so, this criterion is
as clear as that of intention—however imprecise both may
be—and can therefore serve as a criterion of the concept of
action, which agency cannot. Consequently, without debating
the criterion, let us accept making B happen in the endeavor to
make A happen as an intelligible property in order to ask Is it an
omnipresent feature of all human actions?

It seems to me that it is not. To be sure, there are many
recognized, indisputable examples of human action in which we
do make one thing happen in the endeavor to make something
else happen or to prevent it from happening. Yet, even if we
grant that all descriptions of human actions can be paraphrased
into the terms of making B happen in the endeavor to make A
happen, it is simply not true that all redescriptions of actions can
be so paraphrased. To revert to my previous example: I may
clear my walk of ice and snow or not clear it. My act of clearing
it or not clearing it can be redescribed as obeying or breaking the
law. As strained as it is to talk of not clearing my walk as
making something happen in the endeavor to make or to prevent
something else from happening, it is very odd indeed to talk of
obeying or breaking the law in these terms. Making B happen in
the endeavor to make A happen may be a criterion of the
descriptive use of "action"; but it is no criterion of the imputative use, hence it is not a necessary criterion, applicable to all
actions.

Danto's implicit doctrine that all actions include as a necessary
ingredient a basic action does not, I have argued, establish basic
action as either necessary or sufficient. Indeed, as he formulates
it, it is difficult to ascertain whether basic action is a condition at
all. Neither declension nor appeal to our repertoire of acts
provides a necessary or sufficient condition for deciding what is
to count as a basic action. What about Danto's criterion of an
agent's making event e to occur without first making event d to
occur as the cause of e? In the sense that we can and do move our
arm without first causing something else to do it, for example,
by striking it, there are basic acts. But then, on this view, basic
acts and actions include many bodily functions, some very basic

indeed, which functions are usually classified among the processes or movements of nature. Thus, if there are basic acts or basic actions in Danto's causal sense, they cannot serve to distinguish action from movement; consequently, they can furnish no answer to what differentiates action from nonaction in human (and animal) behavior.

Claims that all human actions are goal-directed or are conventional—C. Taylor's and Melden's respective doctrines about necessary properties—are also exaggerated. As we have seen from those examples of action that are neither goal-directed nor governed by conventions but can be rejected as clear cases of human action only by arbitrary stipulation, these two conditions are not necessary; they are only sufficient.

The more important issue raised by this appeal to goals or conventions, in which reasons having to do with these goals or conventions are offered as answers to why a particular action was done or why a particular x is an action, is the issue raised by Davidson: Do these reasons, when they are introduced to explain actions, denote the causes of actions?

I have already discussed this issue. Davidson, I argued, does not show that reasons are causes or that they can function as causes of action. Nevertheless, in spite of his conflation of a mental event as a cause of an action with the primary reason as the cause, the possibility remains that our pro attitudes and beliefs, our goals and conventions, or our wants and beliefs about realizing them—the reasons for our actions—are causes; and, indeed, so does the possibility he urges, that all action is caused by reasons. If it could be shown that nothing is an action without a reason as the cause of the action, this would secure a necessary property, so strongly desiderated by all the theorists.

The most promising candidate for a reason as the cause is a particular want or desire that one has in conjunction with a related belief about how to satisfy it. In his essay, "Actions, Reasons, and Causes," Davidson says that, although a desire or a belief is dispositional, the *onslaught* of a desire or a belief is not. The onslaught is a mental event; therefore it can serve as an identifiable antecedent event of an action. "A desire to hurt your feelings may spring up at the moment you anger me; I may start wanting to eat a melon just when I see one; and beliefs may begin at the moment we notice, perceive, learn, or remember something" (p. 74). These onslaughts of desires and beliefs, like Melden's driver who notices (or thinks he notices) his turn coming up, are mental events—awarenesses, not something we are aware of; these, then, are the reasons that cause the respective actions of hurting your feelings, eating a melon, or signaling a turn.

Is, for example, the onslaught of my desire to hurt your feelings at the moment you anger me the primary reason that causes my hurting you? If it is, it must include a related belief; so let that be my belief that I can hurt you by insulting you. Now the mental state is the specific desire and the related belief about how to satisfy it. This state is my awareness, and it causes my insulting you. "Why did you insult me?" asked by you, is answered by me, "Because you hurt my feelings"; and my answer implies a pro attitude I have about retaliation toward people who hurt my feelings and a belief about how to retaliate in this kind of situation: the primary reason, according to Davidson.

Well, now, the primary reason of my action of insulting you is my pro attitude toward retaliation and my belief that insulting you will satisfy this pro attitude. On Davidson's view, this has to be the cause of the action. But in his example, it is not; the cause of my desire to hurt you is your angering me. Your action of angering me is the cause of my desire to hurt you and of my action of insulting you. Yet, for Davidson, your action cannot be the cause of mine because all that can be the cause of mine is my pro attitude and related belief toward actions like yours.

Thus, what Davidson shows by his appeal to the onslaught of a particular desire is that it is caused by something else (e.g., your angering me) and, in turn, is a cause of my action (e.g., insulting you). He does not show that my particular pro attitude toward, for example, retaliation, and my particular related belief, for example, that insulting you is one way to retaliate—together constituting the primary reason—are *the* cause of my action of insulting you. The primary cause of my action is your action; the primary reason of my action is my attitude toward being angered and toward retaliation. Of course, to repeat what I said before, in explaining my insulting you, there may be, among the reasons *in* the explanation, statements about some of the causes, for example, "You insulted me," "I wanted to retaliate," and so forth; but the explanation contains a statement about my pro attitude and related belief not as a cause but only as a reason.

Davidson, then, does not show that reason as cause is a necessary constituent of all human actions. Nor does he show that specific desires or their onslaughts are *the* causes of action. All he shows is that these onslaughts, along with other mental events, are among the causes of action and, as such, can enter into the explanations of actions as reasons. This reminder is important to the philosophy of mind in its assemblage of mental events. Its contribution to the philosophy of action, however, is limited to the range of causes; it is not extended to reasons as causes.

Are the pro attitudes and related beliefs, given as reasons for actions, reducible to particular desires and related beliefs? If they are, then the reason for an action is the particular desire and related belief that cause the action. Such is the heroic line taken by some philosophers, most recently by Alvin Goldman in *A Theory of Human Action* (1970).[10] Like Davidson, Goldman construes reason-explanation as a species of causal explanation. To explain why *A* did *x*, to give the reason for *A*'s action, is to imply that *A* had the indicated particular want and belief and that his having this want and belief caused his action. Goldman ties reasons to action-plans and adds a provocative logical entailment between want and action. However, of immediate concern here is his overriding thesis that all the reasons cited in the explanation of actions—all our goals, purposes, attitudes, conventions, and convictions that we specify in answering why we do or did what we do or did—are among the causes of our actions. Our reasons for action are the standing wants that become the occurrent wants which cause the action.

These occurrent wants, he says, are mental events or mental processes: goings-on in consciousness. Each of us has privileged access to his own wants and can know, though not with the certainty of one's own, the wants of others. How, then, does one acquire the concept of an occurrent want? Goldman faces this crucial question. His answer is that each of us learns the first-person use in two ways: (1) "The child notices the occasions in which adults ascribe [certain] wants to him [e.g., wanting to play with the ball] and correlates their words with the state he is in. He comes to recognize that when he is attracted to playing with the ball . . . , then the adults say he 'wants' to play with the ball. . . . Thus, he learns to say of *himself* that he wants the ball . . . in the right circumstances" (p. 121; italics in original). (2) The child, having learned to name objects, when he is attracted to the ball and wanting to reach it, says "ball."

> Gradually he acquires the idea of making a *request* . . . . The word "want" is taught to him (or simply learned by him) as part of request behavior. Thus, he learns to say "I want the ball" . . . , instead of simply "ball." . . . Although he *has* these mental events, he has not yet *reflected* upon his consciousness to notice them *as* mental events. Later, however, he comes to recognize that his reaching for the ball, or his asking

someone to give him the ball, results from a *felt attraction* for the ball. At this stage he recognizes wanting as a mental event that tends to cause his behavior [ibid.; italics in original].

The child's learning of the third-person use parallels his learning of the first-person use. In either case, when the child fully understands the term, Goldman concludes that "'want' is seen to apply in the same sense both to himself and to others—viz., to a mental event which tends to lead to action" (ibid.).

This reading of the concept of want, on which Goldman rests his theory of human action, including the doctrine that the reasons for action are the desires that cause action, entails the indefensible thesis that since the word "want" names an inner private event or process—which we are brought to recognize by teaching and learning how to use "want" in external circumstances but where this teaching and learning are only preparatory to grasping the meaning of the word—the sole necessary and sufficient criterion for the understanding (not the teaching and learning) of the concept of want is the innately private experience of wanting. Whatever can be said about such an experience, it cannot be said of it that it is a criterion, sole or not, necessary, sufficient, or not, because it cannot function as a criterion at all. Thus, it seems to me that Goldman's attempt to affirm reason-as-cause as a necessary property of all human actions, depending as it does on his doctrine of wants as causes of action—a doctrine which in turn, rests entirely upon his misreading of the concept of want as criterionless—does not succeed either.

None of our theories establishes a necessary property of human actions. This leaves open the possibility that other theories may succeed where these fail. To foreclose on this possibility and indirectly to rationalize my omission of other theories, past and present, I want now to argue that such a pursuit is not feasible. I do not mean to suggest that it is self-contradictory but rather that the attempt to do so is logically misbegotten in that it lays down necessary criteria for a concept whose use and conditions of use preclude such criteria.

In his essay "Action," Melden writes:

> It is the enormous variety of cases that defeats any attempt to provide a summary account of the nature of action in bodily and psychological factors. Some of my actions are deliberate. I weigh alternatives and choose. Some of my actions are done with a motive but without deliberation and

choice.... Some things I do without any motive.... Some things I do simply because I want to, or on the spur of the moment, and for no reason at all. If we consider the mental processes attending the relevant bodily movements, we find an enormous variation in what transpires. The cases range from those in which nothing that seems at all relevant happens except the occurrence of the bodily movement—one responds to the situation in which one finds oneself almost automatically, guided as it were by habit and the whole accumulation of past experience—to the cases in which force of mind, great effort, or internal struggles are involved as habit is resisted or passions and temptations conquered.... The characteristic philosophic vice of generalizing from special cases is involved in the familiar summary explanation of the concept of action in terms of various psychological factors or processes ["Action," p. 526].

Melden limits his criticism of theories of action to the causal ones because he wishes to counter them with his own noncausal, conventional theory. But the reason he gives for the defeat of the causal theories—the vast variety of cases of human action—defeats all theories, that is, all statements of the necessary and sufficient properties of human action and, what is just as important, all claims about their necessary properties.

That there is this vast variety of cases of human action, ranging from habitual behavior to the deliberation, decision, and execution involved in a complicated plan of action, is indisputable. It is this variety—encompassing actions with or without desires, intentions, motives, causes, mental events, purposes, goals, reasons, and even with or without any ordinary acts or doings, as in certain inactions which we and the law regard as actions—that an elucidation of the concept of a human action must hold constant.

Thus, it is no good starting with a class of core cases (for example, C. Taylor's "strong" cases of intentional behavior), working out a theory of these, and then situating the others on the margins (Taylor's "loose" cases) or throwing them out of the class altogether; for a marginal case of one theorist becomes a core case for another (e.g., wiggling one's finger for no reason at all), or a nonaction for one theorist becomes a core case for another theorist (e.g., killing a man unintentionally).

Instead of talking of core or strong cases of human action, we must talk of undeniable or clear cases. If we do not, we foreclose on the vast variety of cases which it is the philosopher's assigned and accepted task to illuminate. Of course there are enormous and notorious difficulties surrounding the criteria of the identity and individuation of an action; but it does not seem to me that

we cannot talk of clear cases of human action until we can solve
these difficulties. Quite the contrary: we cannot even begin to
formulate the criteria of an action unless we have some clear
cases before us. Indeed, it is because of the clarity of the
cases—of flipping the switch, turning on the light, illuminating
the room, and alerting the prowler—that philosophers such as
Davidson, Anscombe, Goldman, and others can raise questions
about the identity and individuation of these actions: Are they
the same action with different descriptions of it? Or are they
different actions with correspondingly different descriptions?
Whatever the correct answers to these questions are, and
however tied these answers are to the quest for necessary
properties of human actions, philosophers can concentrate on
this search without first settling the problems of identity and
individuation, since answers to these problems derive from what
theorists take to be the necessary (or necessary and sufficient)
properties of human action; or, if there are no such properties,
they can be resolved in other ways.

Now, if we keep before us as many of the clear, undeniable
cases of human action as we can, it does look as if their vast
variety does defeat any putatively necessary property. What,
one must ask, is the common denominator of the following
haphazard list of actions, none of which can be repudiated
without arbitrarily limiting the range of use of the concept of
human action? Moving one's finger for no reason at all; putting
on the left shoe before the right; driving to work; raising one's
arm to signal; polluting the atmosphere by driving; forgetting to
clear the iced walk; refusing to vote on polling day; stopping at
the store for some tobacco; convening an important meeting;
reading a report with the assigned task of making a recommendation regarding future action, with the intention of sorting
out all the issues, painful or not, with the motive of enhancing
the welfare of the institution, and with the goal of making a
better university; getting married; filing for a divorce; falling in
love; resigning one's job; writing a letter of resignation; quitting
one's job; turning on the wrong tap; scalding Watkins; killing a
man unintentionally, impulsively, by accident, mistakenly, or
inadvertently; stalking a bird; hunting a lion; shooting a rabbit;
missing the target; looking for a needle in a haystack; finding a
needle in a haystack with or without looking for it; shaking
hands; brushing elbows; greeting one's friend; murdering someone, etc., etc., etc.

The theorists, of course, do not accept all of these as cases of
action, nor do they offer the same reasons for the ones they
agree are actions. Even so, it remains a fact that each of these

examples is a legitimate member of the class of human actions for one of our theorists or another. The concept of human action accommodates all these cases, in spite of all the disagreements over whether they are cases or not.

If we turn from this vast variety of cases to those disagreements among the theorists about what counts as an action—disagreements about their action-giving reasons—we find the clue both to the concept of human action and to the impossibility of any necessary criterion of that concept. For it is in their disagreements about why x is an action or whether x is an action that the logic of the criteria of the concept can be discerned. What is at issue in these disagreements is not the application of agreed-upon criteria but a debate over the criteria themselves.

The concept of a human action, even as it is employed by the theorists, has many criteria, all manifested in the diverse properties of the vast variety of cases of human action. None of these criteria covers all the cases; each is applicable only to some of the cases. The theorist—in his quest for a common property—opts for at least one among all the extant criteria as a necessary criterion, which then serves as his main action-giving reason in answering why or whether x is an action. In effect, he proffers a necessary criterion of a concept whose use and conditions of use, as these conditions are embodied in their and our collective talk about the vast variety of cases, reveal that the concept has no such criterion. To persist in claiming that it does have a necessary criterion is to violate the logic of a concept which can perform its assigned role only under the second-order condition that it is governed by a multiple, diverse set of first-order criteria, some of which are sufficient but none of which is necessary.

What sort of concept, then, is the concept of a human action? It illuminates nothing to characterize or castigate it as ambiguous, vague, fishy, purely stipulative, or even dummy, for as it is applied to the vast variety of cases of human action, it is predominantly none of these. Rather, as I have tried to show—mainly by pitting the theorists against each other—it is open in the precise sense of having sufficient but no necessary criteria. If this is correct, the concept of a human action is not closed, defeasible, essentially disputable, or a family-resemblance concept. Moreover, the sufficient criteria of the concept of a human action are coextensive with the good reasons—the action-giving reasons—for something's being a human action. Because these action-giving reasons differ radically from those good reasons that are coextensive with definitive criteria, necessary criteria,

disjunctive sets of nonnecessary, nonsufficient criteria, the concept of action is not closed, like that of triangle; or open in Hart's
sense of necessary but no sufficient criteria, like that of contract;
or open in Hampshire's sense of no undebatable criterion, like
the concepts of morality or tragedy (which I call "perennially
debatable"); or open in Wittgenstein's sense of no necessary, no
sufficient, but some unrejectable criteria, such as the concepts of
game or drama (which I call "perennially flexible"). Its openness
of sufficient but no necessary criteria can be assimilated to none
of these. However, although it cannot be modeled on any of the
above concepts, it may nevertheless serve as a model for our
philosophical elucidation of other concepts, especially in psychology, where the quest for the common properties of the
various bits of human behavior continues unabated and unchallenged.

Some contemporary moralists complain that much of twentieth-century ethics is barren and trite, especially Moore's and theories that derive from his or are similar to his in their preoccupation with abstract problems of meaning and definition of moral terms rather than with concrete problems of morality and human action. Let me therefore begin an elucidation of the concept of morality with a number of theses that, barren in their eyes, can hardly be characterized as trite: There is no true theory of morality; there cannot be such a theory; and there need be no such theory in order to explain or to justify morality, or to render moral utterance or action intelligible. **Morality**

That the concept of morality is open in the sense of perennially debatable; that moral concepts, which, in any case, are not the same as the concept of morality, are some of them open, governed by criteria less than definitive, as others of them are closed, governed by definitive sets of criteria; that good reasons, if there are any, in morals and ethics, do not rest on necessary or sufficient properties of the moral or the good; that, though some moral judgments may be true or false, no judgments about what is moral or what is good are true or false—these theses I take to be truths about the concept of morality and some moral concepts. They may be barren, but they are not trite. Indeed, for many, they are not only false, they are immoral.

That they can be characterized and castigated as immoral, in a manner in which no one has yet said, of the rejection of and the need for a theory of art or tragedy, that such rejection is unaesthetic or untragic, shows something about the range of the concept of morality that is missing from other open concepts.

Ethics, it is worth remarking, retains the traditional classical search for real definition even more than its Cinderella sister subject, aesthetics. The terminology has changed. Theorists no longer say that they are seeking true, real definitions of morality; but they do say that they seek the necessary and sufficient conditions or properties of morality, the necessary and sufficient criteria of the concept of morality. Plato's *Euthyphro* remains the model of much twentieth-century ethics—or of what is called "meta-ethics." The platonic assumptions prevail that a necessary condition for an act's or action's being moral is that it satisfies the necessary and sufficient conditions of the moral and that, further, a necessary condition for judging intelligently and truly that an act or action is moral is the formulation, or at least the assumption, of a definition of morality, without which the concept and its applications are incoherent.

Labels, isms, and theories abound and persist in over-all surveys of twentieth-century writings about morality, in regard to both its history and problems. In fact, it is no exaggeration to say that no field of philosophy has been so neatly parceled out, labeled, and systematized as ethics: one is a subjectivist, a relativist, or an objectivist; an egoist or an altruist; a definist, a nonnaturalist, or a noncognitivist; a deontological or teleological intuitionist, an emotivist, or a naturalist; an act-deontologist or act-utilitarian or a rule-deontologist or rule-utilitarian. Although these are not empty labels and do sum up distinctive views on the nature or function of moral and value terms or utterances, they nevertheless encourage the (meta-ethical?) observation that ethics inherently involves the taking of a side in an ongoing game, though it is acknowledged that this game of how to behave and what to strive for is important.

More disconcerting than this penchant for pigeonholing is the employment, by an individual moralist or writer who talks about morality, of "theory" to characterize and cover all doctrines, views, or obiter dicta, however extensive they may be. One is said to have an ethical theory if one states the putatively necessary and sufficient properties of morality or value; if one affirms the simplicity of moral properties or values; if one denies that the moral or the valuable is a property, complex or simple; or if one claims that moral or value terms or utterances have a univocal or multiple function in discourse, whether one affirms or denies moral or value properties. Thus, intuitionism and naturalism are theories in the same sense of "theory" as are emotivism and prescriptivism. Presumably, there is no place or pigeonhole for anti-theory or, even more distressing, for the elucidation of moral concepts and the concept of morality that is not itself a theory of morals and, in this case, not even a meta-ethical theory.

I have already suggested that such wholesale use of "theory"
does less than justice to the rejection of theories of art or tragedy
in aesthetics. If aesthetics can find room for conceptual elucidation that is either anti-theory or, better, other than theory and
anti-theory, why cannot ethics? In any case, it serves no ideal of
clarification to attach the label "theory of morality" to a view
when that view, whether a correct elucidation of its relevant
concept or not, denies rather than affirms definitive properties of
the moral or definitive criteria of the concept of morality.
Moore's doctrine that good is indefinable—that it has no necessary and sufficient properties (even though the word "good"
may have necessary and sufficient criteria for its correct use,
thus raising a problem that no one has yet explored)—and that
right is definable, as is its conveying word, is a clear case of a
theory—as, indeed, are other intuitionist or purely naturalist
views. But are Ayer's or Carnap's early views—that good and
right are not properties at all, hence are not amenable to
definitions of them, and that "good" and "right" are words that
are used (that serve) to evince and stir up emotions—a theory
of morality? Perhaps these views may be said to be a theory—a
statement of the necessary and sufficient criteria—of the functioning of moral or value words, although it is difficult to
establish that their "emotive theory" ever claimed or implied
such a statement. Still, emotivism may be construed to be a
theory about the definitive conditions of the functioning of
moral and value discourse. However, even if it can be so
construed, there is, I believe, no warrant to characterize as a
theory of morality the view that some moral concepts are open,
some are not, and that the concept of morality is open in the
most radical sense of openness—whether this view is true or not,
immoral or not. For it is not a theory of morality or of anything
else. Nor is it a meta-ethical theory. It is what it claims to be: a
description of the logical grammar of the concept of morality
and of moral concepts.

Whether Ayer's or Carnap's early views about the emotional
functioning of ethical terms and utterances add up to an ethical
theory or do not is a verbal question, easily resolvable by a
sorting-out of the ambiguities of "theory." But whether the
denial of the closed character and the affirmation of the openness of the concept of morality is or is not a theory of morality is
not a verbal issue. There is no sense of "theory," ambiguous as
the term is, that warrants as a variant of theory the denial of
theory or, especially, the shift from theory or anti-theory to pure
elucidation. Elucidation of moral concepts or of the concept of
morality is no more a theory of morality than anti-ontology is

just another ontology or than the shift from ontological and anti-ontological assertion to conceptual elucidation is a variant of ontology.

Is there, then, a true theory of morality? Has anyone stated the necessary and sufficient properties of the moral; or proved that the moral is simple; or combined successfully the thesis that the moral is simple but is nevertheless governed by necessary and sufficient criteria of its correct use; or stated the definitive properties of the functioning of ethical terms? To have attempted any of these—not simply to have expressed doctrines, views, or opinions about them, in which nothing definitive is claimed or implied—is an instance of theory, at least in the senses covered by the ambiguous but still manageable notion of theory.

That there is not a true theory of morality, no correct definitive statement about what is moral or about the nature and functioning of moral terms and utterances, is overwhelmingly suggested by the history of ethics. This history, as its successive participants make abundantly clear, is mostly a series of rejections of previously argued-for theories. Plato rejects the Sophists and offers in a series of dialogues a theory or congeries of theories about the moral and the good. Aristotle repudiates much of Plato in order to present his own theory of the moral and intellectual virtues as well as a general reassessment of the relation between the moral and the good. Augustine builds on Plato, Aquinas on Aristotle, but both supplement their borrowings with distinctive Christian doctrines that yield new theories of morality and value. These in turn are changed or repudiated by later theorists—Hobbes and Spinoza, Hume and Kant, Mill and Nietzsche—each of whom proffers a new putatively true theory of the moral, only to be repudiated by later thinkers. In our own century, Moore begins absolutely at the beginning with the wholesale rejection of all previous theories of value and of morality founded on these theories of value, because of their "naturalistic fallacy," and goes on to propound his theory of good as simple and of the good and the moral as complex. Prichard and Ross reject Moore's conception of the moral, modeling the moral on Moore's conception of good. Emotivism demolishes both the nonnaturalism of Moore, Prichard, and Ross and the naturalism of many previous theories, only to be refuted in turn by more refined versions of nondescriptivism.

The incidence of success in the history of ethics, thus, has not been impressive. That this is so needs no reinforcement from outside commentators on this history, since this assessment is voiced by every great theorist in the history. That there is no true theory receives its strongest support from the great theorists themselves in what each has said about the inadequacies of those who came before. However, that there *is* such a true theory also gets its greatest support from the theorists in what each claims to be true about morality in the theory he goes on to propose.

What occurred 2,500 years ago has never ceased; it keeps occurring today. In spite of the agreed-upon failures of almost the entirety of ethics to secure a true theory of morality, certain contemporary moralists try once again to state the correct theory. The passion prevails that there must be such a true theory, consequently that there is one, to be found by further meticulous probing and understanding. The history of failures is said to be remediable: an improved—true—theory is forthcoming, one that exploits the partial successes of the history and integrates these with a new approach.

One of these new approaches is the theory of morality that is based on the moral point of view. Anticipated by Butler, Hume, and Kant, among others, revitalized by Kurt Baier, it has been made central by two contemporary moralists, G. J. Warnock and William Frankena, both of whom introduce it as the *only* alternative to the present impasse in ethical theory.

Morality

In *The Moral Point of View: A Rational Basis of Ethics* (1958),[1] Baier begins—as Moore had, in *Principia Ethica* (1903), or Prichard, in "Does Moral Philosophy Rest on a Mistake?" (1912), or Stevenson, in *Ethics and Language* (1944), or Hare, in *The Language of Morals* (1952), or Toulmin, in *An Examination of the Place of Reason in Ethics* (1950)—with a *wholesale* rejection of previous conceptions of the nature and problems of ethics. According to Baier, the central problem of ethics is our knowledge of right and wrong; and "the scandal is that the principal theories cannot provide a satisfactory solution to this problem" (p. v). Because these theories model moral judgments on other kinds of utterance, they cannot explain how moral judgments can be mutually contradictory, action-guiding, based on good reasons, and known to be true about what particular course of action is right or wrong. Every traditional or previous theory stumbles over one or another of these four logical features of moral judgments. The true theory, Baier proposes, is that moral judgments express natural facts: "they state that the course of action in question has the weight of moral reasons behind or against it" (p. vi). Because moral judgments state facts, knowledge of these facts can guide actions, provided that we are moral agents, that is, persons who are "already determined to do whatever is morally right and to refrain from doing whatever is morally wrong" (p. vii). Being so determined is not a stipulation about "moral agent," since this definition can also be defended by a reason, without which no one is a moral agent, determined to do what is right and to not do what is wrong. "The reason is that a general acceptance of a system of merely self-interested reasons would lead to conditions of life well described by Hobbes as 'poor, nasty, brutish, and short.' These unattractive living conditions can be improved by the general adoption of a system of reasoning in which reasons of self-interest are overruled, roughly speaking, when following them would tend to harm others. Such reasons are what we call 'moral reasons'" (p. vii). Moral reasons thus contrast with reasons of self-interest; they are good, not because they are moral, but because they rest on our rational desire for survival. To know that a given course of action is right or wrong is simply to ask and answer whether that course has behind it the weight of moral reasons—reasons that overrule reasons of self-interest.

Morality then, as Baier conceives it, is essentially the overruling of reasons of self-interest that is justified by the best reason of all, that of self-interest. Instead of beginning as a true theory of morality, Baier's seems to begin as a self-contradictory one: The moral rests on the ruling of self-interest but consists in its being overruled.

However, since I am not interested here in Baier's theory of why we should be moral but rather in his theory of morality, I skip over what is for me, at least, this difficulty to ask whether the moral can be defined in terms of the moral point of view, independently of why we should, or whether it is rational, to take this point of view. For Baier, morality can be and must be so defined. That the moral point of view is central in morality is surely his central thesis and contribution to ethical theory.

Baier, in introducing the concept of the moral point of view in his chapter seven, "Moral Considerations," writes: "It is indeed true that a person must adopt the moral point of view if he is to be moral" (p. 184). Now, I read this as the claim that a necessary condition for being moral is the acceptance of the moral point of view. What, then, is the moral point of view, without which there can be no morality?

Baier first considers the concept of a point of view. Every point of view can be defined by its principle: "When we adopt a certain point of view, we adopt its defining principle" (p. 184). This defining principle is the point of reference for all answers to relevant practical questions. Baier offers as an example of the relation between such a practical problem and a point of view, with its defining principle, the debate over erecting a traffic roundabout. Baier lists a number of competing points of view:

that of the pedestrian, the motorist, the local politician, the manufacturer of roundabouts, the traffic expert, and the town planner. Each has its defining principle: the first four revolve around different principles of self-interest; only the last two rest on the disinterested principle of favoring an easy flow of traffic. The traffic expert and the town planner, acting in the interests of all, are like others in the social order who also act independently of their own advantage.

As this example shows, Baier assumes that every point of view has a principle that not only defines it but cannot be subject to review and possible emendation or rejection without abandonment of that point of view. This may be true of the pedestrian or the motorist; but it need not hold for the politician or the manufacturer, and it especially need not hold for the traffic expert and the town planner should they happen, as one might hope, to be troubled by aesthetic considerations at the same time as they worry about votes, profits, efficiency of traffic flow, or the quality of urban life. What, then, is *the* point of view, for example, of the town planner—as town planner—that parallels *the* point of view of the pedestrian—as pedestrian—which is that of the safety of the walker? The free flow of traffic is a criterion of his point of view that the town planner shares with his traffic adviser, but it is surely not the criterion. Moreover, the town planner may even reject this criterion if he opts for other criteria, such as safety, cost, elimination of pollution, quiet, or beauty— all allowable criteria for the correct use of the concept of town planning. It is, therefore, not enough to distinguish the pedestrian from the town planner by the difference between the interested and the disinterested principles involved, because the points of view in this example are themselves logically different as well. The concept of the pedestrian is closed, the concept of the town planner is not: there are no definitive criteria for town planning, hence there is no principle that defines it as a point of view. The concept of town planning may still have a disjunctive set of sufficient criteria, but it certainly does not have the requisite set of necessary and sufficient ones that provide it, and the point of view it applies to, with its defining principle. On the other hand, the concept or the point of view of the town planner may be as much of a myth as the concept of "*the* aesthetic point of view."

What, now, about the moral point of view? Are it and its corresponding concept not only disinterested but closed, governed by a definitive set of properties or criteria that serves as the defining principle of morality?

Baier devotes his eighth chapter to "The Moral Point of

View." First he states and scrutinizes and then he demolishes the historical and ever popular version of it that identifies the moral point of view with shortsighted or enlightened self-interest. Such a version is, rather, a perversion because, based as it is on ethical egoism, it is not only a false but also an inconsistent thesis about morality, since it precludes the making of moral judgments, especially those which disagree over conflicting interests. "If the point of view of morality were that of self-interest, then there could *never* be moral solutions of conflicts of interest.... But by 'the moral point of view' we *mean* a point of view which is a court of appeal for conflicts of interest. Hence it cannot (logically) be identical with the point of view of self-interest" (p. 190; italics in the original).

Thus the moral point of view, according to Baier, is necessarily nonegoistic, since this point of view entails the falsity of ethical egoism. Adherence to it also presupposes, I think, that all conflicts of interest can be solved only if the moral point of view—defined by its principle—has a definitive set of properties, the appeal to which definitively settles the conflict. However, there is another possibility. Suppose, as I believe is the case, that the moral point of view has no such set of properties but has, rather, a disjunctive set of nonnecessary, nonsufficient, and no unrejectable properties. Could not this logical feature of openness as perennial debatability solve conflicts of interest? For these conflicts are now construed as disagreements over opted-for different sets of properties or criteria, neither necessary nor sufficient; this disclosure would solve the conflict, though, to be sure, it would leave us without the requisite true-false solution, which may be logically unforthcoming anyway, given the openness of the concept of the moral point of view. In any case, even though the moral point of view may entail the refutation of ethical egoism, it does not ensure the truth of its definitive character.

The moral point of view excludes ethical egoism. It is, therefore, necessarily concerned with interests other than our own. Baier lays this down as a formal criterion or condition of the moral point of view. Here is his summary of both the formal and material conditions of this point of view and, consequently, of morality itself:

> The moral point of view is characterized by a formal and a material condition. The formal condition is this: a man cannot be said to have adopted the moral point of view unless he is prepared to treat the moral rules as principles rather than as rules of thumb, that is, to do things *on principle* rather than merely to act purposively, merely to aim at a certain end.

And, furthermore, he must act on rules which are meant for
everybody, and not merely for himself or some favored
group. The material condition is this: the rules must be for
the good of everyone alike. This does not mean that they
must be for the common good of all human beings, past,
present, and future, for such a condition would be impossible
to satisfy. Its meaning can be elucidated by setting forth the
criteria of saying that a rule is for the good of everyone alike.
As far as absolute morality is concerned, only one condition
must be satisfied, namely, that these rules should be "rever-
sible," that is, not merely for the good of the agent, but at
least not detrimental to the persons who are affected by the
agent's behavior [pp. 207–8; italics in the original].

For Baier, then, the formal and the material conditions are the
definitive conditions of the moral point of view; each is necessary, both are sufficient. It and it alone provides the foundations
of morality and the nature and role of the moral agent in it as
"an independent, unbiased, impartial, objective, dispassionate,
disinterested observer" (p. 201).

Certain conclusions follow. One of these is that morality,
which is social, cannot apply to the solitary individual or indeed
to the individual in society when his actions do not interact with
others. Morality, thus, is not only necessarily social; its social
nature excludes any conception of the morality of the self. I have
no duties or obligations to myself; there is nothing that I ought
to do or ought not to do unless others are concerned.

Baier says that we *mean* by the moral point of view the point
of view whose defining principle is the necessary and sufficient
formal and material conditions he specifies. But why does he
accent "mean," not "we"? Because he regards this meaning as a
conceptual truth, not as a choice stipulation that we—to be read
as "I, Baier"—lay down as a condition without which we cannot
characterize morality and distinguish it from all else.

Is the meaning of "the moral point of view" a conceptual
truth, as Baier implies it is? That it is so is, I think, his central
ethical doctrine. Without arguing that the meaning here is the
use, or without enjoining that we turn from meaning to use,
suppose that we just do turn to the use—the role and the
conditions for playing that role—of the concept of morality or
the moral point of view. Do we then as a matter of fact find that
these concepts are governed by Baier's formal and material
conditions that add up to the definitive criteria of their correct
employment? The answer, which is a conceptual truth about
morality and the moral point of view, is a loud and clear NO. For
the concept of morality or the concept of the moral point of

view, with or without their appropriate conveying words—
which, after all, did not create these concepts but rather (and this
includes the concept of the moral point of view) created the
words for them—have performed their roles, as their history
reveals, under less than the formal and material definitive
conditions stated by Baier.

If a theory of morality includes, as it surely does, a statement,
implicit or explicit, of the necessary and sufficient properties or
conditions of the moral, then many theories differ from Baier's;
this he of course recognizes and indeed offers as the reason for
proposing his new theory. However, if different theories turn on
and are to be adjudicated by *the meaning* of "moral," as Baier
construes that meaning, then these theorists not only disagree
with Baier but, worse, they violate the concept of morality by
distorting or contradicting it. Accordingly, ethical egoism is not

the only transgressor; all theories that oppose Baier's, whether
characterized by self-interest or by disinterestedness, contradict
the putatively conceptual truth about morality because they
omit, pervert, or deny one or another of the formal or material
conditions of morality.

Theories of morality fail for many reasons. Their criteria may
be vague or obscure; they may be circular as definitions; they
may be unempirical or untestable; they may mistake incidental
properties for necessary or sufficient ones; and they may, as
Baier says ethical egoism does, yield contradictions, e.g., that a
particular action x is both right and wrong.

Now, according to the view that I propose, all theories of
morality, including Baier's, fail because they try to state the
definitive criteria for a concept whose use shows that it has no
such set. It is, I think, Baier's implied counterclaim that all
theories of morality, except his, fail, not because they attempt
the impossible, but because they do not, in one way or another,
state the formal and material—the necessary and sufficient—
conditions of the moral and, therefore, the definitive criteria of
the concept of morality. Thus, for him, previous theories of
morality violate the definitive criteria of the concept of morality,
i.e., what we *mean* by "moral"; whereas, for me, *all* theories of
morality violate not the criteria, definitive or not, but the
openness of the concept of morality.

Is Baier, then, correct in his assessment of traditional theories,
that they fail to state correctly the two definitive formal and
material criteria of the concept of morality? (Whether my
assessment is correct or not depends in part on whether Baier's
is, so the adequacy of his assessment is the prior issue.) We are
back to Prichard's devastating question: Does moral philosophy

rest on a mistake? For Baier, traditional moral philosophy does
rest on a mistake; but the mistake is not the one Prichard noted,
of trying to justify the self-evident. It is rather a series of
mistakes that converge on the overriding mistake of incorrectly
characterizing or denying the exact nature of the formal and
material conditions of morality. Thus Kant's mistake, Baier
remarks, was to state the formal condition inadequately and to
omit the material altogether. Plato's (presumably, since Baier
says little about his theory of morality) was to miss both the
formal and material conditions in advancing the notion, or at
least intimating it (on one interpretation of Plato), that the moral
life—the life a man ought to live—consists in the cultivation of
his soul, which involves as central the philosophical quest: "The
unexamined life is not worth living." Indeed, on Baier's theory,
unless I misread him here, Plato's moral views, since they are
governed by self-interest (of the highest order, to be sure), are
not properly a theory of morality at all. Nor, presumably, are
Nietzsche's, whether we interpret them as a putative theory of
morality resting, at least in part, on the rejection and tran-
scendence of all disinterested—"herding"—theories of morality
or as a theory of value in which there is no place for morality.
Hume and Mill, Hobbes and Spinoza, Ayer and Stevenson,
Moore and Ross, and so forth, fail for a variety of reasons,
according to Baier, but basically because none of them comes
close to correctly setting forth the two conditions and seeing that
they are definitive.

Now, as Baier interprets traditional theories of morality, it is
indubitable that they disagree with his. It is also clear that each
of the theories, taken by itself, claims or implies that it is a true
theory and that the others, which it opposes, are false; and it is
clear, further, that each contradicts contending theories in such a
manner that at most one of them can be true—the one offered by
the individual theorist—while the others must be false.

But, now, is it indubitable, obvious, and clear that the
disagreements among the theorists or their theories of morality
are contradictory true-false claims about the nature and definitive character of morality or the moral point of view? That it is
rests, I think, on another assumption, also taken as indubitable
(one of the four logical features of moral judgments, Baier says),
that conflicting moral judgments about the same action cannot
all be true since, among contradictories, only one can be, the rest
cannot be, true. Are the disagreements among the theorists
logically like those among competing moral judgments about the
same action? Even if we grant for the moment what is very much
open to question, that conflicting moral judgments are always

true-false, contradictory statements, must it be that the conflicts among theories of morality—which in any case center on the criteria of the moral—are true-false disagreements, contradictories, with only one theory possibly true, the others necessarily false?

What, then, do the conflicts and disagreements—and especially the range of disagreements—tell us about the concept of morality or about the concept of the moral point of view? Whatever else they reveal, they tell us that the use of the concepts is richer than Baier's *meaning* of "moral" or "the moral point of view"; for though each theory of morality or its stated or implied theory of the moral point of view rides on its putative set of definitive criteria, these sets differ and often disagree, sometimes radically, with others (Nietzsche versus Mill, for example). This fact about the logical grammar of "morality" or "the moral point of view" establishes that the concepts under investigation have functioned under definitive sets of criteria all right but that these definitive sets have been multiple and not simply the two formal and material criteria stated by Baier. Can this historical use of the concepts of the moral and the moral point of view—fundamentally characterized by multiple, competing, and sometimes contradictory sets of criteria—be accommodated by Baier's *meaning* of "moral" and "the moral point of view"? Can the disagreements among the theories of morality be resolved by an appeal to the defining principle of the moral point of view when this defining principle is itself but two of the many extant or possible criteria of the moral? Baier's affirmative answers rest on the *meaning* of "moral," not its use; and the meaning dictates the assessment of the correctness of the variations within the use. But his meaning is only one aspect of the use; it is not some ultimate court of appeal, as if it were independent of that use. In effect, then, Baier, like every other theorist, has legislated *a* use as *the* use, among many historical uses, of the concepts of morality and the moral point of view; he has done so by picking out among their multiple, competing, and sometimes disparate sets of criteria two of them, which he proclaims and argues for as the definitive criteria for the correct use—the meaning—of "moral." He, too, attempts to close a concept that is open: a concept whose criteria of use, as its history of competing theories abundantly shows, are perennially debatable. There are, of course, misuses of "moral" or "moral point of view"; but that all uses other than the one specified by the individual theorist, be he Baier, Kant, Plato, or Nietzsche, are misuses of these terms or their conveying concepts leaves us with the intolerable situation in which one theorist's meat of the true meaning of "moral" serves as another theorist's poison of false meaning. Baier's supreme court of appeal is transformed into a trial among competing conceptual litigants in which every participant is a prosecutor or defense attorney and no one is a judge. The meaning of "morality" must be beholden to its use, not the other way round. Accordingly, the moral point of view, if we are to do justice to the history and functioning of that concept, must be seen as a principle, or board of review, not as a principle of reference, or supreme court of appeal, for competing theories of morality. Under these new auspices but rightful proprietorship, it is no misuse of "morality" to define it as Baier or any other theorist does; but it is a misuse of the concept to think that it is amenable to definition in such a way as to generate the correct use of the concept.

Is there a true theory of morality? Is it the same as the moral point of view? Or is it based on the true theory of the moral point of view? Baier argues that any adequate theory of morality rests on a true account of the moral point of view—on what we *mean* by it. That what we mean by it is less than what its multiple uses have been, I have just argued, renders the meaning of both "moral" and "moral point of view" legislative, not reportive of the criteria of these two concepts. We must therefore look elsewhere in order to see whether there is a true theory of morality which is the same as, or based on, the true theory of the moral point of view.

First come two books by G. J. Warnock, *Contemporary Moral Philosophy* (1967) and *The Object of Morality* (1971),[2] in which Warnock claims, among other things, that morality is not based on the moral point of view: it is the moral point of view. It is based on the human predicament that, according to him and as suggested by Hobbes, things are, as they are, likely to go badly for us human beings. Morality is one way of dealing with this predicament: by formulating action-guiding principles for the amelioration of at least those human ills that are remediable. The whole point of morality—"the object of morality"—is such betterment of the human condition. It is here, in the identification and understanding of the remedial character of the human predicament, which character determines the range and type of considerations that are moral, that the subject matter of morality—what it is about—is to be secured. It is not to be secured in the esoteric objects of morality or in its language, which in any case empties morality of any subject matter. The foundations of morality are situated in this contingent general fact about human life, not in some superreal realm of indefinables or in a nonexistent projection of deep but illusory desires.

Warnock also begins, as Baier and others do, with a statement of general disaffection with the way things have been going in moral philosophy—with the ethical predicament, one might say. He finds intuitionism, emotivism and prescriptivism—the big three of twentieth-century ethical theories—variously barren, empty, bald, jejune, and remarkably free of pressing concerns for the content of morality, especially its nature and basis, the grounds and reasons of moral judgments. These major theories, obsessed either by the search for the exact nature of ethical propositions or their predicates or with the language of morality, have concentrated on what ethical discourse denotes or what it does or what it does it in; they have thus neglected, for the most part, the role of reasons in morality and even why anyone should do a particular thing, x, rather than y.

Only prescriptivism—which, like emotivism, recognizes that moral judgments guide actions, though it has misdescribed this guidance as the creating of influences—has attempted to explain as well as describe this action-guiding feature of moral judgments. The explanation—that moral judgments entail universalizable imperatives—fails, Warnock claims, because universalizability is not sufficient for *moral* judgments, and implied imperatives are neither necessary nor sufficient for moral judgments. But prescriptivism fails for another, deeper, reason, Warnock contends: it construes both the moral judgment and its reason or reasons as decisions or choices, thereby rendering the relation between moral judgment and its evidence otiose. He points out that Hare, the leading exponent of prescriptivism,

> is saying, not only that it is for us to decide what our moral opinions are, but also that it is for us to decide what to take as grounds for or against any moral opinion. We are not only, as it were, free to decide on the evidence, but also free to decide what evidence is. I do not, it seems, decide that flogging is wrong because I *am* against cruelty; rather, I decide that flogging is wrong because I *decide to be* against cruelty. And what, if I did make that decision, would be my ground for making it? That I am opposed to the deliberate infliction of pain? No—rather that I *decide to be* opposed to it [*CMP*, p. 47; italics in original].

Hare's conflation of judgment with evidence is no model of morality or moral reasoning; rather, it is a menace, because it abstains from reasons based on evidence.

However vehement Warnock is against prescriptivism and its conversion of reasons to decisions or to choices of principles, he too (I think but do not fear) comes dangerously close to this conversion when he shifts from the justification of particular moral judgments to the general question Why be moral? Why adopt the moral point of view (which for him makes "Flogging is wrong" true and founded on the moral reason that flogging inflicts pain, which aggravates rather than ameliorates the human predicament)? For he allows that one not only can be ignorant of the moral point of view but can, being cognizant of it, *decide* that it is not important, for one reason or another, and *choose* to abandon it altogether.

> In short: while a rational being, merely *qua* rational, may possibly be obliged to concede that what moral argument adduces as reasons really are reasons, I do not see that he can be obliged to concede—could not rationally deny—that morality really "works," so to speak, as it is supposed to work, or that, in the balance with other reasons for and against doing things, moral reasons must be accorded very great or preponderant cogency. He may see what morality is, and think that there is not much in it [*OM*, p. 164].

As I understand Warnock here, one cannot decide or choose what is evidence for one's moral judgments as one can decide or choose one's moral judgments, but one can decide or choose—or not—to play the moral game; however, one does so by using its built-in criteria of what is to count as evidence. How, then, we must ask, can "Flogging is wrong" be true, founded on facts, and not deniable and be, as well, a moral conviction that we "should not let ourselves be bullied out of" (*CMP*, p. 60)?

In this connection, Warnock notes (throughout his two books) a number of similar moral judgments that he says are matters of fact, not of opinion, decision, or choice. For example, it is wrong to torture people, to humiliate people, to induce one's children to take heroin; it is bad to starve, to suffer; it is good to help people; it is better that people be loved than that they be hated or neglected; and so on. In *OM* (pp. 123–24) he produces "a plain specimen of a moral truth": that of a dictator contemplating a whole series of wrong actions, including an initial assassination of his ambassador in a neighboring state in order to intensify the passions of his subjects so that they will engage wholeheartedly in the war he will start, using as a pretext the "murder" of his ambassador by inhabitants of the neighboring state. The dictator confides to his adviser, whom Warnock allows, for the purposes of his example, to exclaim: "What you propose is wrong!" The adviser, Warnock says, is absolutely right: it *is* undeniably wrong to assassinate, lie, fabricate evidence, cause gratuitous death and wanton injury, and, in general, contribute to the further worsening of the human predicament.

That this contemplated action is wrong, and wrong because of the reasons given, is not contestable, Warnock adds; nor can there be any counterbalancing moral justification of it. One can say of it that it is not wrong, but one cannot say of it that it is not morally wrong.

> Why not? Well, if the phrase "morally wrong" is not abso-
> lutely meaningless; if it is possible to say, in elucidation of
> what it means, what sort of things rank semantically as
> morally wrong; then there are some things, such as those
> described, from which that appellation *could* not be withheld
> by anyone not unaware of the meaning of the expression,
> or not deliberately misusing it [*OM*, p. 124].

Just here I shall not ask whether the dictator's adviser's moral judgment, or any other, is contestable. Rather, what puzzles me is how Warnock can claim that some moral judgments are incontestable, and as true as "Snow is white," and yet are rationally rejectable, which he says they are. How can a rational person reject what is uncontestably true? How can he opt to cop out of the moral game, with its inherent moral point of view? Why, on Warnock's theory of moral knowledge, is not such a rejecter immoral rather than amoral or nonmoral, which he allows him to be? I cannot see that Warnock can have it both ways: that there are moral truths and that you can choose to reject them but not to contest them. His notion of the moral point of view as identical with morality begins to waver, if not to totter: the moral point of view rests on a choice, a decision; morality, the decision once made, does not, since it rests on facts. If morality is the evaluation of the human condition from the moral point of view, and if that point of view is an option—a decision of principle to assess human actions in a certain way— Warnock's theory of morality is as prescriptive as Hare's, at least on the issue of the foundations of morality.

What, now, is Warnock's theory of morality and of the moral point of view? First he says, following the classical tradition about the correct use of concepts and their conveying terms, that a necessary condition of their intelligible use is a true account of morality, of what "moral" means. This question of the meaning of "moral" is fundamental, Warnock says, yet it is given little attention.

> When philosophers discuss moral principles, moral judgment,
> moral discourse generally, *what* are they discussing? What
> does "moral" mean? What distinguishes a moral view from

views of other kinds? I think it must be quite clear that there is no easy answer to these questions: and yet, until they are answered, it seems that moral philosophers cannot really know what they are talking about, or at any rate, perhaps no less importantly, cannot be sure whether or not they are all talking about the same thing. It is, indeed, pretty clear that, historically, they have not been [*CMP*, p. 52].

Second, instead of exploring these different historical meanings of "moral," and of what they reveal about the debatability of the concept of the moral, Warnock states and tests certain putative defining properties of the moral—the criteria of "moral." He lists four of these conditions: (1) the presence or absence of certain feelings, especially guilt; (2) the dominant principles of conduct; (3) the universalizability of certain principles; and (4) the content, or the range or type, of considerations on which morality is founded. Warnock dismisses the first three on the grounds that they are neither necessary nor sufficient; instead, he claims, they are at best consequential on the fourth. His rejection of (2) is especially relevant to his treatment of the meaning of "moral." For, in accordance with (2), individuals, such as Nietzsche, or societies, such as the Homeric, said to be moral even though they live by standards different from our own, may also be said to be nonmoral, as their dominant principles of conduct reveal.

Condition (2)—that one's moral principles are best exemplified in one's actions—troubles Warnock, I suspect, more than (1) or (3), for he returns to it in different ways in his two books. In *CMP* he questions (2) by dissociating actions or conduct from moral principles by considering the plausibility of a man who acts but, on no principles at all, acts only whimsically or capriciously. Or he considers a man who acts on principles but not moral ones the egoist, for example. For Hare, but not for Baier, this man has a morality—ethical egoism. For Baier, he may be able to universalize his imperative, but only at the expense of self-contradictorily affirming that the same action is both right and wrong. It is not clear whether Warnock rules out the egoist as a moralist because he rejects (4); rules him in as an immoral moralist because he accepts (4) and does not mitigate the human predicament; or rules him out as moral because he satisfies (2) and has no moral principles. So, too, for the man whose conduct is dominated by ideals; he may be said to satisfy (2), but his ideals are said to be not moral ones. Or are they? Warnock allows that this man can be seen either as a moral idealist or as an idealist who, like Nietzsche—at least in one of his moods—goes beyond cramping morality. In *OM* (pp. 89 ff.),

Warnock considers the Socratic-Platonic conception of the moral as their specific answer to How ought one to live? But instead of rejecting their answer, Warnock rejects their question, saying that it is not a question of morality at all, not because it is irrelevant to morality, but because it is senseless, like the similar senseless question How ought one to cook? Morality has to do with assessment of means to ends, not with ends, goals, life-styles—evaluation of the good—except when good conduct or character is at stake.

Condition (4), and only (4), is necessary, essential, to morality or to what "moral" means. However, that it is necessary, Warnock acknowledges, reflects what he calls an "option in ethics." Condition (4), thus, is necessary to morality relative to one way of looking at morality, at defining "moral." Shifting from the putative criteria of "moral," which yields only (4) as
necessary criterion, to the larger question of the various possi-bilities for the meaning of "morality," Warnock considers a number of options for its meaning and for the consequent doing of moral philosophy. In OM (chap. 1), he sums up three major options—"different lines to take" (p. 8)—each legitimate. One may survey historically and anthropologically the tremendous diversity of views about good and bad, right and wrong, in human conduct and character, employ and confirm "moral" as applying to all these views, however wide this renders the term, and infer from this survey the perfectly respectable doctrine that moral ideas change with changes in social life. Or one may seek general principles common to the evolution of moral ideas, interpreting these changes as instances of moral appraisal; in this case one arrives at a different doctrine, namely, that moral concepts are timeless and do not change as their applications do. Ethics here becomes in effect the general theory of practical appraisal. A third option is to construe

> "morality" . . . as a *particular* way, or ways, of looking at issues of character and conduct; these things can be looked at from what is called "the moral point of view"—which is not just *any* point of view the adoption of which issues in practical judgements, but a particular point of view that can be posi-tively identified and described [p. 10; italics in original].

Warnock, of course, chooses the third option with regard to what "moral" means and with regard to doing moral philoso-phy. It is this decision that provides him with what I have ascribed to him as a decision of principle: the decision to take as foundational in morality, not moral truths, but the moral point of view. It is also crucial to understand that Warnock, right at the very beginning of his inquiry into the nature of morality, has also made a fundamental choice about how to treat the agreed-upon vagueness of morality and its concept or term. He recognizes this vagueness, perhaps even the ambiguity, of "moral." But, once more, instead of exploring the possibility of an irreducible kind of vagueness or of a radical kind of openness that is suggested by the ambiguity and vagueness of "moral," Warnock chooses to mitigate this vagueness by turning to indisputable or clear cases of morality that defeat the charge that the term is inherently "woolly, or vague, or indeterminate" (*OM*, p. 2). Perhaps this compromise with the vagueness of "morality" is better than the rejection of attributed vagueness on the grounds that the concept of morality is fixed by the clear cases of morality although its range of application is not; for what, then, is unclear are not the definitive criteria of the moral but whether any particular act or action satisfies these criteria. Warnock, unlike other ethical theorists, will not have moral matters so neat: "but then 'moral' is surely not, on any showing, a very exact word, or a word to be always very confidently applied or withheld" (*CMP*, p. 59). However, his compromise with this vagueness does reflect seriously on the true character of his theory of morality or of the moral point of view, since, at best, these rest on initial choices regarding the subject matter of morality, the meaning of "moral," and the vagueness of the concept and phenomenon of morality. His theory is true, if true, only from a certain point of view about both the language and the data of morality, in spite of the fact that some of these data are hard-core "moral truths," which may, according to Warnock, be rejected but not contested.

Let us return to (4), the content of morality. The content of morality, what "moral" is about, and what identifies and distinguishes morality from feelings, dominant principles of conduct, or universalizable principles (conditions [1], [2], and [3]) "is what is good or bad for people, what they want or need, what promotes or detracts from their happiness, well-being, or satisfaction" (*CMP*, p. 56). Warnock suggests but does not affirm in *CMP* that it is a priori that moral views are concerned with content, not with (1), (2), or (3) or even with (5), the formal character of moral discourse; condition (4), thus, is not only a necessary condition of "moral," it is integral to the concept of morality. Hence, no theory of morality can neglect the central importance of this content.

In *OM* Warnock presents a detailed picture of (4), the content of morality, as based on the human predicament but seen and assessed from the moral point of view. In *CMP* he offers instead a series of objections (and his answers to them) to (4) as essential to morality, thereby preparing the way for his later theory.

Condition (4), it may be objected, makes the concept of morality reasonable by definition, thereby ruling out as moral those codes of conduct, either barbarous or benighted, that not only do not promote human interests but damage them. This objection, he replies, does not apply to (4) because (4) does not claim that a code of conduct, to be moral, actually satisfies human interests if the code is observed; it claims only that this code is supposed to do so. Nor does (4) deny that some moral codes are used for harm; it claims only that it is pretended by its perpetrators to do good.

Further, it is said that (4) does not accommodate the morality that consists wholly or primarily in a life lived according to lofty ideals. To this Warnock reiterates that even these ideals must be

submitted to moral assessment as defined by (4), for otherwise the storm trooper, for example, devoted as he is to his *Führer*, would be as moral in his idealism as the artistic soul who produces little harm to others and much good to some. In any case, there is something perverse about calling moral an ideal that destroys or damages, that is pointless or even insane. (Warnock says nothing about the obvious riposte to his reply, that such ideals, which generate harm, are wrongly called "ideals" rather than wrongly called "nonmoral," "immoral," or "amoral.")

Another objection is that (4) is viciously circular, since the well-being or happiness that morality is about is not independently identifiable; that is, (4) defines "moral," not in terms of a fact at all, but in terms of another inherently evaluative phrase. To this Warnock replies that well-being is not a matter of evaluation but of fact: some things are, quite simply, good or bad for people, and moral truths about them are not contestable. Moreover, (4) is circular, not if its *definiens* is not independently identifiable, but only if it is itself a moral judgment. Condition (4) thus need not rest on neutral facts; all that is required is that it not itself be a value judgment—as indeed, according to Warnock, it is not:

> That a certain person, or a certain community of persons, would, if certain things were done, be in a better or worse condition, advantaged or disadvantaged, helped or harmed, may be partly or even wholly a matter of judgment; but it is, I submit, quite clear that it is not always, not wholly or necessarily, a matter of *moral* judgment [*CMP*, p. 61; italics in original].

Finally, it is objected, (4)—that moral judgment is concerned by definition with human good—commits the naturalistic fallacy in Moore's or Hume's formulation of it. Facts about human needs, interests, or well-being do not, it is objected, entail any moral judgment, as (4) claims or implies they do. Warnock dismisses this charge mainly by attacking the only plausible version of it he recognizes: that description and evaluation are not only different but are independent in the sense "that, though we often do not, we always *could* so 'state the facts' of any case that evaluation of that case would be a logically independent operation" (*CMP*, p. 64; italics in original). Central to this thesis is that evaluation, but not description, implies the acceptance and employment of certain standards or criteria of merit.

Instead of meeting this thesis head-on, Warnock asks whether, even if we grant it, it follows from it that anything might be a standard or criterion of merit. It does not, he rightly insists. Nor does it follow from the thesis, or from Warnock's rejected inference from it, that there are over-all criteria which determine the range or limits of the particular criteria of merit for particular kinds of evaluation, including moral ones. Yet Warnock offers, as such an over-all criterion for setting the limits of criteria for moral evaluations, the over-all criterion of the "*relevance* of considerations as to the welfare of human beings" (*CMP*, p. 67; italics in original). That what is relevant to human welfare sets the range and limits of those features we describe and employ as criteria of merit in making moral judgments is not itself a decision in principle—something we choose—but an analytic truth about "moral." We are, therefore, obliged to accept certain features as criteria of moral merit; what we are not obliged to do is to engage in moral evaluation at all.

> That there are, as it were, necessary criteria of moral value does not imply that anyone, let alone everyone, necessarily evaluates things with reference to those criteria; it is only that we *must* do so *if* we are prepared, as we may not be, to consider the question "from the moral point of view" [*CMP*, p. 68; italics in original]

Here again Warnock contrasts an analytic truth about "moral" with a prescription about "moral," where, though the contrast is not something we choose but find, the analytic truth, resting as it does on the adoption of the moral point of view, is, it seems to me, a matter of choice for Warnock. For him, we can choose to be moral or not; but having chosen to be moral, we must accept as necessary, in what we have chosen, that being moral means being concerned with the welfare of others. Accordingly, for him, we can choose or not choose to adopt the moral point of view; but we cannot choose the criteria of that point of view. They are as incontestable and unrejectable as the criteria of the moral, themselves secured by the analytic truth regarding the over-all criterion of concern for human welfare. If this is a correct reading of Warnock, it does seem that his theory of the moral point of view is, like his theory of morality, more a piece of legislation about how he proposes to use certain terms than it is a true account or report on the nature of the moral point of view or of morality. Condition (4), then, does not identify the subject matter of morality; rather, it proposes a way—an option—of doing so. Why one cannot propose differently about "the moral point of view" and, subsequently, about "moral," which Warnock will not allow, as one can reject his

proposed identification, which he does allow, remains unclear, dangling. And we seem to be left with only two possibilities, neither of which satisfies Warnock: Either we start with the determinate range of application of "moral point of view" and "moral" and formulate a theory from them; or we swallow the indeterminacy of the range of application of both "the moral point of view" and "moral" and, thereby, accept that even the determinate cases are contestable, not merely rejectable by abandoning all of morality.

In *OM*, Warnock fills in his theory of morality as defined by (4)—by the content of morality, rather than by its psychological, sociological, or formally linguistic surroundings ([1], [2], and [3]). The content consists of action-guiding principles for the amelioration of the human predicament. What is moral has to do—analytically—with what is good or bad for people. That this is what "moral" means follows from the practical appraisal of conduct and character from the moral point of view. And, if I am right about Warnock, this point of view is for him not the same as the moral (as, I think, Warnock claims that it is) but is (as it is for Baier) a necessary condition for the moral. Their great difference is that for Warnock we can rationally reject this necessary condition for moral assessment and thus reject morality altogether, whereas for Baier it is irrational—a violation of the concept of morality, of what "moral" means—to reject this condition. If, then, the moral point of view is, for both moralists, the main, perhaps the only, pillar of the foundations of morality, the destruction of that pillar shatters the foundations; but for Baier we cannot rationally destroy or even disregard the pillar, as we can, according to Warnock. Nevertheless, in spite of this difference, both agree that the moral point of view is as closed a concept—governed by necessary and sufficient conditions—as is the concept of morality. And for neither is there even a taint of vagueness in the moral point of view, as there is in morality.

In effect, then, Warnock, in filling in (4) in *OM*, draws a picture of morality whose outline is already sketched by his prescriptive cartoon or option. The moral point of view, once adopted, dictates, because of its definitive, uncontestable, though rejectable, character, what shall count as moral, namely, the range and type of considerations about conduct and character as they revolve around the amelioration of the human condition. The analyticity of "the moral" follows from the prescriptivity of "the moral point of view."

What, then, is moral? Warnock starts with moral discourse and moral concepts. He asks what they are about and identifies their subject matter as issues having to do with certain kinds of evaluation, in particular the evaluation of the actions of *rational* beings, not just *human* beings; for only those who are rational are able to perceive and consider alternative courses of action.

Why, now, do we evaluate morally? What is morality for? What is its point?

> The general object of moral evaluation must be to contribute
> in some respects, by way of the actions of rational beings,
> to the amelioration of the human predicament [*OM*, p. 16].

What, then, in this predicament requires amelioration, and how can morality help? If the human predicament is, as Warnock says it is, "inherently such that things are liable to go badly" (p. 17), and if we are hampered in trying to make them go less badly by what Warnock calls "limiting factors"—of resources, information, intelligence, and sympathies—the primary problem is that of reducing these limiting factors as much as we can, especially the factor of limited sympathies, which he regards as the most important. The reduction of this one factor is where and how morality can help, by trying to get us to expand these limited sympathies. To illuminate this effort is to elucidate at the same time the moral point of view.

A theory of morality is thus, inter alia, a theory about how morality contributes to the betterment of the human situation. Different, competing, theories of morality are or contain different answers concerning the need to countervail limited sympathies and the role of morality in doing so. For example, utilitarianism is the theory that one's limited concern for the welfare of others can be mitigated or rather defeated by a morality that makes central the welfare of all. Warnock infers from such a view that there is only one basic virtue, that of universal beneficence. He then shows—as others have shown on other considerations—that since this virtue may conflict with justice viewed as fairness, it cannot be the only or even the basic virtue, i.e., the only principle that should guide actions if we are to better the human condition. The sole concern of the moral, as seen from the moral point of view, cannot then be the promotion of the happiness of the greatest number.

Rule-utilitarianism, on Warnock's reading, seeks to counter limited sympathies by rules rather than by the principle of beneficence; he demolishes it, not by showing that it, too, conflicts with other principles that ameliorate our predicament, but by showing that its conception of rules is incoherent and that, in the end, it is no different from simple utilitarianism. Indeed, the whole idea of "moral rules" as distinct from "moral views" is a confusion.

That things are likely to go badly for us is the human predicament. That they are likely not to go as badly as they might calls for an expansion of our sympathies, and for this we require, among other things, good dispositions: "some degree of readiness voluntarily to act desirably, and to abstain from behaving otherwise" (*OM*, p. 76). Good dispositions to endure the disagreeable engender the virtues of industriousness, courage, and self-control. These, while necessary for moral virtues, are clearly not themselves *moral* virtues, since they may be self-profiting, damaging to others, or possessed by a bad man. These virtuous exercises in good dispositions help reduce human weaknesses, not limitations of sympathies. The moral virtues, then, are only those good dispositions that attempt to expand our sympathies, therefore, that are good for others, not for oneself. These comprise nonmaleficence, fairness, beneficence, and nondeception. It is these, and only these, four moral virtues that can serve as fundamental moral standards or moral principles in both judgment and decision. They also serve to define "moral reason":

> It is a consideration, about some person, or some person's character, or some specimen of actual or possible conduct, which tends to establish in the subject concerned conformity or conflict with a moral principle. That your act would inflict wanton damage on some other person would be a "moral reason" for judging that—at least "from the moral point of view"—you ought not so to act, since it tends to establish that your act would be in conflict with the moral principle of non-maleficence [*OM*, p. 86].

These principles, Warnock insists, are independent, not reducible to one another; their independence explains and warrants conflicts among moral reasons and the insolubility of some moral disputes. They also, as moral virtues, render irrelevant the platonic question (if not all the platonic virtues), How should one live? even if that question were intelligible (and Warnock, as we have seen, does not think it is). Adherence to these principles, by practicing the moral virtues they guide and define as well as the moral reasons they provide and justify, is what morality is all about—but only if it is looked at from the moral point of view, the univocal option that brings morality into proper focus. If one does not like what one then sees—because one thinks it a fraud, too cramping for one's own life-style, a bore, or perhaps not the important thing in life, one can change the focus by exchanging the moral point of view. What one cannot do is to focus on morality from the moral point of view and reject morality as the predominant effort to better the human condition through the exercise of one's disposition to expand human sympathies. Nor can one reject or contest the definitive nature of the moral point of view, whether one adopts it or not. Nor, presumably, can one, in rejecting the whole realm of morality from the moral point of view, contest, any more than one's opposing adherent to this point of view can contest, the objective truth of at least some moral judgments. The adoption of the moral point of view may be an option; but it remains difficult to understand how it can be rejected rationally if there are some moral judgments that are true independently of any point of view or option.

Whether Warnock has provided a theory of morality, or—what is perhaps needed more—a theory of ordinary common decency, by recasting the specifically moral virtues almost as drastically as the early Christians did the Greeks', I leave to the moralists to decide. What Warnock's list of the moral virtues reveals, at least as far as the concept of a moral virtue is concerned, is that that concept also seems as open and debatable as the concepts of morality and the moral point of view. Whether, for example, courage is a virtue, a moral virtue, or a vice is no less and no more an open question than whether rudeness, about which we have heard so much these days, is a vice, a moral vice, or a virtue, even though we agree with some contemporary philosophers that the criteria of both courage and rudeness are fairly fixed.

Neither Warnock nor Baier has solved the main problem, nor have they raised it. Is it so clear that the concept of the moral point of view is closed—that it is not rationally contestable but rejectable, according to Warnock; that it is neither rationally contestable nor rejectable, according to Baier? The moral point of view cannot serve as a necessary condition of morality or as definitive for morality unless it is itself exact, not subject to those debates we associate with the vagueness of morality or the distinctively moral virtues.

William Frankena also probes morality from the moral point of view in his essay "Recent Conceptions of Morality" (1963) and his book *Ethics* (1963; 2d ed., 1973).[3] In his essay, Frankena begins by noting a recent shift of concern in moral philosophy from the traditional analysis or elucidation of first-order ethical terms and utterances—followed by the debates among the intuitionists, naturalists, and various forms of antidescriptivists

about these terms—to the definition or elucidation of the second-order terms "moral" and "nonmoral" as applied primarily to discourse, not to acts. Much of very recent moral philosophy, thus, centers on the nature of morality as an institution rather than as a quality of conduct. Alternative conceptions of morality have supplanted alternative theories of right and ought. However, since conceptions of morality as an institution are at least implicit in much traditional first-order moral philosophy, there has been a shift within traditional moral philosophy, not a wholesale break from it. Accordingly, Frankena does not share with Baier and Warnock the sense of persistent failure on the part of previous moral philosophy to come to grips with any putatively central neglected problem, such as our knowledge of right and wrong (Baier) or the content of morality (Warnock). This recognition of continuity and change, rather than insistence on discontinuity and break, bears directly on the concept of the moral point of view as well as on the concept of morality as an institution, since it allows that the first concept, like the second, has application to views preceding, and independent of, the articulate use of it. Does it also allow that there are different, alternative conceptions of the moral point of view, as there are different, alternative conceptions of morality as an institution? Baier and Warnock, at least on my reading of them, claim that, though there are different conceptions of morality as an institution, only one of which can be true, there cannot be different conceptions of the moral point of view; only one conception must be true—analytically, necessarily, conceptually true. It is this truth that guarantees the meaning of "moral"—both as a first-order predicate applied to conduct and character and as a second-order term applied to morality as a whole. According to them, one either has the concept of the moral point of view or one does not (however they disagree about the rationality of rejecting the concept). If one has the concept, and only if one does, one can then assess all competing theories of morality by asking whether any of them satisfies the necessary and sufficient formal and material criteria of the moral point of view. If any of them does, that one is the true theory of morality. Thus for them there may be different conceptions of morality, but there are not different conceptions of the moral point of view; there is only the *concept* of the moral point of view, which one either grasps and comprehends or does not.

Frankena lists different conceptions of morality, concentrating in his essay on three recent different, alternative, and competing conceptions of morality as an institution or as a whole. Does he also list or allow for different, alternative, competing concep-

tions of the moral point of view? Does he even allow, among the traditional and recent conceptions of morality as institutional, those that fail to grasp and state the defining characteristics of morality—what it is that makes them conceptions of morality at all? Are these incorrect conceptions of morality, or are they putatively correct conceptions of something else?

The first recent conception of morality he considers is individualistic. He distinguishes two versions, the existentialist, as exemplified by Sartre, and the prescriptivist, as formulated by Hare. However, Sartre's view, because it makes morality a matter of individual commitment, freely and arbitrarily chosen, neither to be defended nor attacked, yet self-justifying, thereby transforming "morality beyond recognition," is, according to Frankena, "perhaps best understood as a proposal to replace morality by an 'ethos' of activism or heroism, which is so different from morality that it can be called an ethic only because it takes the same room in our lives" ("RCM," p. 3). So, for Frankena, Sartre's conception of morality is, according to one set of criteria—the formally universalizable and the materially social—no such conception at all but a proposal about (a persuasive definition of?) an "ethos of activism"; yet, on another criterion—personal authenticity, sincerity, integrity—Sartre's is a conception of morality. In any case, whether it is or is not a conception of morality is presumably to be decided by whether or not that conception satisfies certain recognized criteria of "morality"; those criteria are either definitive or definite enough to mark off the moral from the other-than-moral. That the criteria of "morality" are less than necessary or sufficient (so that Sartre's criterion, however we express it—as other than the formal or the material—is an intelligent contender among the legitimate criteria of "morality" as an open concept) is not ruled out, but only because it is not even whispered as a cogent possibility.

No such problem arises with Hare. He, too, is an individualist in his conception of morality; but this is so because his conception includes universalizability of the principle of individual choice. Hare's may be, as Frankena thinks it is, an inadequate conception of morality, but at least it is an indisputable example of a conception of morality and is not to be read as a conception of something else. Hare does not satisfy all the definitive criteria of "morality"; but because he recognizes at least one of them, his theory is a conception of morality. Hare is wrong in thinking that being moral is acting on universalizable imperatives, and is wrong in particular in regarding universalizability as sufficient

and imperatives as necessary or self-imperatives as coherent; and Sartre is wrong in thinking that being moral is committing oneself to a certain course of action or way of life. Even so, Hare is still a moralist with a conception of morality, whereas Sartre is not, because his criterion, while overriding or total in a man's life, is not moral and can be considered to be so only by analogy with the commitment to principles in morality. Applying the term to Hare and withholding its application to Sartre rest more on morality as an establishment than on morality as an institution. Can Sartre join as a respectable member of the establishment and achieve the status of proclaiming a theory of morality, a conception of morality, not a conception of something else, only when he belatedly adds that one chooses for all, not only for oneself, and that, moreover, one can make that kind of choice intelligible? Hare, with his notion of self-imperatives that no one understands except himself, is not required to do this to stay in the club.

Individualism, whether in Sartre's form (moral or nonmoral), in Hare's form (an adequate conception of morality or not), or in the strongest form (recognizing and allowing for an individual to choose for all), denies that morality is intrinsically social in its concern. Individualism thus accepts the formal criterion of the universalizability of principles; but since it does not accept the material criterion of social concerns, it does not accept any transindividual justification or validity of moral judgments. Even if an individualist advocates a social principle of benevolence or utility in its strongest form, he must allow that the denial of the principle by others is equally valid. In other words, the validity of an individualist's advocacy of such a social principle and his condemnation of its rejection depends entirely on his commitment, just as the validity of the opposite advocacy and condemnation depends entirely on the opposite commitment.

The second recent conception Frankena discusses is that morality is necessarily transindividual. Here again he distinguishes two versions. The first version holds that moral judgments claim not only that everyone should do likewise but that others who take the moral approach agree that they should do likewise, that is, that moral judgment is valid for all. In its weak form, this first version holds that a judgment is moral only if it claims such intersubjective validity; in its strong form, it adds that this judgment is corrigible if consensus about it does not obtain. The second version holds that moral judgments (or moral principles, moral reasoning) are moral because of their form, not because of their content. In all versions, however, this second conception of morality, according to Frankena,

> maintains that there is something which may be called the moral point of view. This point of view can be described in purely formal terms—readiness to think and to make practical decisions by reference to principles which one is willing to take as supreme and to see everyone else take as supreme, even in the light of the best available knowledge, etc. ["RCM," p. 8].

According to this second conception, then, morality is governed by the moral point of view; but that point of view, to be moral, has no content and indeed is compatible with any content, whether concern for the welfare of others, self-love, pure aestheticism, or even a combination of sadism and masochism.

These two recent conceptions of morality concur in holding that the definition of morality includes nothing about the content of morality. It is this denial that the third conception of morality rejects.

> This [third conception] again is a family of positions, but they all hold that our judging and deciding is moral if and only if it is done from a certain point of view which is not definable in purely formal terms; its definition may include purely formal features but it must also include a material one. This material condition, moreover, must reflect a concern for others or a consideration of social cohesiveness and the common good; even if morality be limited to "justice," as distinct from "benevolence," it still must involve something of this sort ["RCM," p. 9].

As we saw in connection with Baier and Warnock, who are firm advocates of this third conception of morality, concern for the interests of others is part of the meaning of both "moral" and "the moral point of view." Therefore, a conception of either that omits the welfare of others may be honored as a conception of morality, inadequate though it is; but it may not be honored as a conception of the moral point of view, since it is not *the* conception of that point of view. Frankena is more liberal. He allows that there are different conceptions of both. The three conceptions he lists and a fourth which he invents all have a morality and a moral point of view: (1) the formal and individualistic; (2) the formal and social; (3) the material and social; and (4) the material and individualistic.

Having acknowledged that the concepts of morality and the moral point of view function under disparate sets of conditions, Frankena does not then go on to ask, What does this logical feature tell us about these concepts? For example, do they have multiple, conflicting criteria for their correct use? He asks, instead, What issues are involved in their disagreements, and which conceptions of morality and the moral point of view, if any, have the correct solution? Elucidation of the logical grammar of "moral" and "moral point of view" thus gives way to adjudication of conflicting theories of them.

There are, Frankena says, two basic issues: whether a claim to intersubjective validity is essential to moral judgment and whether a material social concern is intrinsic to morality. In regard to the first issue, Frankena argues that because we do invite similar responses on the part of others when we make moral judgments, we do claim the agreement of others, at least those who subscribe to the moral point of view; and, most important, because we cannot be "a party to an ultimate disagreement and still assert that both parties are taking the moral point of view" ("RCM," p. 14), a claim to intersubjective validity is essential to moral judgment.

If to this affirmative answer it is objected that any such claim about a transindividual validity is illusory, Frankena counters by distinguishing between actual consensus, sometimes realized, and hypothetical consensus, not yet realized (by definition), but certainly not illusory. Indeed, this claim is on a par with a similar claim in science; those who share the moral point of view will agree in the end on their moral judgments, as those who share the scientific point of view will agree in the end on their scientific judgments. The claim to intersubjective validity, then, may be an act of faith. "Perhaps," Frankena adds, "it is even a part of the moral point of view itself to keep this faith" ("RCM," p. 15).

In regard to the second issue—whether a material, social

concern is intrinsic to morality—Frankena begins by asking whether such a concern is a necessary condition of morality. That it is not a necessary condition gets support from those varied uses of "moral" by religious, formal, egoistic, and intuitionist positions that do not regard this condition as necessary or even as relevant. Frankena generalizes from this evidence that a material, social condition is not in fact necessary; at most, it is a sufficient condition or a proposal about a future use of "moral."

The denial also gets support from certain anthropological considerations about certain cultures in which other than social concerns are paramount; but the argument from this support— that the morality of such cultures, without the social concerns, *is* a morality and not merely a code of conduct—assumes what must be proved, namely, that these cultures have a morality in our sense of the term. For example,

one cannot say that the Navaho have a morality until after one has formed some conception of morality and found that the Navaho have such an institution. The fact that they have some kind of code which partakes of certain formal properties proves that they have a morality only if these properties suffice to define morality. But this is our question ["RCM," p. 17].

According to Frankena, then, this argument against the social and material as necessary begs the question Is morality defined, or can it be defined, in terms of an overriding code of conduct? One can play Frankena's game and ask, in turn, whether his charge does not itself beg the question Is morality definable by any set of properties? In order to dissociate codes of conduct from morality, he assumes that the concept of morality is closed. But—to put it his way—the definable, closed character of "morality" is precisely the question at issue. The claim that a material and social concern is not necessary to morality because some moralities do not so recognize it stands unless Frankena can prove that morality is definable by some set of properties and, by implication, that the concept of morality is and must be closed.

Though he thinks that a material and social concern is not a necessary condition of morality, Frankena nevertheless defends another view that claims it is necessary. Toulmin, for example, holds that concern for social harmony is necessary to—part of the meaning of—"moral." Nietzsche, it is objected to Toulmin, denied this; and, in denying it, he did not deny morality but instead gave it a different, yet legitimate, meaning. Frankena challenges this objection to Toulmin, arguing that Nietzsche can be interpreted as going beyond morality rather than as challenging it and that Nietzsche's rejection of the material and social concern as necessary versus Toulmin's acceptance of it as necessary need not be regarded as an issue within morality but can be seen as an issue between morality and some would-be successor. "Indeed, anyone who maintains that some particular requirement is essential to morality will have his Nietzsche, as Toulmin has his; and he must either give up his position or deny that his opponent's is a moral position, just as Toulmin must" (RCM, p. 19).

Is a material, social condition sufficient? The major objection, according to Frankena, is that the affirmative answer allows as sensible the senseless question "Why should I live like that?" This objection, Frankena replies, if taken as the factual claim that "moral" has no application to codes of conduct in which such a motivational question can be asked, is mistaken, since "moral" does not have this motivational meaning in all of its uses; on the other hand, if it is construed as a proposal to define "moral" in such a way as to rule out as sensible the question "Why should I?" the objection has little going for it, since the motivational "Why?" question is possible for, and consonant with, all conceptions of morality as systems of guidance "to which we do not automatically conform" ("RCM," p. 20).

At the conclusion of his essay, Frankena says that the issues raised by the disagreements among the different conceptions of morality and of the moral point of view, difficult and weighty as they are, cannot be solved "simply by looking to see how we use the expressions 'moral' and 'morality'" ("RCM," p. 21); they must be solved by further clarification and discussion. Yet the two issues he regards as central, the three or four conceptions of morality he expounds and assesses, and the two conceptions of Sartre and Nietzsche that he questions as conceptions of morality all turn on the use of "moral" or "morality." Central in his essay are these questions: What are the defining conditions of morality as an institution or as a whole? and Which conception of morality has stated them best? These questions, I have argued throughout this book, entail the questions: What are the defining criteria of the concept of morality? and, by further entailment, What are the criteria of the correct use of "morality"? Frankena's dichotomy—between, on the one hand, probing and solving the two issues he raises by looking at the use of "morality" and, on the other hand, clarifying them, seems a false dichotomy, since any clarification of these issues (or any other) must proceed by elucidating the actual functioning of certain concepts and their conveying words and the sets of conditons or criteria for such functioning and, thereby, in his case, for the use of "morality." Every conception, every issue, every objection, every reply that Frankena discusses in his essay is conceptual, not factual, except in the sense that it is about certain facts having to do with what some say we can or cannot say with or about "moral" and with what Frankena agrees or disagrees with in their claims about the possible and actual uses of "moral" or "morality." Thus, Frankena's clarification and discussion probe the respective claims or implications of these recent conceptions of morality as an institution that they do state the necessary and sufficient conditions of morality. Each, he argues, has failed to state this definitive set. Each nevertheless remains an indisputable example of a conception of morality, not because it states truly these requisite conditions, but rather because it subscribes to the doctrine that there are such conditions—that "morality" is definable, that "morality" has a correct use—even though it does not succeed in its attempt at such formulation. It is this over-all criterion of the assumption of a definitive set of formal or material and social criteria for the concept of morality—not the criterion of a true or adequate statement of the set—that determines what counts and what does not as a conception of morality. Thus Sartre and Nietzsche fail, not because they go wrong about the necessary and sufficient formal or material, social criteria, but simply because they do not subscribe or show signs of subscribing to the over-all criterion. They are ruled out as moralists because they introduce putatively true criteria for the correct use of "moral" that are neither formal nor material and social; they are not ruled out because they think, as their judges also think, that the concept of morality is strictly definable; nor are they ruled out because they think, as their judges do not, that the formal and material, social are one thing when they are something else. So, it *is* by looking at the use of "moral" that Frankena clarifies and discusses these conceptions or would-be conceptions of morality; in each case, he tests them against an assumed correct use of "moral."

That the use or logic of "moral" is central in his essay, including his clarifications of issues, can also be seen in his rejection of the argument against social and material concerns as necessary to morality by anthropological considerations; for his rejection proceeds by way of a clarification that converges on what "suffices to define morality," that is, the use of "moral," if it is to be used correctly. Moreover, how else are we to interpret Frankena's persistent reading of a contention in or about morality as either false or as a proposal if not a contention about the actual as against the recommended use of "moral"?

When we turn from Frankena's exposition and criticism of others' conceptions of morality to his own (which, to be sure, is only sketched in this essay), we find further support for the observation that Frankena's preoccupation, perhaps sole occupation, in the clarification of issues in morality is conceptual, hence is about the uses of "moral" and "morality." He states one necessary condition of morality: the claim to intersubjective validity of moral judgments, principles, or reasoning. This claim is equivalent to or entails the statement that a necessary criterion of the concept of morality or of the correct use of "morality" is intersubjective validity of utterance, a condition, Frankena says, "morality" shares with "science." He also argues and states that the concern for welfare is neither necessary nor sufficient for morality; this claim, again, is the same as or entails that the criterion of welfare—the material and social criterion—is not a necessary or a sufficient criterion of the concept of morality and, therefore, of the correct use of "morality." Frankena does not then go on to deny or to doubt that "morality" is definable, that it has a definitive set of criteria for its correct use; all he denies or doubts is that these have been secured, not that they can be or, indeed, must be if moral philosophy is to pursue the most pressing of its weighty problems.

The basic issues raised by the recent conceptions of morality that Frankena surveys and scrutinizes, are not, then, the two that he specifies. What is basic is what these two—in conjunction with the conceptions, their disagreements, the objections to them as conceptions, the replies to these objections, and the refusal to countenance certain conceptions as conceptions of morality—point to, namely, What kind of concept is the concept of morality? Is it open or closed? Is it governed by a definitive set of criteria or a set less than definitive? For, unless we can settle this issue, we cannot solve the problems raised in Frankena's essay. And the only way we can begin to settle it is to look at the use of "morality" and "moral," a procedure Frankena discounts as inadequate. However, if we do look at that use, and especially at the disagreements over the criteria—its different ones and the different characterizations of the same ones—we will find, I submit, that "morality," either as a second-order or as a first-order term, has functioned and continues to function—that is, to describe, enjoin, prescribe, proscribe, emote, persuade, assess, or whatever—but has done so and continues to do so under conditions other than definitive and, in particular, under sets of nonnecessary, nonsufficient conditions, each of them emendable, debatable, or rejectable. This—above all—is the logical,

the history of ethics, with its never-ending succession or sequences of theories. That the concept of morality is an open,
perennially debatable concept is a fact about that concept: its
use. That that fact can be disregarded, challenged, or repudiated
by something called "the moral point of view," neither Baier nor
Warnock is able to show. Nor, at least in the essay we have
discussed, does Frankena. Indeed, it is not even clear exactly
what role Frankena finds for, or assigns to, the concept of the
moral point of view in morality as an institution.

As he employs the concept, every recent conception has a
moral point of view; and, if each of these, why not all traditional
conceptions of morality as well? On this use, "the moral point of
view" seems to be simply another designation for the conception
of morality held by the individual moralist, or at least not a
necessary condition for such a conception's being moral as
against nonmoral. There are, then, different, competing conceptions of morality, each having its distinctive moral point of
view that does little more than sum up its conception of
morality. That *the* moral point of view is fixed, definitive (not
merely definable), and incontestable and thereby an overriding,
independently existing, or statable standard for the adequacy of
a putative conception of morality (Baier's and Warnock's conception of the concept of the moral point of view) Frankena
seems no more to accept than he does the concept of morality as
so fixed, definitive, and incontestable in its particular characterizations of the formal and material criteria that it can serve as
the standard for assessing contending conceptions of morality.
"What is the moral point of view?" cannot, then, be answered
prior to or independently of "What is morality?"; for these
questions and their answers proceed together. Moreover, the
introduction of the concept of the moral point of view, on this
conception of the concept, adds nothing to the clarification of a
conception of morality; for the egoist's conception of morality—
which for Frankena is, as it is for Hare, a conception of
morality—is no different from the egoist conception of the moral
point of view, and even the sadist-masochist conception of
morality—which Frankena also allows, as long as it satisfies the
formal requirement of universalizability—is its moral point of
view; and so on. There are, thus, as many legitimate moral
points of view as there are legitimate moralities. The criteria of
their truth, not their adequacy or legitimacy, are, to be sure,
definitive in character; but the definitive criteria of the one are
not a necessary condition for the definitive criteria of the other.

But Frankena also refers to the moral point of view as

something more than, over and above, separate from, independent of if not prior to, a moral point of view or the moral point of view of the individual conception of morality. Here, the moral point of view seems to function as an ideal or ideal principle that is definable, necessarily universalizable, and intersubjectively valid in form and necessarily socially concerned with human welfare in its content, which two necessary features are sufficient for the moral point of view (though not, we must remind ourselves, definitive for the true conception of morality, according to Frankena). Perhaps one might characterize Frankena's conception of the moral point of view as an ideal principle that is a hypothetical rather than categorical imperative: If you want to see morality from the moral point of view, employ and appeal to this principle, but not, as Baier or Warnock hold, with varying degrees of stringency; you must look at morality from

the moral point of view if you want to look at morality. On this use, then, "the moral point of view" denotes for Frankena a principle among principles in morality; it is not, as it is for Baier or Warnock, the overriding—one might say, second-order— principle that serves as the standard for determining moral principles. That Frankena distinguishes the moral point of view from a moral point of view or from the moral point of view embodied in a particular legitimate conception of morality, and that he holds the moral point of view to be an ideal principle, fixed by its formal and social defining components, *in* morality rather than a defining principle *for* morality—this is at least suggested not only by his defense of intersubjective validity as necessary, not illusory, in morality but by his arguments in favor of the second conception of morality, in its strong version, with its moral point of view, both defined in terms of formal and social features. What remains unclear is how the moral point of view as an ideal principle in morality can be claimed to have a definitive form and content that have already been truly stated when the morality of which it is an important, though not determining, part cannot be claimed to have a definitive form and content, since the latter have not yet been truly stated. Yet, this is Frankena's claim. Thus the role of the moral point of view as an ideal principle in morality is not as clearly delineated as one might wish. But a more fundamental question, I think, remains. Whatever role the moral point of view is claimed to have—as a principle in morality or as a principle for determining what morality is—what is the status of such a principle? For Baier and Warnock, the moral point of view is tied analytically to morality: it is what we mean by "moral." For Frankena, it is contingently related to only certain conceptions of morality, as an ideal principle among other principles. So we cannot clarify it by clarifying morality. Is it, then, simply self-evident for Frankena that the moral point of view, as against a moral point of view or a conception of morality, is the principle of being ready to think, argue, act and judge about conduct and character by reference to supreme principles that everyone should accept and would accept as supreme for everyone else (the formal feature)? And are these supreme principles social (the material feature)? The moral point of view, however it is formulated, in all its detail, is surely no less vulnerable to objections to self-evidence than any other principles in morality. It is not a self-evident defining principle for morality, according to Frankena; nor does it seem to be a self-evident ideal principle in morality for Frankena. What, then, is its status? Frankena does not say; and I cannot find an answer in his essay. In any case, it is difficult to see how it could be foundational for or in morality if it were not, as it is not, self-evident.

Does Frankena's book *Ethics* provide an answer to the nature and role of the moral point of view? *Ethics*, of course, is a textbook; nevertheless, in its lucid, masterly presentations, analyses, and solutions of traditional problems of morality and moral philosophy, it is an original and important contribution to the subject. Of immediate relevance to our topic—the concept of morality—are Frankena's theory of morality and the nature and role of the moral point of view in it.

He distinguishes early in his book between morality as an instrument of society and as a personal code and, later (pp. 61 ff.), between a normative theory of obligation and a normative theory of moral value. Presumably, the latter distinction has application to morality as a personal code, having to do with human conduct and character rather than with morality as a whole, in contrast with other institutions. Moreover, because this second distinction involves complementaries, not rivals, he treats conduct and character together under the rubric "morality as personal" (to be distinguished from "morality as institutional").

Morality, in both senses, is not prudence, however alike they are and however much prudence may be a moral virtue. Why is morality not prudence? Because "it is not characteristic of the moral point of view to determine what is right or virtuous wholly in terms of what the individual desires or of what is to his interest" (*E*, p. 7). If the moral point of view can determine what is an incorrect theory of morality, or of right and wrong, or of the virtuous and vicious, can it also determine the correct theory? If it can, what must this imply about the status of the moral point of view?

Extant or prevalent sets of rules, because they conflict, are diverse, and some of them are downright bad; thus they cannot serve as the standard of the morally right or wrong. What, then, can serve as the standard? Certainly not the principle or rule of acting and assessing conduct and character by enlightened self-interest; indeed, not only is this principle false in morality, but it is nonmoral and so cannot be used to characterize morality. (Here, as against his essay, Frankena seems to agree with Baier that egoism cannot be an ethical theory because it violates a defining principle of ethical theory, namely, that it must be disinterested; and, he adds, ethical egoism has no good argument, factual or moral, to recommend it as a replacement

of morality.) Frankena then considers in turn various forms or versions of deontological and teleological theories that revolve around different and competing standards of the morally right and wrong, the virtuous and vicious, each of which he rejects as inadequate in one way or another. Because he thinks that there is such a standard and that there must be such a standard in order for there to be any morality at all, he offers as his own standard and theory what he calls a mixed deontological one, in which two principles, not one, are ultimate; these two principles can serve as standards of the morally right or wrong, the virtuous or vicious, and appeals to them can solve all moral problems except those having to do with an irresolvable conflict over the priority of these two principles. The two principles are those of beneficence (not benevolence) and justice as equality. From these, all other principles and duties can be derived; and the two principles themselves, which he offers as his theory of obligation, are the "most satisfactory from the moral point of view" (E, p. 43). According to this theory and its two principles, all of us have a prior prima facie obligation to do good and prevent harm and another such obligation to treat everyone equally. Since both duties rest on good and evil—"Morality was made for man, not man for morality" (E, p. 44)—both presuppose the existence of good and evil and concern about them. Since this dependence on good and evil makes Frankena's theory of obligation a mixture of deontological and teleological elements, he labels it a "mixed deontological theory."

Why is this theory the most satisfactory one from the moral point of view? Because "everyone who takes the moral point of view can agree that the ideal state of affairs is one in which everyone has the best life he or she is capable of. Now, in such a state of affairs, it is clear that the concerns of both the principle of justice or equality and the principle of beneficence will be fulfilled'" (*E*, p. 53).

This theory, however, is not only satisfying and most satisfactory from the moral point of view; it is also true, and justified as true, from the moral point of view. Since the truth and justification of the theory of morality—of the principles or standards of the morally right or wrong, the virtuous or vicious—are much more important than whether the theory satisfies, from any point of view, Frankena's justification requires greater detail. If the argument for the truth of his theory of obligation rests on his theory of the moral point of view, it is crucial to determine whether this theory is also true and, if it is true, what its truth status implies about the moral point of view as a principle in morality or as a condition of morality.

Kant, according to Frankena, identified the moral point of view with one's being willing to universalize one's maxims. Frankena accepts this, but only as a necessary, not a sufficient, condition. Baier's conception is better: "one is taking the moral point of view if one is not being egoistic, one is doing things on principle, one is willing to universalize one's principles, and in doing so one considers the good of everyone alike" (*E*, p. 113). Hume regarded the moral point of view as sympathy, a conception Frankena develops. In general, the point of view, whatever it is, can be identified by the kind of reason given for a judgment when it is made or challenged; thus, it is the kinds of reasons, not kinds of judgments, that determine the kinds of of points of view, whether prudential, aesthetic, or moral. The moral point of view, then, can be identified by the kind of reasons given in moral judgments when these are made or challenged. These are moral reasons; and they "consist of facts about what actions, dispositions, and persons do to the lives of sentient beings, including beings other than the agent in question" (*E*, p. 113).

The moral point of view is the concern for these facts that function as reasons in moral judgments. It is this concern that identifies the moral point of view. But it does not define it or characterize it; however, that is precisely what Frankena proceeds to do:

One is taking the moral point of view if and only if (a) one is making normative judgments about actions, desires, dispositions, intentions, motives, persons, or traits of character; (b) one is willing to universalize one's judgments; (c) one's reasons for one's judgments consist of facts about what the things judged do to the lives of sentient beings in terms of promoting or distributing nonmoral good and evil; and (d) when the judgment is about oneself or one's own actions, one's reasons include such facts about what one's actions and dispositions do to the lives of other sentient beings as such, if others are affected. One has a morality or moral action-guide only if and insofar as one makes normative judgments from this point of view and is guided by them [E, pp. 113–14].

For Frankena, this *is* the moral point of view. How, then, does it justify moral judgments, including his two basic principles of beneficence and justice? It justifies them—indeed, shows them to be true—not by proving them, as other moralists claim, but by holding them up to scrutiny from the moral point of view. And to be able to do this, one must be free, impartial, and logical and must know "all that is relevant about himself, mankind, and the universe" (E, p. 112). Once the moral judgment or principle, basic or derived, is argued for, coolly and rationally and from the moral point of view, ideal, not actual, consensus or objectivity—what Frankena refers to as "intersubjective validity" in his essay—is also guaranteed.

Why, finally, should we adopt the moral point of view? Why should we be moral? There may be a conclusive answer to this question if it is taken as one about motives, Frankena says, but there is no conclusive answer if it is a demand for justification by nonmoral reasons. Such reasons may justify taking the moral point of view to some but need not to others, even though these others, remaining rational, remain so by giving reasons for preferring a different point of view and a different way of life, not by demanding, irrationally, why they should be rational.

In *Ethics*, then, Frankena seems to resolve the ambivalence (which I attribute to him) over the role of the moral point of view in relation to morality—that is, whether it is a necessary condition for morality or is, instead, an ideal principle in morality—in favor of its being a necessary condition for morality. It is a species of the genus the evaluative point of view, which latter also includes the species of the prudential and aesthetic points of view. It is also a species of a larger genus, point of view, and it shares membership in this genus with the economic, historical, scientific, educational, prudential, and aesthetic points of view. It is not a species of morality.

Rather, the moral point of view sets the over-all standard for morality, both as an institution and as a personal code of conduct and character, so that nothing counts as moral as against nonmoral or moral as against immoral without satisfying that over-all standard. It also sets the over-all standard for one and only one correct conception of morality as a whole and of morality as right and wrong, virtuous and vicious. Moreover, the moral point of view not only serves to assess different, competing, or conflicting conceptions of morality, but it also determines that beneficence and justice as fairness are the basic principles or standards of morality. Indeed, the moral point of view justifies these two as true, basic principles. To revert to the previous distinction I borrowed from Kant, of the hypothetical and categorical imperative, Frankena in *Ethics* seems to be saying: you must look at morality from the moral point of view if you want to look at morality—thereby agreeing with Baier and Warnock—rather than, as he intimates in his essay: if you want to see morality from the moral point of view, employ and appeal to that point of view. The moral point of view, Frankena allows in the *Ethics*, may be an option from the evaluative point of view, but it is no option for the understanding of morality: it is the only way.

Morality, on this view, is not the same as the moral point of view. Rather, morality is based on the moral point of view, and in at least two ways: that point of view sets the over-all criterion of what is moral, and it justifies that what is claimed to be moral is moral. The moral—acting and judging in accordance with the principles of beneficence and justice—is objective, perhaps absolute, being true and true for all, independently of our opinions about it. The concept of morality, consequently, is governed by definitive criteria, criteria that are themselves unambiguous and not contestable; the concept, thus, is closed, not open in any sense.

The moral point of view is also fixed, consisting of the four constituents Frankena lists on pages 113–14 of his *Ethics*, already quoted. This implies that the concept of the moral point of view is also closed: governed by a set of necessary and sufficient criteria, each incontestable. Presumably, unlike the moral principles it sets and justifies, it is not itself true (or false) and is not justifiable, since it is the ultimate criterion of justification of other—moral—principles. What, then, is its status, if its role is to serve as a necessary condition for morality? I gather that Frankena rules out that it is self-evident or that it is a postulate, an assumption, a stipulation, or a synthetic a priori judgment. Is it, then, a conceptual truth about the meaning of "the moral point of view"? It seems to me that the truth of the moral point of view for Frankena is a conceptual truth about its meaning. For, in claiming that the moral point of view involves the making of certain kinds of normative judgments that we are willing to universalize, and that the reasons for these judgments, including the reasons for first-person normative judgments, have to do with the promotion and distribution of good and evil among human beings—the formal and material, social conditions—Frankena states the *definiens* of "the moral point of view" as the *definiendum*. Thus, the four conditions he lays down he takes as equivalence conditions for "the moral point of view."

But, now, if the truth of the moral point of view is an analytic truth (consisting of a *definiens*) of that point of view (its *definiendum*), the moral point of view is analytically tied to morality, and morality is similarly tied to the moral point of view. The concept of the one entails the concept of the other. Although one can be moral or even make moral judgments without adopting the moral point of view, one cannot have a conception of morality without adopting the moral point of view; nor, if the equivalence conditions hold, can one adopt the moral point of view without having a conception of morality.

How, then, can the moral point of view be a condition, necessary or not, for morality that can be argued for independently of morality and can serve to set the standards and truth of moral principles? It cannot be, for the moral point of view cannot be distinguished from (correct) morality. It is a species of morality, indeed, an *infima* species.

That Frankena does not in *Ethics* resolve the ambivalence about the role of the moral point of view is suggested by this description of it:

> It seems to me that everyone who takes the moral point
> of view can agree that the ideal state of affairs is one in which
> everyone has the best life he or she is capable of. Now, in such
> a state of affairs, it is clear that the concerns of both the
> principle of justice or equality and the principle of beneficence
> will be fulfilled [*E*, p. 53].

The natural way to read this is that the moral point of view is itself a principle in morality, indeed, the basic principle, from which beneficence and justice can be derived. The moral point of view is a requirement of neither an ideal state of affairs nor of agreement on it; it consists of this principle of an ideal state of affairs. The principle is claimed to be true; we do not need the moral point of view to see that it is true or to agree that it is; we need only the ability to see that it is true and, indeed, foundational to and in morality. On such a reading of the moral point of view as a true principle about an ideal state of affairs for human beings, Frankena's theory of obligation becomes purely teleological, since our duties are defined in terms of this ideal state of affairs. The truth of the moral point of view as the truth of this principle of what is an ideal state of affairs for human beings cannot even pretend to be an analytic truth about the meaning of "the moral point of view"; its status is exactly that of the principles of beneficence and justice, except that, as the basic principle, it cannot be justified, rendered true, by any more basic principle or point of view.

Frankena, thus, it seems to me, has not answered satisfactorily the question What is the role of the moral point of view in relation to morality? That it is a prior, necessary condition for morality, which determines and justifies its principles, leaves it an analytic truth whose truth conditions foreclose on any distinction between morality and the moral point of view. That it is a principle in morality—indeed, the basic one—leaves it without a creditable truth status.

Perhaps these difficulties can be resolved; perhaps Frankena has resolved them elsewhere or would not agree that they are difficulties at all. But, as they stand, these difficulties about the role of the moral point of view seem insuperable. For any introduction and employment of the concept of the moral point of view, if that concept is to be informative and illuminating, must distinguish it from the concept of morality. But if the criteria of the one are the criteria of the other, they cannot be distinguished; and, if their criteria are different, the criteria of the one are determining and justifying criteria of the other, and the criteria of the one—in this case, of the moral point of view—must have other criteria to determine and to justify them. There are no such criteria, and there cannot be such criteria without falling back on stipulation, self-evidence, or analytic truth, none of which is acceptable and the last of which, as Frankena's *definiens* shows, collapses the distinction between morality and the moral point of view.

Although I believe that the moral point of view has not been given an intelligent role in morality and cannot be given one, my greater reservation is about the criterion of the identification, rather than the criteria of the characterization or definition, of the moral point of view. Baier, we remember, proposed as the criterion of the identification of the moral point of view its defining principle, just as, indeed, he offered its defining principle as the criterion for recognizing and distinguishing any point of view from others. Frankena rejects this criterion, as well as the putative criterion of the kind of judgment made. For him, the criterion for the identification of any point of view is the kind of reasons proffered when a judgment is made or challenged:

Consider three judgments: (a) I say that you ought to do X and give as the reason the fact that X will help you succeed

in business; (b) I say you should do Y and cite as the reason
the fact that Y will produce a striking contrast of colors;
and (c) I say you should do Z and give as the reason the fact
that Z will keep a promise or help someone. Here the reason
I give reveals the point of view I am taking and the kind
of judgment I am making [*E*, pp. 110–11].

It is the reasons given that identify the prudential, aesthetic, and
moral points of view of these three examples. These examples,
and the criterion of their different reasons as the criterion of the
identification and differentiation of three different points of
view, are illustrative, but are they definitive of a point of view?
What would Frankena say if (b) were offered from the diver-
sionary point of view of a would-be thief who wished to shift
attention from him and his colleagues to an ensemble of
contrasting colors so that they could get at the till unnoticed?

Does the same reason for the same advice—"Paint a large canvas
of red and black!"—identify the same point of view? Hardly.
Nor is it indisputable that the reason given in (b) identifies the
aesthetic point of view. It may identify the aesthetic point of
view of some artists, critics, or aestheticians, whose reasons are
regarded by other artists, critics, and aestheticians as bad or as
not aesthetic reasons at all; therefore (b), as it stands, is not an
aesthetic judgment but a psychological one: striking contrasts,
after all, may be strident; what we want is a contrast that comes
off. For them, then, it is the judgment, not the reason, that
identifies the aesthetic point of view.

Frankena, too, wavers in his claim that the reason given
identifies the point of view. In his essay he compares the moral
with the scientific point of view, pointing out that they share the
belief in the intersubjective validity of their utterance; in this
instance, their similarity and identification of separate points of
view are determined not by the criterion of kinds of reasons for
judgments but by the criterion of an ideal consensus of their
judgments.

Moreover, when we turn from the moral point of view to the
scientific, historical, aesthetic, or, for that matter, any point of
view, including the philosophical, and ask, as Frankena bids us,
What are the kinds of reasons that identify and differentiate
these points of view? we find that his criterion is either suspect or
inadequate. What, for example, are scientific reasons? And why,
even if we could specify them or their kind, do they, and not
certain procedures, assumptions, or aims, identify science as a
point of view in contrast, say, to the religious point of view?
"What is a scientific reason?" is as central and suspect in science
as "What is the scientific point of view?" Debate about both is

vehement in science and the philosophy of science. How, then, can we identify or define the scientific point of view by its kind of reason when the very concept of a scientific reason is subject to a seemingly interminable scrutiny? How can we possibly identify this point of view by a criterion whose own criteria are up for fundamental debate? The scientific point of view—if there is such a thing—may be identifiable and distinguishable from other things. But it is not identifiable by its kind of reasons, especially when these, vague as they are, are unaccompanied by other criteria of kinds of questions asked or askable, kinds of procedures followed, kinds of assumptions made, and kinds of aims pursued.

If the scientific point of view is one kind of myth, the aesthetic point of view is another. The former may, with some justice, claim at least a hard core at the center of its point of view or enterprise. The latter cannot claim even that. How can we Morality identify the aesthetic point of view by a kind of reason when, as is the case, aesthetic reasons are themselves defined by what counts as aesthetic and where the answers to that question are as varied as opposing theories of the aesthetic? The prevailing criterion of the identification of the aesthetic point of view in every case is not a kind of reason offered in support of a kind of judgment but a putative true theory of the aesthetic, whether stringently defined as orders within sensuous surfaces (Prall), or extravagantly defined as the quality of completed experience (Dewey), or defined according to the hundreds of views in between. In aesthetics as nowhere else, what counts as an aesthetic reason and what identifies the aesthetic point of view is nothing short of what is claimed to be the true theory of the nature of the aesthetic: the aesthetic determines the aesthetic point of view and acceptable aesthetic reasons. Whether the moral point of view and moral reasons, like their aesthetic counterparts, rest on a putatively true theory of the moral, where everything is putative and nothing is true, is precisely the great issue. One thing, however, is sure: Do not model the moral point of view or moral reasons on the aesthetic point of view or aesthetic reasons; that way points only to the undeniable openness of both.

As far as the philosophical point of view is concerned—a point of view neither Baier, Warnock, nor Frankena mentions (why not?)—it seems to dissolve into a morass when one asks for its kind of reason. What is a philosophical reason? cannot identify philosophy or the philosophical point of view, since it is already a philosophical problem to be solved or, more likely, to be resolved as the puzzle it is.

The clue to what has gone terribly wrong in the introduction of the moral point of view as a new panacea for the ethical predicament can be seen if we turn to history. Frankena talks about the historical point of view. But what can this mean if it is to be identified by its kind of reason? What is a historical reason unless it is the same as What are past-tense statements?—which is, of course, absurd. Yet we do talk intelligently about the Marxist and the Augustinian and the Freudian points of view. These are properly points of view in and of history; and they are this because they describe and explain the past from a particular point of view that is a set of interpretive categories. We can ask whether historian *A* looks at history from the Marxist or Augustinian or Hegelian or even no point of view; and we can get, we think, a straight answer once we determine what that point of view is and whether its exponent employs it according to its founder. But this has nothing whatever to do with seeing history from the historical point of view. "See history from the historical point of view!" is at most a *cri de coeur* of the working historian to look at the past without dubious and unnecessary assumptions, whether of a metaphysical or a methodological sort.

What, finally, of the moral point of view? Is it intelligible on its own, without backing from very different or very suspect points of view? I have already argued as best I can that it cannot serve as a necessary condition for morality without resting on an analytic truth about the meaning of "the moral point of view" which renders the distinction between morality and the moral point of view otiose; and I have argued, further, that it cannot serve as the basic principle in morality without becoming a proposition whose truth status is as indeterminate as it is unacceptable.

Can it, unlike other points of view, be identified by its reasons? Only if, like the prudential point of view or the pedestrian point of view (in Baier's example of the roundabout), the moral point of view is identifiable by a fixed or definitive set of reasons that consist of a similar set of facts about the promotion and distribution of good and evil for human beings— only if, that is, the concept of the moral point of view is closed. That it is closed, governed by a set of necessary and sufficient criteria, none of them contestable, has to be shown. But it cannot be shown by appealing to its use, which reveals, instead, that the concept, if not the phrase, functions under diverse, competing sets of criteria; and it cannot be established by appealing to its meaning, which, if different from its use, consists of a stipulated restriction of the criteria of its use and is given the status of a dubious or self-defeating analytic truth about the concept.

The reasons that identify the moral point of view or could intelligently identify it are as diverse, competing, and conflicting as the reasons that identify morality. Both, therefore, are open concepts; their reasons, their criteria, even their facts, show that they are. What has not been shown, needs to be shown, and, I think, cannot be shown is that the concept of the moral point of view is the foundational, buttressing concept of or in morality; it is not merely a summative concept for a particular conception of morality, either as an institution or as a code of personal conduct and character (a view that Frankena suggested in his essay but discarded in *Ethics*). That morality is based on the moral point of view or that it is the moral point of view or that its prime principle is the moral point of view is a mistake. But this mistake is different from, and in addition to, the mistake it shares with all theories of morality: the mistake of construing the concept of morality—which is open—as closed.

In the preceding chapters, I have argued as best I could that there
are open concepts. Five of these were detailed: the concepts of
art, tragedy, style, human action, and morality. Each of these, I
stressed, is an open concept, not a vague, woolly, or ambiguous
word. As their uses—their functioning, or roles, and the conditions under which they play their roles—reveal, all are governed
by criteria that are less than definitive sets of them. The concept
of art or of a work of art functions under a disjunctive set of
conditions or criteria in which none is necessary and none is
sufficient but each is not rejectable and each is a good reason for
saying of something that it is a work of art. The concept of
tragedy, like the concept of art, is perennially flexible, because
the history of its set of nondefinitive criteria shows that this set
and the concept accommodate new examples with their new
properties; but the concept of tragedy, unlike the concept of art,
is perennially debatable as well, because each of its criteria is
subject to emendation, rejection, or replacement by other criteria. The concept of morality also is perennially debatable;
however, given the relative stability and continuity of the
human condition, it is not perennially flexible. The concept of
style or, better, of certain style concepts, whether in art history
or history proper, where period-style concepts occur, is irreducibly vague and open in the sense of functioning under disparate
and exchangeable sets of criteria, none of them definitive. The
concept of human action—a concept that ranges over metaphysics, morality, and psychology—unlike the others detailed,
functions under a disjunctive set of sufficient conditions but with
no necessary ones.

Other open concepts were mentioned. Among these is the
concept of contract and Hart's elucidation of it as defeasible,

that is, governed by necessary but no sufficient conditions. Hart characterized many legal and some ordinary concepts as defeasible rather than definitive, as traditional jurisprudence and philosophy wrongly assumed them to be. His further generalization about the defeasibility of all action concepts, including the concept of action itself, were questionable (as he came to see), but his logical mapping of legal concepts, including the concept of the law, remains a solid contribution to jurisprudence and to the inventory of open concepts.

Stevenson's elucidation of the concept of a cultured person—an elucidation that served his immediate purpose of introducing the notion of persuasive definition—though couched in an unacceptable theory of meaning, is, in its intimation of the logic of the conditions or criteria of "cultured" and similar terms, especially in ethical discourse, one of the great discoveries in the development of open concepts. That "cultured" or "good" or "right" or "poet" is amenable to persuasive definitions is rendered possible by its particular sets of criteria. These terms he called "vague," and I suggested that they are vague, not in the sense of "obscure" or "without boundaries," but in the sense of what I called "irreducible vagueness"—the vagueness of the inadequacy or incompleteness of their individual *sets* of criteria, not of their individual criteria.

In this connection, it may not be amiss to comment on recent criticisms of Stevenson's implicit notion of irreducible vagueness. Certain philosophers, among them Philippa Foot,[1] have argued that some concepts or words we use for evaluating—words such as "rude"—are not governed by exchangeable sets of criteria, as Stevenson's example and elucidation of "cultured" allow. "Rude" expresses (mild) condemnation all right, but not on any criterion or set of criteria; it does so only on the criterion of a kind of behavior that causes offense by indicating lack of respect. Thus, the concept of rudeness, which is a moral concept, is not open but closed. To say that someone was not rude, though he caused someone else offense by showing a lack of respect for him, is to misuse or to be ignorant of the concept of rudeness. Now, just as Stevenson offered a wholesale theory of moral and evaluative terms as amenable to persuasive definition, made possible by the (irreducible) vagueness of the criteria of these terms, Philippa Foot also generalizes from some terms, such as "rude" or "pride" (an example she uses in another essay), to all moral terms' being governed by fixed, unchallengeable sets of criteria, tied to facts and features of the world, which criteria count as the rules of evidence for our moral judgments. No "private enterprise" theory of moral criteria for her; every moral concept, to be used correctly at all, must abide by established rules for its use.

So far as I am aware, Stevenson has not replied to Foot's objection; I am not even sure that he would accept the criticism as I have put it. At any rate, it is the issue that is important to me, namely, whether all moral concepts are closed in the same way that rudeness is (if it is). Rudeness is certainly fixed in its criteria of correct use, so that it cannot be joined, say, with politeness in any utterance of the form "I am being rude only to be polite." If I am rude, I cannot be polite. Rudeness cannot accommodate politeness as one of its criteria; nor can politeness accommodate rudeness as one of its criteria, whether rudeness or politeness has definitive criteria or not. That being rude is not being polite is one of the rules of evidence, one of the rules of correct use, of "rudeness."

But what then of, say, cruelty? Can cruelty be joined with, say, kindness, as rudeness cannot be with politeness? I cannot be rude to be polite; I cannot be polite to be rude. Can I be kind to be cruel? Can I be cruel to be kind? Shakespeare's Hamlet thought he could join them: "I must be cruel only to be kind" (3.4.178). In context, it is not unambiguous whether he refers to his killing of Polonius or to his chastisement of his mother or to both, although it is clear that he is not punning on "kind," as he does earlier in his parenthetical aside on Claudius' "But now my cousin Hamlet, and my son— / (A little more than kin and less than kind)" (1.2.64–65). Hamlet's "only" need not be read as "in order to," to produce a straightforwardly intelligible rationale or explanation of the behavior he is offering to his mother; for he does not seem to be saying, "I am being cruel in order for me to bring about a state of affairs prompted by kindness" but, rather, "My kindness includes my cruelty" or "My cruelty is kind." In any case, he does not say, "My kindness is cruel." Maybe the latter is as much an infringement on the rules of "kindness" as "I am rude in being polite" or "I am polite in being rude" is on the rules of "rudeness" and "politeness." But Hamlet's observation seems in absolutely impeccably good linguistic order: a criterion for "kindness" may be "cruelty"; a criterion of "cruelty" may be "kindness." I cannot produce a convincing example of "I must be kind only to be cruel"—but then I am not Shakespeare. However, I wonder whether even he could come up with convincing contexts that joined politeness with rudeness.

Well, now, if Philippa Foot's generalization about the rules of evidence for all moral terms breaks down so early in the game—on the level of "rudeness" and "cruelty," so that certain linguistic moves are possible with the one and not the other, and where the criteria of the one are not as fixed as the criteria of the other, which allow for these aberrant linguistic moves—why must we subscribe to her wholesale doctrine about the closed character of evaluative terms or to her wholesale rejection of Stevenson's reading of moral terms as (irreducibly) vague? Both philosophers, it seems to me, are right about some evaluative concepts and wrong about all—which is exactly as things should be if we are to do justice to the varieties of concepts, both open and closed.

Wittgenstein—to go on with some of the open concepts we merely mentioned but did not explore—establishes the openness of the concept of game as well as the openness of the concepts of understanding and pain, among many others. The concept of pain is especially interesting since it is one that we can apply in some cases with absolute certainty—with no reason to doubt—

and yet which has no sufficient conditions that entail the correct application of the concept; nevertheless, the conditions that there are furnish criteria and good reasons for the correct application or withholding of the concept of pain. Although Wittgenstein did more than anyone else to destroy the myth that all concepts are and must be closed, he did not do as much, for example, as Stevenson did in suggesting the possibility of open concepts in the radical sense of perennial debatability.

Gallie, too, uncovered a number of important open concepts, which he called "essentially contested concepts" but which he needlessly identified with appraisive ones. "Democracy," "work of art," and even "Christian" are open, but in different ways; and none of them, though employed primarily to appraise, requires the ruling-out of "game" as an open concept and as one that does not primarily appraise. Waismann and Sibley also provide interesting examples of different kinds of open concepts; but the reading of them as "open-textured" or "noncondition-governed" does not do justice to their examples or to the variety of open concepts. Hampshire, in *Thought and Action* (1959), opened up a new world in arguing that the concept of the moral and its related concepts of human nature and mind are essentially disputable; but I cannot find that he did not abandon this world in his later writings and criticism of similar views. The implication that morality and the moral point of view are both essentially disputable, present in this early book, was not revived, at least so far as I can determine, until Henry Aiken called into question the definitive character of the moral point of view in his essay "The Concept of Moral Objectivity" (1963).[2] Whether Aiken would infer from there being "no definitive principle of moral right and wrong" to the openness, even

radical perennial debatability, of both the concepts of morality
and the moral point of view, I do not know; nor, I suspect,
would he want to be saddled with such openness in his elucidation of objectivity in morality.

Besides the open concepts I have detailed and the ones that I
have mentioned throughout this volume, there are others that
await scrutiny. Among these are certain concepts in politics and
ethics, such as those of equality, freedom, liberty, democracy,
fascism, communism, ideology, sovereignty, the state, and even
justice—Rawls' *A Theory of Justice* notwithstanding. Who
among the classical or recent theorists about these concepts does
not regard them as closed—as perhaps not amenable to real
definitions of their essences but surely definable or characteriz-
able by their necessary and sufficient conditions? Who among
them does not assume or assert that, unless and until we
determine such a set of criteria, each of these concepts is
deficient and their uses without proper foundations? That they
are open in any sense is unacceptable; that way lies incoherence,
not understanding. Even though each theorist recognizes both
agreement and disagreement, each nevertheless persists in thinking that the disagreements can be ideally resolved by a forthcoming true theory that will reduce competing conceptions to
the best conception of the relevant concept. I do not wish to
claim that these concepts are or are not open; I devoutly hope
that they are closed and that, with sufficient skill and luck, they
can be truly defined. But my strong conviction is that they are
open in varying degrees of openness and that the disagreements
among the theorists over the individual definitive sets of criteria
for their correct use lead to nothing else but their openness,
which cannot be swept away by dubious appeals to meanings or
analytic truths about these concepts and their meanings. If it
turns out that some of them—all of them, we may hope—are
closed, but because their histories of use establish this, not their
intuited meanings, so much the better; however, we cannot
simply begin by assuming that they are governed by definitive
sets of conditions, state them, argue for them by anything other
than the history of their uses, and utilize this definitive set as a
final court of appeal in the adjudication of all contending views,
conceptions, or theories of these concepts.

Among the concepts of the social sciences—for example,
anthropology, sociology, and history—there are, besides the
concepts that provide their distinctive domains—man, society,
the past—the concepts of explanation, understanding, and
causality, which, of course, they share with other disciplines,
but with avowed shifts in meaning and use. These three concepts

have been of special mutual concern to philosophers as well. Radical divisions, even cleavages, exist among different theories of these concepts, ranging from those that reduce or identify them to those that distinguish sharply between scientific, causal explanation and teleological understanding, with many permutations of causality, explanation, and understanding in between.

Some of this controversy, I believe, converges on the logical character of these concepts: on their closure or openness. Positions are taken and theories are promulgated about them, but I have yet to hear any full-blown discussion of whether any or all of these are only ambiguous, vague, a family of cases, or whether they may be, instead, open in any one of the senses we have detailed. Is, for example, the concept of causality governed by necessary and sufficient conditions, as the tradition, including the big three—Descartes, Hume, and Kant—assumed, in spite of their enormous differences on the specific set of conditions? So, too, with the concept of explanation: is it definable by a set of necessary and sufficient conditions? Is it indeed reducible to a deductive model that covers all explanations, from physics to history? Is understanding—which Wittgenstein regarded as a family of similar cases—like one of its related concepts, interpretation, especially as the latter functions in art and literary criticism? Directly related to this problem of the open or closed character of interpretation as, or different from, explanation or understanding is the concept of centrality, i.e., the concept of what is most important in the *explicandum*, whether this is a work of art, a person, a historical epoch, or an atomic blast. At the very least, I submit, it is an open question whether these concepts are open or closed. And it cannot be overemphasized that the best way to find out, perhaps the only way, is to turn from what social scientists say they are doing in their first or last chapters, or their separate essays on their methods and concepts, to what they do with their concepts when they work with them in practicing their crafts. The contrast between what they do and what they say they do may be as great and glaring in the social sciences as it is—as I hope I have showed—in the humanities.

Religion also has a number of concepts that beg for elucidation of the sort I am proposing: God, faith, creed, worship, and religion itself. Is each of these a closed concept or is each, as some claim, vague? Or are some of them at any rate open, with varying degrees of the absence of definitive criteria? I think, myself, that the concept of God, whether God exists or not, is a closed concept and that the traditional philosophical conception of him as a perfect being is correct in implying that the concept of God is governed by definitive criteria, as strict as those that

govern the concept of a Euclidean triangle or of entailment as
against implication. These criteria can be stated in such a way
that omniscience, omnipotence, and infinity, among others, but
not his existence, follow from his perfection.

But even if I am wrong about the concept of God as a closed
concept, there are some closed concepts in religion. The concept
of a Roman Catholic, for example, fluid and flexible enough in
its long history, from the Council of Nicaea on, from which it
derives its doctrinal authority if not its name, has performed its
primarily classificatory role of dividing the true Christian sheep,
whether separated or excommunicated from the flock or not,
from the false, heathen, blind, or heretical goats, under a set of
necessary and sufficient conditions which, though different at
different times, perhaps even contradictory from one time to the
next, is absolutely closed at any particular time. Much like a
game played according to strict rules, formulated to aid in the
solving of questions that arise during the game and especially to
block doubts about possible moves in the game, Roman Catholicism, unlike other versions of Christianity, functions under
criteria or rules that, ideally at any rate, defeat doubts about the
application or withholding of the concept.

What about the concept of a Christian? Is it closed? A belief in
the divinity of Christ seems to be a necessary condition, and yet
there have been people who claim they are Christians who do
not accept the divinity of Christ but only his historical presence
as an inspired or less-than-divine figure. Are they really Christians? We remember Frege's answer: we must know what being a
Christian is—we must have the exact concept—before we can
decide definitely and definitively whether A is a Christian or
not. Even so, this debate about belief in the divinity of Christ
centers on one necessary condition, not a definitive set; and it
leaves unsolved the problem of what it is to be a Christian.
What, then, is the absolute minimum the concept demands? Can
one be a Christian if one rejects the divinity of Christ as well as
his historicity? Can one remain a Christian by dismissing Christ
even as a real figure in history? Presumably, one can retain one's
religion or can remain religious or become religious without
believing in Christ as the Son of God if one adheres to belief in
Christ as a certain kind of man. But can one then be or remain a
Christian? The range of answers says something about the
relevant concept and, through these answers, about what the
concept applies to: what it is to be a Christian.

What, now, about Judaism? Is this a closed concept, or is it
vague or even open? Is the concept of a Jew like the concept of
an Orthodox, Conservative, or Reformed Jew? The history of

Judaism, I dare say, is also fluid and flexible; but is it, like Roman Catholicism, governed by necessary and sufficient criteria? Or is it, like the concept of a Christian, governed only by a necessary criterion that may itself be difficult to determine? Perhaps the concept of a Jew is more than religious, somewhere in between the concept of a Christian and the concept of a Black. Russell, for example, wrote a book, *Why I Am Not a Christian*, thereby repudiating Christianity; he could just as well have written a book, *Why I Am Not a Communist* or *Why I Am Not a Buddhist*. A Black can write a similar book, but he cannot write a book *Why I Am Not a Black* and not remain black as Russell can write his book and not remain a Christian. A Jew cannot write a book *Why I Am Not a Jew* and thereby give up being a Jew: he is and remains a Jew whether he says he is or is not. Being a Jew is more like being a Black than it is like being a

Christian; yet, the concept of a Jew is governed by criteria that are more complicated than those of physical characteristics. They are social, for a Jew is one who is not permitted—by Jews and non-Jews—to become a non-Jew. A Christian can choose not to be a Christian; a Black cannot choose not to be black; but a Jew cannot choose not to be a Jew, not because *he* cannot, but because *others* will not let him. The concept of a Jew, then, is more than a religious or physical one. And the concept of an authentic Jew—about which we hear so much these days, in which the Diaspora borrows from existentialism—need not be identical with the concept of a devout Jew, which is on a par with the concept of an authentic Christian; for the concept of an authentic Jew has application also to those Jews whose authenticity consists only in the acceptance of the complex absurdity of trying to write a book on why they are not Jews. Indeed, this acceptance of the logic of the concept may be a deeper rejection of *la mauvaise foi* than any devotion, total or not, to a creed.

What, now, about religion? Is the concept of religion or of the religious governed by a definitive set of criteria? No one, I think it would be accurate to say, has yet come up with such a set that others do not reject for still other sets. Is there even a necessary condition for the correct use of the concept? Since no one (thus far) has attempted to state such a necessary condition by deriving it from, or identifying it with, the religious point of view—a move as fashionable as it would be fatuous—the serious contenders for such a condition are worship, faith, a creed, a church, or a belief in God or gods. Even if we grant the distinction between literal and metaphorical uses of "religious" or "religion"—so that, for example, communism can be said to be a religion, but only in a metaphorical sense—is anything

necessary for religion? A belief in God or the gods, or in the
divine in some sense, seems the least deniable of the contending
necessary conditions. But Rousseau's Savoyard Vicar and Tolstoy's Fyodor, who converts Levin to religion without God,
both of whom find in Nature what others have found in God, do
not seem to accept a belief in God or the divine as necessary; and
indeed, even without these two fictional possibilities, why
cannot one insist that one is religious without falling back on
any condition that one claims, or is forced to acknowledge, as
necessary? The concept of religion, thus, may be as open as
other perennially flexible concepts; that is, it may be governed
by disjunctive sets of nonnecessary, nonsufficient conditions,
each of which can serve as a good reason for saying of *A* or *B*
that he is religious, since it is not rejectable. At any rate, the
question whether the concept is closed, open in the sense of
perennially flexible, or (and this we must investigate) even
perennially debatable, is eminently worth pursuing, since much
of great importance to many is at stake.

Education, too, has its interesting problems and concepts,
each of which deserves the kind of scrutiny I am proposing.
What, for example, is a liberal education? What is it to be
educated? Is the concept of being educated like the concept of
being literate or like the concept of being cultivated, each of
which is governed by a necessary condition or by exchangeable
sets of conditions? What is a discipline? How does it distinguish
itself from a department of studies? Academicians need only
reflect on the agonizing sessions of faculty meetings in which
these questions are debated with more heat and fury than
understanding and, in particular, on the logic of these basic
concepts. Here again the beginning of wisdom is not so much
wonder as it is a thorough inquiry into the different theories of
education and its subconcepts, with an especial concentration on
the kinds and range of disagreements among the theorists about
what education is, what a discipline is, what a department is,
and so on. It may be, as I am convinced it is, that the concept of
education and its subconcepts or related concepts are not all of
them closed, ambiguous, or vague, demanding only tightening-
up and real definitions to attain their maturity and efficacy, but
are instead open in varying degrees of openness.

The physical or natural sciences and mathematics also contain
many different sorts of concepts. But whether they are open in a
variety of ways or closed in a number of different ways is itself
an open question, well worth exploring but hardly broached by
scientists or philosophers of science as they warm over or
discard the old chestnuts of concept formation and concept

change. Frege's dictum, having replaced Plato's about the hegemony of mathematics in the study of the sciences, hovers over all: "A concept that is not sharply defined is wrongly termed a concept." Behind the worry and debate lie certain questions: Where does science end and metaphysics or nonsense begin? Are there observation as against theoretical terms? Are the concepts of one paradigm of science commensurate with the concepts of another, even if, as with "mass," they have the same name? Each of these questions revolves around the Fregean notion of the concept as exact, with its directive to establish either by stipulation or contextual definition this exactness. Accordingly, the assumption that all concepts in science, including the concept of science, are and must be closed—governed by sets of necessary and sufficient criteria—has become so entrenched that to question it is to commit heresy. Science, it is strongly urged, is the

search for the necessary and sufficient conditions of things and the consequent formulations of definitive, exact sets of criteria for the concepts employed to talk and theorize about these things. Thus, that some concepts, not merely some eliminable words, are open—are not and need not be governed by definitive criteria—seems a lost cause right at the very beginning of any plea to reopen the question whether all concepts are or must be closed. Maybe all of them are closed, in one way or another, and must be in order for them to be scientific at all; but maybe they are not. We ought to look at this as a possibility, and do so with competence in, and first-hand knowledge of, some of these hard sciences that provide flesh as well as blood to the elucidation of these concepts. Since I do not have the competence or knowledge, or even the requisite energy, to try, all I can do is to express a deep dissatisfaction with the present lack of interest in this possible shift from concept formation and concept change to the logic of the sets of conditions that prevail among concepts in science. One of the surprises that may await us is to find that some likely candidates for openness, like the concept of mass, are not open at all but are best understood in Lockean terms as different concepts, each closed, governed by its stipulated nominal essence, but each with the same name.

The only scientific concept I have been able to discuss—that of human action—touches psychology along with, of course, metaphysics and morality. At the end of my chapter on that concept, I suggested that perhaps it could serve as a model for the elucidation of other concepts in psychology, especially because of its specific nondefinitive character of being governed by a disjunctive set of sufficient conditions but no necessary ones. Some philosophers, such as Anthony Kenny, have raised ques-

tions about the definitive character of both emotional concepts
and the concept of the emotions as against the concept of
motives.[3] Ryle, on the other hand, at least in *The Concept of
Mind*, offered a program for the elucidation of psychological
concepts that, though revolutionary in its rejection of the
hidden, inner, mental criteria for these concepts, nevertheless
subscribed throughout to the hard-edged character of each of
them, so that, for example, the emotions are clearly delineated
from motives, as are feelings, moods, agitations, and inclina-
tions distinct from each other. In this insistence on public,
behavioral criteria for psychological concepts and on their
distinctive hard-edgedness, Ryle is closer than Kenny is to
contemporary psychologists' assumptions about the kinds of
acceptable criteria for their concepts and about the definitive
character of them. Ryle, of course, recognizes different kinds of
psychological statements and concepts: the categorical, the
hypothetical, and the mongrel-categorical. But I think it is true
that he is impatient with family-resemblance concepts or other
kinds of open concepts. The most he allows are what (subsequent to *The Concept of Mind*) he called "polymorphous
concepts"; these include concepts, such as work, farming, or
thinking, that apply to different activities but to none in
particular, such as bricklaying, apple-picking, or adding two
large numbers. Whatever their logic is, these polymorphous
concepts are not vague or open; they are only incomplete.

It seems to me that on this issue of the logical character of the
concepts of psychology, Kenny's is the more fruitful approach
and that psychology and the philosophy of psychology, engaged
in by either psychologists or philosophers, ought to ask of each
of these concepts, especially those that are not technical and
invented, just what its logical status is: open or closed? The
merging and vagueness of the phenomena dealt with by psychology call for clarification and explanation; it remains mere
conceptual fixation, however, to suppose that this clarification
and explanation must not reflect in their logic the logic of the
phenomena themselves. To clarify is not necessarily to render
definitive.

What, finally, about the concepts in philosophy and the
concept of philosophy? Does not the history of philosophical
theories of concepts reveal—if it reveals anything—that the
major tradition has been that all concepts are closed? Philosophers have disagreed over the ontological nature of the concept
and over the roles of all or some particular concepts; but on the
logic of the conditions under which concepts function they have
been unanimous, or almost so, in assuming that these conditions

must be definitive. Accordingly, though philosophers have notoriously differed on the nature of truth, knowledge, value, and meaning and even on the nature of validity and of philosophy itself, they have differed scarcely, if at all, on the closed character of the corresponding concepts.

Now, it may very well be that many philosophical concepts—perhaps such major concepts as truth, validity, and knowledge—are governed by sets of necessary and sufficient conditions and that the perennial quest for their definitive criteria, though perennially frustrated, is a realizable goal. Maybe Tarski's definition of truth is the truth about truth; perhaps knowledge is warranted true belief after all, and validity is consistent inference, guaranteed by the logical principle that A cannot be both A and not-A. Certainly, it would be as egregious to insist that all philosophical concepts are open as it is to assume that

they must all be closed in order for them to be concepts. Is the concept of reason, for example, open or closed? What counts as a reason? Only a reference to a necessary or sufficient property of something? Is the concept of a concept open? For many, it has not been; for others, it is vague—so much so that it ought to be dispensed with altogether; for me, it is a family. What about the concept of a person or of personal identity? Has anyone laid down the definitive criteria for either? Can they be stated? Or are both open in ways that have yet to be explored? What about reality and existence? It is notorious that both have been construed as properties, even by philosophers as acute as Moore. Are these concepts indefinable, definable, or perhaps, at least in the case of existence, systematically ambiguous, as Waismann, among others, has claimed? Philosophers have been debating the nature of causality at least since Aristotle; when we turn from this debate to ask, What does it tell us about the concept of causality? is it so clear that, though each theory of causality embodies its putative set of definitive criteria for the concept of causality, the concept is closed and that not more than one contending theory can be correct? Perhaps, as recent philosophers, such as Hart and von Wright, have suggested but not developed, the concept of causality is not fixed by a definitive set of criteria that has application to all cases of causality, whether in natural or human phenomena. It is not clear whether either philosopher, in rejecting the Humean conception of causality, is proffering a new conception—one in which causality is identified with agency viewed as interference with nature—or is instead simply reminding us that agency, viewed in this way, is as legitimate a criterion of the concept of causality as regularity is and that perhaps the concept of causality functions under a less-than-definitive set of criteria. At any rate, central in this debate over the adequacy of the Humean conception of causality is the logical character of the concept of causality: are the conditions for its employment an open or a closed set?

Of course, many concepts in philosophy are closed, for example, those that are technical or labeling terms, such as "sense datum," "sensibilia," and "neutral monism," among many others. But there are also technical terms that cut across ordinary discourse as well: "substance," "event," "space," "relation," and "evidence," among others. Are each of these and the concept it conveys open or closed, or what? And what about the concept of philosophy itself? What are its definitive criteria? Think of all the differing historical conceptions of philosophy: do these add up to a definitive set of criteria that enables us to say what counts as philosophy as against something else? Philosophy may be joined with science or with a way of life; but philosophers perennially ask, What is distinctive about philosophy? Ryle and, if Ryle is right, Wittgenstein, in both the *Tractatus* and his later work, raise, as the fundamental problem of philosophy, What is proprietary to philosophy? For both, at least according to Ryle, it is the search for the logical categories and their irreducible and distinctive types as these are embodied in, and to be extracted but not abstracted from, discourse.

Is philosophy activity? Others claim that it is theory or theory-building, either joined with science or based on it. Philosophy, like science, is statement about the world, not statement about the forms of discourse. And for still others, regarded by their despisers as disreputable or as no philosophers at all, philosophy is either commitment, or verbalization of commitment, and its accompanying existential penumbra. How convenient and wonderful it would be if we could transform that will-o'-the-wisp—the philosophical point of view—into an analytic truth that would then determine what is and what is not philosophy. But, deprived of this good fortune, all we can hope for is a necessary condition, not a definitive set of conditions, for the correct use of "philosophy." The obvious contender is the criterion of consistency; for whatever else philosophy is, it must adhere to the law of noncontradiction. But now, what do we say to a philosopher like Kierkegaard (and there must be others), and not just to Walt Whitman (and poets like him), who proclaims, when told he contradicts himself: "But, of course, I contradict myself, I'm a philosopher"? We may cheer ourselves up by ruling him out as a philosopher, but that will only make him smile. I wish I knew the way out of this depressing situation;

but, because I cannot take the high road of real definition or even the middle road of a minimum necessary property of philosophy, I am willing to grant that the concept of philosophy is as perennially debatable as the concepts of tragedy or morality. Thus, what I have been doing in this book—logical grammar, or elucidation of the concept of concept—or what others, such as Ryle or Wittgenstein, have also done in doing philosophy, is not and cannot be claimed to be what philosophy *really* is. What we do—or at least what I have been doing—in doing philosophy as elucidation is at most one option among others, some directly opposed to mine—an option that is made possible but is not demonstrated by the openness of philosophy. That the concepts I have detailed, that some of the concepts I have mentioned and others have detailed, and that many of the ones I offered for further examination are all open in varying degrees of openness

is not an option but a truth about the logic of certain concepts. What is an option is that philosophy should concern itself with such matters as the roles, and conditions of roles, of certain concepts. The justification of such an option, though not secured by a true definition of philosophy, is based on a further option: that truth, including conceptual truth, is a precious thing, whose fragility rests, not on any openness of truth, but on the openness of philosophy.

1. Gilbert Ryle, "Phenomenology versus 'The Concept of Mind,'" in French translation in *La Philosophie Analytique, Cahiers de Royaumont Philosophie*, no. 4 (Paris: Minuit, 1962); original English text in Ryle, *Collected Papers*, 2 vols. (London and New York, 1971), 1:182.

2. Bertrand Russell, "Logical Atomism," *Contemporary British Philosophy*, 2d ser.; reprinted in *Logic and Knowledge: Essays 1901–1950*, ed. Robert C. Marsh (London and New York, 1956) pp. 323–43.

3. Gilbert Ryle, "Systematically Misleading Expressions," *Proceedings of the Aristotelian Society*, 1931–32; reprinted in Ryle, *Collected Papers*, 2:39–62.

1. C. L. Stevenson, "Persuasive Definitions," *Mind* 47 (1938); reprinted in Stevenson, *Facts and Values* (New Haven, 1963), pp. 32–54.

2. Stevenson, *Facts and Values*, p. 32.

3. I discuss this third form of vagueness in chapter 5.

4. F. Waismann, "Verifiability," *Proceedings of the Aristotelian Society*, suppl. vol. 19 (1945). Reprinted in A. Flew, ed., *Logic and Language*, 1st ser. (Oxford, 1951), pp. 117–44.

5. Waismann, in *Logic and Language*, p. 122.

6. Ibid., p. 120.

7. I discuss perennial flexibility and perennial debatability more fully in *Hamlet and the Philosophy of Literary Criticism* (Chicago 1964, and London, 1965), chap. 17.

8. H. L. A. Hart, "The Ascription of Responsibility and Rights," *Proceedings of the Aristotelian Society*, 1948–49. Reprinted in Flew, ed., *Logic and Language*, 1st ser., pp. 145–66.

9. L. Wittgenstein, *Philosophical Investigations* (Oxford, 1953), Part 1, § 97 (p. 44e).

10. Ibid., § 65 (p. 31e).

11. W. B. Gallie, "Essentially Contested Concepts," *Proceedings of the Aristotelian Society*, 1945–46, pp. 167–98.

12. Ibid., p. 172n.

13. Ibid., p. 174n.

14. F. Sibley, "Aesthetic Concepts," *Philosophical Review* 68, no. 4 (October, 1959): 421–50. Reprinted and revised in J. Margolis, ed., *Philosophy Looks at the Arts* (New York, 1962), pp. 63–87.

Chapter One
Words, Concepts
and Things

Chapter Two
Open Concepts

252   15. Sibley, in Margolis, ed., *Philosophy Looks at the Arts*, p. 65.

    16. R. Bambrough, "Aristotle on Justice: A Paradigm of Philosophy," in R. Bambrough, ed., *New Essays in Plato and Aristotle* (London, 1965), pp. 159–74.

Chapter Three   1. M. Weitz, "The Role of Theory in Aesthetics," *Journal of Aesthet-*
Art   *ics and Art Criticism* 15, no. 1 (1956): 27–35: reprinted in a number of anthologies of readings in aesthetics, including, M. Weitz, ed., *Problems in Aesthetics*, 2d ed. (New York, 1970), pp. 169–80.

    2. M. Mandelbaum, "Family Resemblances and Generalization Concerning the Arts," *American Philosophical Quarterly* 2, no. 3 (1965): 219–28; reprinted in Weitz, ed., *Problems in Aesthetics*, pp. 181–97.

    3. M. H. Abrams, "What's the Use of Theorizing about the Arts?" in M. W. Bloomfield, ed., *In Search of Literary Theory* (Ithaca, 1972), pp. 3–54. All page references in the text are to this edition.

    4. John M. Ellis, *The Theory of Literary Criticism: A Logical Analysis* (Berkeley, 1974). All page references in the text are to this edition.

    5. George Dickie, *Art and the Aesthetic: An Institutional Analysis* (Ithaca, 1974). All page references in the text are to this edition.

    6. The example is derived from Harold Rosenberg, *The De-definition of Art: Action Art to Pop to Earthworks* (New York, 1972). This book is full of aesthetic gold, especially for those who seek and those who deny a theory of art.

    7. Rosenberg cites the whole document ibid., p. 28. The other page reference in the text to Rosenberg is to this book. A more complete account of Rosenberg on the problems and the "crisis" of modern art, as well as an attempt to resolve the crisis by means of the perennial flexibility and the perennial debatability of open concepts, may be found in my review of his *De-definition of Art*; see Weitz, "Art and Nonart," *Partisan Review* 40, no. 1 (1973): 126–30.

Chapter Four   1. G. W. F. Hegel, *Lectures on the History of Philosophy*, edited and
Tragedy   translated by E. S. Haldane and F. H. Simson (London, 1955), vol. 1, pp. 446–47.

Chapter Five   1. See, e.g., M. C. Bradbrook, "Fifty Years of the Criticism of
Style in Art   Shakespeare's Style: A Retrospect," *Shakespeare Survey* 7 (1954): 1:
History   "There is no question relating to Shakespeare as a writer that does not involve his style. . . . Yet on this central problem comparatively little has been written."

    2. Meyer Shapiro, "Style," first published in A. L. Kroeber, ed., *Anthropology Today* (Chicago, 1953); reprinted in M. Philipson, ed., *Aesthetics Today* (New York, 1961). All page references in the text are to this Meridian reprint.

    3. James S. Ackerman, "A Theory of Style," *Journal of Aesthetics and Art Criticism* 21 (1962). Reprinted in M. C. Beardsley and H. M. Schueller, eds., *Aesthetic Inquiry* (Belmont, Calif., 1967). All page references in the text are to this reprint.

    4. Arnold Hauser, *The Philosophy of Art History* (New York, 1963), and *Mannerism*, 2 vols. (London, 1965.)

    5. Hauser, *Mannerism*, 1:111.

    6. Hauser, *Philosophy of Art History*, p. 209.

    7. Hauser, *Mannerism*, 1:18–19.

8. Both essays are collected in E. H. Gombrich, *Norm and Form:*
Studies in the Art of the Renaissance (London, 1966).
9. George Kubler, *The Shape of Time* (New Haven, 1962), p. 130.
10. Inaugural lecture, 1914. Published in translation in 1925, under the full title, "The Rise of the Anticlassical Style in Italian Painting in 1520." Reprinted in Walter Friedlaender, *Mannerism and Anti-Mannerism in Italian Painting* (New York, 1965). All page references in the text are to this Schocken reprint.
11. The full title of the translated essay is "The Anti-Mannerist Style around 1590 and Its Relation to the Transcendental" (1930). Reprinted in Friedlaender. I quote from p. 48.
12. First delivered as a lecture in 1920 and published in Max Dvořák, *Kunstgeschichte als Geistesgeschichte* (1953). Translated in *Magazine of Art* 46 (1953). All references are to this translation.
13. Dvořák, p. 21.
14. Ibid.
15. Lionello Venturi, *From Leonardo to El Greco* (New York, 1956). All page references in the text are to this edition.
16. On the history of *"maniera,"* see esp. Marco Treves, "Maniera, the History of a Word," *Marsyas* 1 (1941); Sir Anthony Blunt, *Artistic Theory in Italy* (London, 1940), chap. 7; and R. Klein and H. Zerner, eds., *Italian Art, 1500–1600*, Sources and Documents in the History of Art Series (Englewood Cliffs, N.J. 1966), esp. pp. 53–91.
17. C. H. Smyth, "Mannerism and *Maniera,*" pp. 174–99 in *The Renaissance and Mannerism*, vol. 2 of *Studies in Western Art: Acts of the Twentieth International Congress of the History of Art* (Princeton, 1963).
18. Quoted by Smyth, ibid., p. 177.
19. Quoted by Smyth, ibid.
20. Ibid., p. 181.
21. Ibid., p. 194.
22. Ibid., p. 198.
23. John Shearman, "*Maniera* as an Aesthetic Ideal," in Meiss, ed., *The Renaissance and Mannerism;* and Shearman, *Mannerism* (Baltimore, 1967).
24. Shearman, "*Maniera* as an Aesthetic Ideal," p. 213.
25. Shearman, *Mannerism*, p. 23.
26. Shearman, "*Maniera* as an Aesthetic Ideal," p. 215.
27. Ibid., p. 217.
28. Ibid.
29. Shearman, *Mannerism*, p. 35.
30. Ibid., p. 84.
31. Giuliano Briganti, *Italian Mannerism*, trans. M. Kunzle (Leipzig, 1962), p. 6. Cf. Blunt, *Artistic Theory in Italy*, chap. 7.
32. Sydney J. Freedberg, "Observations on the Painting of the Maniera," *Art Bulletin* 47 (1965). Freedberg discusses Mannerism also in *Parmigianino* (Cambridge, Mass., 1950); *Painting of the High Renaissance in Rome and Florence*, 2 vols. (Cambridge, Mass., 1961); and *Painting in Italy, 1500–1600*, Pelican History of Art (Harmondsworth, Eng., 1970). All page references in the text are to the *Art Bulletin* article.
33. On Mannerist architecture, a concise study is Nikolaus Pevsner, *An Outline of European Architecture* (Baltimore, 1951), chap. 5; on Mannerism as an International Style, see F. Würtenberger, *Mannerism:*

The European Style of the Sixteenth Century, trans. M. Heron (New York, 1963). Both contain good bibliographies on their subjects.

34. See, e.g., M. Salmi, "Tardo Rinascimento e primo Barocco, Manierismo, Barocco, Rococò: Concetti e termini," Convegno int., Rome, 1960 (Rome: Academia nazionale dei Lincei, 1962), pp. 305–17.

35. Shearman, Mannerism, p. 15.

36. Friedlaender, Mannerism and Anti-Mannerism, p. 13.

37. Shearman, Mannerism, p. 84.

38. On centrality as an explanatory concept, see my Hamlet and the Philosophy of Literary Criticism (Chicago 1964, and London, 1965), chap. 15.

Chapter Six
Human Action

1. Charles Taylor, The Explanation of Human Behaviour (London, 1964). The page reference in the text is to the second impression, 1965.

2. Cf. J. L. Austin's discussion of the complexities of action in relation to responsibility in "A Plea for Excuses," Proceedings of the Aristotelian Society, 1955–56; reprinted in J. O. Urmson and G. J. Warnock, eds., Philosophical Papers (Oxford, 1961).

3. Richard Taylor, Action and Purpose (Englewood Cliffs, N.J., 1966). The page references in the text are to this edition.

4. Roderick M. Chisholm, "Freedom and Action," in K. Lehrer, ed., Freedom and Determinism (New York, 1966). The page references in the text are to this reprinting of Chisholm's lecture, Human Freedom and the Self (1964), and to his paper "The Descriptive Element in the Concept of Action," Journal of Philosophy 61 (1964): 613–25.

5. Arthur Danto, "Basic Actions," American Philosophical Quarterly 2 (April, 1965): 141–48.

6. A. I. Melden, "Action," Philosophical Review 65 (October, 1956): 523–41. The first quotation is from p. 538; subsequent page references in the text are to this publication.

7. A. I. Melden, Free Action (London, 1961). All page references in the text are to the second impression, 1964.

8. Donald Davidson, "Actions, Reasons, and Causes," Journal of Philosophy 60, no. 23 (1963): 685–700; reprinted in M. Brand, ed., The Nature of Human Action (Chicago, 1970). All page references in the text are to this reprinting.

9. John L. Austin, "A Plea for Excuses." The page references in the text are to the reprinting in Philosophical Papers.

10. Alvin I. Goldman, A Theory of Human Action (Englewood Cliffs, N.J., 1970). The page references in the text are to this edition.

Chapter Seven
Morality

1. Kurt Baier, The Moral Point of View (Ithaca, 1958). All page references in the text are to this edition.

2. G. J. Warnock, Contemporary Moral Philosophy (London and New York, 1967), and The Object of Morality (London, 1971). All page references in the text are to these editions, abbreviated as CMP and OM.

3. William Frankena, "Recent Conceptions of Morality," in Hector-Neri Castañeda and George Nakhnikian, eds., Morality and the Language of Conduct (Detroit, 1963), and Ethics (Englewood Cliffs, N.J., 1963; 2d ed., 1973). References to these works in the text are

abbreviated *RCM* and *E*; page references to the latter are to the second edition.

1. See, especially, the two articles by Philippa Foot, "Moral Arguments," *Mind* 67 (1958): 502–13, and "Moral Beliefs," *Proceedings of the Aristotelian Society*, 1958–59, pp. 83–104. Both have been reprinted in various anthologies of readings in ethics.

2. Henry David Aiken, "The Concept of Moral Objectivity," *Reason and Conduct: New Bearings in Moral Philosophy* (New York, 1962). The phrase quoted in the text is from page 166.

3. Anthony Kenny, *Action, Emotion and Will* (London, 1963), esp. chaps. 2–4.

Articles from periodicals referred to in the text or notes are not listed here, since the full facts of their publications are given in the notes. All other articles and all books cited in the text or notes, or articles or books that relate to the issues in the text, are listed here. Readers who wish more extensive bibliographies or who wish to probe further may consult the bibliographies appended to the separate articles on relevant issues and concepts in *The Encyclopedia of Philosophy*, editor-in-chief, Paul Edwards, 8 vols. (New York: Macmillan and Free Press; London: Collier-Macmillan, 1967); unfortunately, there is no separate article on "Human Action," nor is the bibliography to "Concept" adequate.

General, and Chapters One and Two

Aaron, R. I. *The Theory of Universals*. Oxford: Oxford University Press, 1952.

Armstrong, D. M. *Belief, Truth and Knowledge*. Cambridge, Eng.: At the University Press, 1973.

Austin, John. *Philosophical Papers*. Edited by J. O. Urmson and G. J. Warnock. Oxford: Clarendon Press, 1961.

Carbonara, C. "Concetto." In *Enciclopedia Filosofica*. Florence: Sansoni, 1957.

Carnap, Rudolf. *Meaning and Necessity: A Study in Semantics and Modal Logic*. Chicago: University of Chicago Press, 1950.

Church, Alonzo. "A Formulation of the Logic of Sense and Denotation." In *Structure, Method, and Meaning: Essays in Honor of H. M. Sheffer*, edited by P. Henle, H. M. Kallen, and S. K. Langer. New York: Liberal Arts, 1951.

———. "The Need for Abstract Entities in Semantic Analysis." In *Contributions to the Analysis and Synthesis of Knowledge*, Proceedings of the American Academy of Arts and Sciences 00, no. 1 (1951). 100–112.

Eisler, R. "Begriff." *Wörterbuch der philosophischen Begriffe*. Berlin: E. S. Mittler & Sohn, 1927.

Feyerabend, P. K. *Against Method: Outline of an Anarchistic Theory of Knowledge*. Atlantic Highlands: Humanities Press, 1975.

Frege, Gottlob. *Grundgesetze der Arithmetik*. 2 vols. Jena, 1893–1903. Parts translated by P. T. Geach and Max Black in *Translations from the Philosophical Writings of Gottlob Frege*.

———. *Die Grundlagen der Arithmetik*. Translated as *The Foundations of Arithmetic* by J. L. Austin. Oxford: Blackwell, 1950.

———. *Translations from the Philosophical Writings of Gottlob Frege*. Translated and edited by P. T. Geach and Max Black. Oxford: Blackwell, 1952.

258   *From Frege to Gödel: A Source Book in Mathematical Logic.* Edited by Jean Van Heijenhoort. Cambridge, Mass.: Harvard University Press, 1967.

Geach, P. T. *Mental Acts: Their Content and Their Objects.* London: Routledge & Kegan Paul, 1957.

Goodman, Nelson, and Quine, W. van. "Steps Toward a Constructive Nominalism." *Journal of Symbolic Logic* 12 (1947): 105–22.

Haller, R. "Begriff." In *Historisches Wörterbuch der Philosophie,* edited by Joachim Ritter. Basel: Schwabe, 1971.

Hamlyn, D. W. *The Theory of Knowledge.* London: Macmillan, 1970.

Hampshire, Stuart. "The Interpretation of Language: Words and Concepts." In *British Philosophy in the Mid-Century,* edited by C. A. Mace. London: George Allen & Unwin, 1957.

———. *Thought and Action.* London: Chatto & Windus, 1959.

Hanson, Norwood. *Patterns of Discovery.* Cambridge, Eng.: At the University Press, 1958.

Hare, R. M. "Philosophical Discoveries." *Mind* 69 (1960): 145–62.

Hart, H. L. A. *The Concept of Law.* Oxford: Clarendon Press, 1961.

———. *Definition & Theory in Jurisprudence.* Inaugural lecture. Oxford: Clarendon Press, 1953.

Heath, Peter. "Concept." In *The Encyclopedia of Philosophy.*

Hempel, Carl G. *Fundamentals of Concept Formation in Empirical Science.* Vol. 2, no. 7, of Foundations of the Unity of Science: Toward an International Encyclopedia of United Science, edited by Otto Neurath, Rudolf Carnap, and Charles Morris. Chicago: University of Chicago Press, 1952.

Kenny, Anthony. *Wittgenstein.* Cambridge, Mass.: Harvard University Press, 1973.

Kneale, W., and Kneale, M. *The Development of Logic.* Oxford Clarendon Press, 1962.

Körner, Stephan. *Conceptual Thinking: A Logical Enquiry.* New York: Dover, 1959.

Kuhn, Thomas S. *The Structure of Scientific Revolutions.* Chicago: University of Chicago Press, 1962.

Lakatos, Imre. "Criticism and the Methodology of Scientific Research Programmes." In *Proceedings of the Aristotelian Society,* 1968–69, pp. 149–86.

Lewis, C. I. *An Analysis of Knowledge and Valuation.* La Salle, Ill.: Open Court, 1946.

———. *Mind and the World-Order.* New York: Charles Scribner's Sons, 1929.

Logic and Language. Edited by A. Flew. 1st and 2d ser. Oxford: Blackwell, 1951, 1953.

Moore, G. E. "The Nature of Judgment." *Mind* 8 (1899): 176–93.

———. *Philosophical Papers*. London: George Allen & Unwin, 259
1959.
———. *Philosophical Studies*. London Routledge & Kegan Paul,
1922.
———. *Principia Ethica*. Cambridge, Eng.: At the University
Press, 1903.
———. *Some Main Problems of Philosophy*. London: George
Allen & Unwin; New York: Macmillan, 1953.
Pears, D. F. *Wittgenstein*. London: William Collins, 1971.
Peifer, J. F. "Concept." In *New Catholic Encyclopedia*. New
York: McGraw Hill, 1967.
———. *The Concept in Thomism*. New York: Bookman Associ-
ates, 1952.
Pitcher, George. *The Philosophy of Wittgenstein*. Englewood
Cliffs, N.J.: Prentice-Hall, 1964.
Popper, Karl R. *The Logic of Scientific Discovery*. London:
Hutchinson, 1959.
———. *The Open Society and Its Enemies*. 2 vols. London:
Routledge & Kegan Paul, 1945. 2d ed., rev. and enl., 1952.
———. *The Poverty of Historicism*. London: Routledge & Kegan
Paul, 1957.
Price, H. H. *Thinking and Experience*. London: Hutchinson's
University Library, 1953.
Quine, Willard van Orman. *From a Logical Point of View:
Logico-Philosophical Essays*. Cambridge, Mass.: Harvard
University Press, 1953.
———. *Mathematical Logic*. Rev. ed. Cambridge, Mass.: Har-
vard University Press, 1951.
———. *Ontological Relativity and Other Essays*. New York:
Columbia University Press, 1969.
———. *Philosophy of Logic*. Englewood Cliffs, N.J.: Prentice-
Hall, 1970.
———. *The Roots of Reference*. La Salle, Ill.: Open Court, 1973.
———. *Word and Object*. Cambridge, Mass.: MIT Press, 1960.
Robinson, Richard. *Definition*. Oxford: Clarendon Press, 1950.
———. *Plato's Early Dialectic*. 2d ed. Oxford: Clarendon Press,
1953.
Russell, Bertrand. *Logic and Knowledge: Essays 1901–1950*.
Edited by Robert C. Marsh. London: Allen & Unwin; New
York: Macmillan, 1956.
——— and Whitehead, Alfred North. *Principia Mathematica*.
3 vols. Cambridge, Eng.: At the University Press. Vol. 1,
1910; 2d ed., 1925. Vol. 2, 1912. Vol. 3, 1913.
———. *The Principles of Mathematics*. Cambridge, Eng.: At the
University Press, 1903; 2d ed., New York: Norton, 1937.
———. *The Philosophy of Bertrand Russell*. Edited by P.A.
Schilpp. Evanston: Northwestern University Press; Cam-
bridge, Eng.: At the University Press; Toronto: Macmillan,
1944.

260   Ryle, Gilbert. *The Concept of Mind.* London: Hutchinson's University Library, 1949.

———. *Collected Papers.* 2 vols. London: Hutchinson's University Library; New York: Barnes & Noble, 1971.

———. *Dilemmas.* Cambridge, Eng.: At the University Press, 1954.

Stevenson, C. L. *Ethics and Language.* New Haven: Yale University Press, 1944.

———. *Facts and Values: Studies in Ethical Analysis.* New Haven: Yale University Press, 1963.

Strawson, P. F. *Introduction to Logical Theory.* London: Methuen, 1952.

Toulmin, S. E. *Human Understanding.* Princeton: Princeton University Press, 1972.

Urmson, J. O. *Philosophical Analysis: Its Development between Two World Wars.* Oxford: Clarendon Press, 1956.

———. "Polymorphous Concepts." In *Ryle: A Collection of Critical Essays,* edited by D. P. Wood and G. Pitcher. New York: Doubleday, 1970.

Weitz, Morris. "Oxford Philosophy." *Philosophical Review* 62 (1953): 187–233.

Wittgenstein, Ludwig. *The Blue and the Brown Books.* Oxford: Blackwell, 1958.

———. *Tractatus Logico-Philosophicus.* Translated by C. K. Ogden. London: Routledge & Kegan Paul, 1922. Newly translated by D. F. Pears and B. F. McGuiness. London: Routledge & Kegan Paul, 1961.

———. *Philosophical Investigations.* Translated by G. E. M. Anscombe. 3d ed. New York: Macmillan, 1968.

———. *Wittgenstein: The Philosophical Investigations: A Collection of Critical Essays.* Edited by G. Pitcher. New York: Doubleday, 1966.

Chapter Three   Abrams, M. H. *The Mirror and the Lamp: Romantic Theory and **Art**   the Critical Tradition.* New York: Oxford University Press, 1953.

Aesthetic Inquiry. Edited by M. C. Beardsley and H. M. Schueller. Belmont, Cal.: Dickenson, 1967.

Aesthetic Theories: Studies in the Philosophy of Art. Edited by K. Aschenbrenner and A. Isenberg. Englewood Cliffs, N.J.: Prentice-Hall, 1965.

Aesthetics Today. Edited by M. Philipson. New York: Meridian, World Publishing Co. 1961.

Aristotle. *Poetics.* Translated by S. H. Butcher. London: Macmillan, 1895. Rev. ed., 1911.

Beardsley, M. C. *Aesthetics from Classical Greece to the Present: A Short History.* New York: Macmillan, 1969.

———. *Aesthetics: Problems in the Philosophy of Criticism.* New York: Harcourt, Brace, 1958.

Bell, Clive. *Art*. New York: F. Stokes, 1913.

Coleridge, S. T. *Coleridge's Shakespearean Criticism*. Edited by T. Raysor. 2 vols. Cambridge, Mass.: Harvard University Press, 1930.

Danto, Arthur. "The Artworld." *Journal of Philosophy* 61 (1964): 571–84.

Dewey, John. *Art As Experience*. New York: Minton, Balch, 1934.

Dickie, George. *Art and the Aesthetic: An Institutional Analysis*. Ithaca: Cornell University Press, 1974.

Ellis, John M. *The Theory of Literary Criticism: A Logical Analysis*. Berkeley: University of California Press, 1974.

Goodman, Nelson. *Languages of Art*. Indianapolis and New York: Bobbs-Merrill, 1968.

Hirsh, E. D. *Validity in Interpretation*. New Haven: Yale University Press, 1967.

Philosophy Looks at the Arts: Contemporary Readings in Aesthetics. Edited by J. Margolis. New York: Charles Scribner's Sons, 1962.

Prall, David. *Aesthetic Analysis*. New York: Thomas Crowell, 1936.

———. *Aesthetic Judgment*. New York: Thomas Crowell, 1929.

Problems in Aesthetics: An Introductory Book of Readings. Edited by M. Weitz. New York: Macmillan, 1959. 2d ed., rev. and enl., 1970.

Rosenberg, Harold. *The De-definition of Art: Action Art to Pop to Earthworks*. New York: Horizon Press, 1972.

In Search of Literary Theory. Edited by Morton W. Bloomfield. Ithaca: Cornell University Press, 1972.

Weitz, Morris. *Hamlet and the Philosophy of Literary Criticism*. Chicago: University of Chicago Press, 1964; London: Faber & Faber, 1965.

Wittgenstein, Ludwig. *Lectures & Conversations on Aesthetics, Psychology and Religious Belief*. Edited by Cyril Barrett. Berkeley: University of California Press, 1967.

Alexander, Peter. *Hamlet: Father and Son*. Oxford: Clarendon Press, 1955.

Bradley, A. C. *Oxford Lectures on Poetry*. London: Macmillan, 1909.

———. *Shakespearean Tragedy*. London: Macmillan, 1904.

Campbell, Lily B. *Shakespeare's Tragic Heroes: Slaves of Passion*. Cambridge, Eng.: At the University Press, 1930. Reprinted, New York: Barnes & Noble, 1952.

Castelvetro, Lodovico. *Poetica d'Aristotele Vulgarizzata, et Sposta*. 1570.

Corneille, Pierre. *Examens* and *Discours*. 1660.

Dryden, John. *Essays of John Dryden*. Edited by W. P. Ker. 2 vols. Oxford: Clarendon Press, 1926.

Chapter Four
Tragedy

262   Ellis-Fermor, Una. *The Frontiers of Drama*. London: Methuen, 1945.

Else, G. F. *Aristotle's Poetics: The Argument*. Cambridge, Mass.: Harvard University Press, 1957.

Farnham, Willard. *The Medieval Heritage of Elizabethan Tragedy*. Oxford: Blackwell, 1956.

Goethe, J. W. von. *Nachlese zu Aristoteles Poetik*. 1827.

Hegel, G. W. F. *Lectures on the History of Philosophy*. Edited and translated by E. S. Haldane and F. H. Simpson. 3 vols. London and New York, 1892–95. Reprinted, London: Routledge & Kegan Paul, 1955.

———. *The Philosophy of Fine Art*. Translated by F. P. B. Osmaston. 4 vols. London: G. Bell & Sons, 1920.

Henn, T. R. *The Harvest of Tragedy*. London: Methuen, 1956.

Johnson, Samuel. *Johnson on Shakespeare*. Edited by W. Raleigh. Oxford: Oxford University Press, 1908.

Kitto, H. D. F. *Greek Tragedy*. London: Methuen, 1950.

Krook, Dorothea. *Elements of Tragedy*. New Haven: Yale University Press, 1969.

Krutch, J. W. *The Modern Temper*. New York: Harcourt, Brace, 1929.

Lessing, G. E. *Hamburgische Dramaturgie*. 1767–69.

Lucas, F. L. *Tragedy*. Rev. ed. London: Hogarth Press, 1957.

Nietzsche, Friedrich. *The Birth of Tragedy*. Translated by Francis Golffing. (Together with *The Genealogy of Morals*.) New York: Doubleday, 1956.

Nurse (Hampshire), Peter. "Quelques réflexions sur la notion du tragique dans l'oeuvre de Pierre Corneille." *Travaux de Linguistique et de la Littérature* 13, no. 2. Strasbourg: Centre de Philologie et de la Littératures Romaines, 1975.

Quinton, A. M. "Tragedy." In *Proceedings of the Aristotelian Society*, Supplementary volume 34 (1960): 145–64.

Schiller, Friedrich. *Essays Aesthetical and Philosophical*. London: Bohn, 1916.

Schlegel, A. W. *A Course of Lectures on Dramatic Art and Literature*. Translated by J. Black and A. Morrison. London: H. G. Bohn, 1846.

Schlegel, Friedrich. *Lectures on the History of Literature, Ancient and Modern*. Translated by J. Lockhart. 2 vols. Edinburgh: Blackwood, 1818.

Schopenhauer, Arthur. *The World as Will and Idea*. Translated by R. B. Haldane and J. Kemp. Reprinted, New York: Doubleday, 1961.

Tillyard, E. M. W. *Shakespeare's Problem Plays*. London: Chatto & Windus, 1957.

Chapter Five   Baldinucci, F. *Vocabolario toscano dell'arte del disegno*. 1681.
Style in Art   Becherucci, Luisa. "Mannerism." In *Encyclopedia of World*
History   *Art*, editor-in-chief, Massimo Pallottino. New York:

McGraw-Hill. 1959–68.

Bellori, Pietro. *Le vite de'pittori, scultori et architetti moderni.* Rome, 1672.

Berenson, Bernard. *The Italian Painters of the Renaissance.* London: Oxford University Press, 1930.

Blunt, Anthony. *Artistic Theory in Italy, 1450–1600.* Oxford: Clarendon Press, 1940.

Briganti, Giuliano. *Italian Mannerism.* Translated by M. Kunzle. Leipzig: Volkseiger Betrieb, 1962.

Chambray, R. Fréart de. *Ideé de la perfection de la peinture.* Le Mans, 1662.

Clark, Kenneth. *A Failure of Nerve: Italian Painting 1520–1535.* Oxford: Clarendon Press, 1967.

———. *Landscape into Art.* Harmondsworth, Eng.: Penguin Books, 1956.

———. *The Nude.* London: John Murray, 1956.

Dvořák, Max. *Kunstgeschichte als Geistesgeschichte.* Munich: R. Piper, 1924.

Ferguson, W. K. *The Renaissance in Historical Thought: Five Centuries of Interpretation.* Cambridge, Mass.: Harvard University Press, 1948.

Frankl, Paul. *The Gothic: Literary Sources and Interpretations during Eight Centuries.* Princeton: Princeton University Press 1960.

———. *Gothic Architecture.* Harmondsworth, Eng.: Penguin, 1962.

———. *Das System der Kunstwissenschaft.* Leipzig: R. M. Rohrer, 1938.

Freedberg, Sydney J. *Painting of the High Renaissance in Rome and Florence.* 2 vols. Cambridge, Mass.: Harvard University Press, 1961.

———. *Painting in Italy 1500–1600.* Harmondsworth, Eng.: Penguin, 1970.

———. *Parmigianino.* Cambridge, Mass.: Harvard University Press, 1950.

Friedlaender, Walter. *Mannerism and Anti-Mannerism in Italian Painting.* New York: Schocken Books, 1965.

Friedländer, Max J. *Landscape, Portrait, Still-Life: Their Origin and Development.* Translated by R. F. C. Hull. Oxford: B. Cassirer, 1949.

Gombrich, E. H. *Norm and Form: Studies in the Art of the Renaissance.* London: Phaidon, 1966.

———. *The Story of Art.* 11th ed., rev. and enl. London: Phaidon, 1966.

Hauser, Arnold. *Mannerism: The Crisis of the Renaissance and the Origin of Modern Art.* 2 vols. London: Routledge & Kegan Paul, 1965.

———. *The Philosophy of Art History.* New York: Alfred A. A. Knopf, 1963.

264   *Italian Art, 1500–1600.* Sources and Documents in the History of
Art. Edited by R. Klein and H. Zerner. Englewood Cliffs,
N.J.: Prentice-Hall, 1966.

Janson, H. W. "The Art Historian's Comments." In *Contemporary Philosophic Thought,* vol. 3, edited by H. E. Kiefer and
M. K. Munitz. Albany: State University of New York Press,
1970.

Kubler, George. *The Shape of Time.* New Haven: Yale University Press, 1962.

Malraux, André. *Les Voix du silence.* Paris: NRF, 1953.

Panofsky, Erwin. *Meaning in the Visual Arts.* New York:
Doubleday, 1955.

————. *Renaissance and Renascences in Western Art.* Stock-
holm: Almquist & Wicksells, Gebers Forlag AB, 1960; New
York: Harper & Row, 1969.

————. *Studies in Iconology: Humanistic Themes in the Art of
the Renaissance.* New York: Oxford University Press, 1939.

Pevsner, Nikolaus. *An Outline of European Architecture.* Harmondsworth, Eng.: Penguin Books, 1951.

Reigl, Alois. *Die Entstehung der Barrockkunst in Rom.* Vienna:
Akademische Vorlesung, 1908.

The Renaissance and Mannerism. Vol. 2 of *Studies in Western
Art: Acts of the Twentieth International Congress of the His-
tory of Art,* edited by M. Meiss. 4 vols. Princeton: Princeton
University Press, 1963.

Rosenberg, Harold. *The De-definition of Art: Action Art to Pop
to Earthworks.* New York: Horizon Press, 1972.

Shearman, John. *Mannerism.* Harmondsworth, Eng.: Penguin
Books, 1967.

Vasari, Giorgio. *Le opere di Giorgio Vasari.* Edited by G.
Milanesi. Florence, 1878–1906.

————. *Lives of the Most Eminent Painters, Sculptors, and
Architects.* Translated by Gaston DuC. DeVere. 10 vols.
London: The Medici Society, 1912–14.

Venturi, Lionello. *From Leonardo to El Greco.* New York:
World, 1956.

Wölfflin, Heinrich. *Die klassische Kunst.* 1889. Translated as
The Art of the Italian Renaissance. New York: Schocken
Books, 1963.

————. *Kunstgeschichtliche Grundbegriffe.* 1915. Translated as
Principles of Art History by M. D. Hottinger. New York:
Dover, n.d.

————. *Renaissance und Barock.* 1888. Translated as *Renaissance and Baroque* by K. Simon, with an introduction by
Peter Murray. London: Collins, 1964.

Würtenberger, F. *Mannerism: The European Style of the Sixteenth Century.* Translated by M. Heron. New York: Rine-
hart & Winston, 1963.

Anscombe, G. E. M. *Intention.* Oxford: Blackwell, 1957.

Beardsley, M. C. "Actions and Events: The Problem of Individuation." *American Philosophical Quarterly* 12, no. 4 (1975): 263–76.

Brown, D. G. *Action.* London: Allen & Unwin; Toronto: University of Toronto Press, 1968.

Brown, Robert. *Explanation in Social Science.* Chicago: Aldine, 1963.

Davidson, Donald. "Action and Reaction." *Inquiry* 13 no. 1–2 (1970): 140–48.

———. "The Individuation of Events." In *Essays in Honor of Carl G. Hempel,* edited by Nicholas Rescher et al. Dordrecht: D. Reidel, 1969.

———. "The Logical Form of Action Sentences. In *The Logic of Decision and Action,* edited by Nicholas Rescher. Pittsburgh: University of Pittsburgh Press, 1967.

———. "Mental Events." In *Experience and Theory,* edited by L. Foster and J. W. Swanson. Amherst: University of Massachusetts Press, 1970.

Donnellan, Keith S. "Reasons and Causes." In *The Encyclopedia of Philosophy.*

Dray, William. *Laws and Explanation in History.* Oxford: Clarendon Press, 1957.

Edgley, Roy. *Reason in Theory and Practice.* London: Hutchinson's University Library, 1969.

Essays in Philosophical Psychology. Edited by D. F. Gustafson. New York: Doubleday, 1964.

Explanations in the Behavioural Sciences: Confrontations. Edited by R. Borger and F. Cioffi. Cambridge, Eng.: At the University Press, 1970.

Feinberg, Joel. "Action and Responsibility." In *Philosophy in America,* edited by Max Black. Ithaca: Cornell University Press; Cambridge, Eng.: At the University Press, 1965.

Fodor, Jerry A. *Psychological Explanation: An Introduction to the Philosophy of Psychology.* New York: Random House, 1968.

Gauthier, D. *Practical Reasoning.* London: Oxford University Press, 1963.

Goldman, Alvin I. *A Theory of Human Action.* Englewood Cliffs, N.J.: Prentice-Hall, 1970.

Hampshire, Stuart. *Freedom of the Individual.* London: Chatto & Windus, 1965.

———. *Thought and Action.* London: Chatto & Windus, 1959.

Hart, H. L. A. *Punishment and Responsibility: Essays in the Philosophy of Law.* Oxford: Clarendon Press, 1968.

The Human Agent. Royal Institute of Philosophy Lectures for 1966–67. London: Macmillan; New York: St. Martin's Press, 1968.

266   Kenny, Anthony. *Action, Emotion and Will.* London: Routledge & Kegan Paul, 1963.

Louch, A. R. *Explanation and Human Action.* Oxford: Blackwell; Berkeley: University of California Press, 1969.

MacIntyre, A. C. "The Antecedents of Action." In *British Analytical Philosophy,* edited by B. Williams and A. Montefiore. London: Routledge & Kegan Paul, 1966.

Melden, A. I. *Free Action.* London: Routledge & Kegan Paul, 1964.

The Nature of Human Action. Edited by M. Brand. Chicago: Scott, Foresman, 1970.

Pears, D. F. "Are Reasons for Actions Causes?" In *Epistemology,* edited by A. Stroll. New York: Harper & Row, 1967.

Peters, R. S. *The Concept of Motivation.* London: Routledge & Kegan Paul; New York: Humanities Press, 1958.

The Philosophy of Action. Edited by A. R. White. Oxford University Press, 1968.

Taylor, Richard. *Action and Purpose.* Englewood Cliffs, N.J.: Prentice-Hall, 1966.

Taylor, Charles. *The Explanation of Human Behaviour.* London: Routledge & Kegan Paul; New York: Humanities Press, 1964.

Wright, Georg H. von. *Explanation and Understanding.* Ithaca: Cornell University Press, 1971.

Chapter Seven
Morality

Aiken, H. D. *Reason and Conduct: New Bearings in Moral Philosophy.* New York: Alfred A. Knopf, 1962.

Anscombe, G. E. M. "On Brute Facts." *Analysis* 18 (1958): 69–72.

Baier, Kurt. "Good Reasons." *Philosophical Studies* 4, no. 1 (1953): 1–15.

———. *The Moral Point of View: A Rational Basis of Ethics.* Ithaca: Cornell University Press, 1958.

Broad, C. D. *Five Types of Ethical Theory.* London: Kegan Paul, Trench, Trubner & Co., 1930.

Essays in Moral Philosophy. Edited by A. I. Melden. Seattle: University of Washington Press, 1958.

Ewing, A. C. *The Definition of Good.* New York: Macmillan, 1947.

Frankena, William. *Ethics.* Englewood Cliffs, N.J.: Prentice-Hall, 1963. 2d ed., 1973.

———. "The Naturalistic Fallacy." *Mind* 48 (1939): 103–14.

Geach, P. T. "Ascriptivism." *Philosophical Review* 69 (1960): 221–25.

Hare, R. M. *Freedom and Reason.* Oxford: Clarendon Press, 1963.

———. *The Language of Morals.* Oxford: Clarendon Press, 1952.

Moral Concepts. Edited by Joel Feinberg. London: Oxford University Press, 1969.

Morality and the Language of Conduct. Edited by G. Nakhnikian and H. Castañeda. Detroit: Wayne State University Press, 1961.

Prior, A. N. *Logic and the Basis of Ethics.* Oxford: Clarendon Press, 1949.

Prichard, H. A. *Moral Obligation.* Oxford: Clarendon Press, 1949.

Ross, W. D. *Foundations of Ethics.* Oxford: Clarendon Press, 1939.

———. *The Right and the Good.* Oxford: Clarendon Press, 1930.

Singer, Marcus. *Generalization in Ethics.* New York: Alfred A. Knopf, 1961.

Stevenson, C. L. *Ethics and Language.* New Haven: Yale University Press, 1944.

Theories of Ethics. Edited by Philippa Foot. Oxford: Oxford University Press, 1967.

Toulmin, S. E. *An Examination of the Place of Reason in Ethics.* Cambridge, Eng.: At the University Press, 1950.

Warnock, G. J. *Contemporary Moral Philosophy.* London: Macmillan; New York: St. Martin's Press, 1967.

———. *The Object of Morality.* London: Methuen, 1971.

Wright, Georg H. von. *The Varieties of Goodness.* London: Routledge & Kegan Paul; New York: Humanities Press, 1963.

Berlin, Isaiah. *Four Essays on Liberty.* London: Oxford University Press, 1969.

Beyond the Edge of Certainty: Essays in Contemporary Science and Philosophy. Edited by R. S. Colodny. New York: Prentice-Hall, 1965.

Braithwaite, R. B. *Scientific Explanation.* Cambridge, Eng.: At the University Press, 1953.

Braybrooke, David. *Three Tests for Democracy: Personal Rights, Human Welfare, Collective Preference.* New York: Random House, 1968.

Bunge, Mario. *Causality: The Place of the Causal Principle in Modern Science.* Cambridge, Mass.: Harvard University Press, 1959.

Campbell, N. *What Is Science?* New York: Dover, 1952.

Caws, Peter. *The Philosophy of Science: A Systematic Account.* Princeton: D. van Nostrand, 1965.

Collingwood, R. G. *The Idea of History.* New York: Oxford University Press, 1956.

Cranston, Maurice. *Freedom: A New Analysis.* London: Longmans, Green, 1953.

Feynman, Richard P. *The Character of Physical Law.* Cambridge, Mass.: MIT Press, 1965.

Fischer, David H. *Historians' Fallacies: Toward a Logic of Historical Thought.* New York: Harper & Row, 1970.

Chapter Eight
Other Concepts— Open or Closed?

268   Fox, Marvin. "Judaism, Secularism and Textual Interpretation." In *Modern Jewish Ethics: Theory and Practice*, edited by Marvin Fox. Columbus, Ohio: Ohio State University Press, 1975.

Frankfurt, Harry G. "Freedom of the Will and the Concept of a Person." *Journal of Philosophy* 68, no. 1 (1971): 5–20.

Gallie, W. B. *Philosophy and the Historical Understanding.* London: Chatto & Windus, 1964.

Gardiner, Patrick. *The Nature of Historical Explanation.* London: Oxford University Press, 1952.

Gasking, Douglas. "Causation and Recipes." *Mind* 64 (1955): 479–87.

Gibson, Q. *The Logic of Social Inquiry.* London: Routledge & Kegan Paul, 1960.

Hart, H. L. A. *The Concept of Law.* Oxford: Clarendon Press, 1961.

———. and Honoré, A. M. *Causation in the Law.* Oxford: Clarendon Press, 1953.

Hempel, Carl G. *Aspects of Scientific Explanation and Other Essays in the Philosophy of Science.* New York: Free Press, 1965.

Hick, John. *Philosophy of Religion.* Englewood Cliffs, N.J.: Prentice-Hall, 1963.

Hospers, John. "What Is Explanation?" In *Essays in Conceptual Analysis*, edited by A. Flew. London: Macmillan: New York: St. Martin's Press, 1968.

Jammer, Max. *Concepts of Force: A Study in the Foundations of Dynamics.* Cambridge, Mass.: Harvard University Press, 1957.

———. *Concepts of Mass in Classical and Modern Physics.* Cambridge, Mass.: Harvard University Press, 1961.

———. *Concepts of Space: The History of the Theories of Space in Physics.* Cambridge, Mass.: Harvard University Press, 1954.

Kelsen, H. *General Theory of the Law and the State.* Cambridge, Mass.: Harvard University Press, 1945.

Mabbott, J. D. *The State and the Citizen.* London: Hutchinson, 1948.

Mackie, J. L. *The Cement of the Universe.* Oxford: Clarendon Press, 1974.

MacPherson, C. B. *The Real World of Democracy.* Oxford: Clarendon Press, 1966.

Malcolm, Norman, *Dreaming.* London: Routledge & Kegan Paul; New York: Humanities Press, 1959.

Nagel, Ernest. *The Structure of Science: Problems in the Logic of Scientific Explanation.* New York: Harcourt, Brace & World, 1961.

New Essays in Philosophical Theology. Edited by A. Flew and A. C. MacIntyre. New York: Macmillan, 1955.

Nozick, Robert. *Anarchy, State, and Utopia.* New York: Basic
Books, 1975.
Plamenatz, J. P. *Man and Society.* London: Longmans, 1963.
Rawls, John. *A Theory of Justice.* Cambridge, Mass.: Harvard
University Press, 1971.
Russell, Bertrand. *Why I Am Not a Christian.* Edited by Paul
Edwards. London: Allen & Unwin; New York: Simon &
Schuster, 1957.
Scheffler, Israel. *The Anatomy of Inquiry: Philosophical Studies
in the Theory of Science.* New York: Alfred A. Knopf, 1963;
London: Routledge & Kegan Paul, 1964.
Smart, Ninian. *The Philosophy of Religion.* New York: Random
House, 1970.
Strauss, Leo. *What Is Political Philosophy?* Glencoe, Ill.: Free
Press, 1959.
Strawson, P. F. "Persons." In *Concepts, Theories, and the Mind-
Body Problem.* Minnesota Studies in the Philosophy of Sci-
ence, vol. 2, pp. 330–53. Edited by H. Feigl, M. Scriven, and
G. Maxwell. Minneapolis: University of Minnesota Press,
1958.
Tarski, Alfred. "The Concept of Truth in Formalized Lan-
guages." *Logic, Semantics, Metamathematics: Papers from
1923 to 1938.* Translated by J. H. Woodger. Oxford: Claren-
don Press, 1956.
Tawney, R. H. *Equality.* 4th ed. London: George Allen &
Unwin, 1952.
Tillich, Paul. *The Courage To Be.* New Haven: Yale University Press, 1952.
Toulmin, S. E. *The Philosophy of Science.* London: Hutchinson,
1953.
Waismann, Friedrich. "How I See Philosophy." In *Contempo-
rary British Philosophy,* 3d ser., edited by H. D. Lewis. Lon-
don: George Allen & Unwin; New York: Macmillan, 1956.
Walsh, W. H. *An Introduction to Philosophy of History.* Lon-
don: Hutchinson's University Library, 1951. Rev. ed. 1950.
Williams, B. A. O. "The Idea of Equality." In *Philosophy,
Politics and Society,* 2d ser., edited by P. Laslett and W. G.
Runciman. Oxford: Blackwell; New York: Barnes & Noble,
1962.
Winch, P. *The Idea of a Social Science.* London: Routledge &
Kegan Paul; New York: Humanities Press, 1970.